''Deny All Knowledge''

"Deny All Knowledge"

READING THE X-FILES

EDITED BY

David Lavery, Angela Hague,

AND

Marla Cartwright

faber and faber

First published in 1996
by Faber and Faber Limited
3 Queen Square London WC1N 3AU

Printed in England by Clays Ltd, St Ives plc

'How to Talk the Unknown into Existence:
An Exercise in X-Filology' © Alec McHoul, 1996
Syracuse University Press is hereby identified as author of this
work in accordance with Section 77 of the Copyright,
Designs and Patents Act 1988.

A CIP record for this book is
available from the British Library

ISBN 0–571–19141–X

2 4 6 8 10 9 7 5 3 1

Contents

Contributors

Linda Badley is professor of English at Middle Tennessee State University. She is the author of a two-volume study, *Film, Horror, and the Body Fantastic* and *Writing Horror and the Body: The Fiction of Stephen King, Clive Barker, and Anne Rice.*

Marla Cartwright is an instructor in the English department at Middle Tennessee State University.

Susan J. Clerc is a doctoral candidate in American Cultural Studies at Bowling Green State University. Her essay "Estrogen Brigades and 'Big Tits' Threads: Media Fandom Online and Off" was published in *Wired Women: Gender and New Realities in Cyberspace.*

Michael Epstein is a Ph.D. candidate in American Culture at the University of Michigan.

Allison Graham is associate professor of communication at the University of Memphis. She is the author of a book on Lindsay Anderson and coproducer/director/writer of the 1993 Emmy-nominated film *At the River I Stand.*

Angela Hague is professor of English at Middle Tennessee State University and is author of *Iris Murdoch's Comic Vision.* She is a state section director for Tennessee MUFON.

Leslie Jones earned the Ph.D. in Folklore and Mythology from UCLA. A professional writer and independent scholar, she is the author of several essays and of *Happy is the Bride the Sun Shines On: Wedding Beliefs, Traditions, and Customs* and *Druids, Shamans, and Priests.*

Elizabeth B. Kubek earned her Ph.D. at the University of Rochester. She is an instructor in the English and Textual Studies program at Syracuse University.

David Lavery is professor of English and chair of the English department at Middle Tennessee State University. He is the author of *Late for the Sky: The Mentality of the Space Age* and editor of *Full¯of Secrets: Critical Approaches to "Twin Peaks."*

Michele Malach teaches communication at Fort Lewis College in Durango, Colorado, and is a doctoral candidate at the University of Texas.

Alec McHoul is professor of linguistics at Murdoch University, Austra-. lia, and author of numerous articles on cultural matters.

Lisa Parks is a doctoral candidate in communication at the University of Wisconsin.

Jimmie L. Reeves is assistant professor of communication at Texas Tech University. He is the author (with Dick Campbell) of *Cracked Coverage: Television News, the Anti-Cocaine Crusade, and the Reagan Legacy.*

Mark C. Rodgers is a Ph.D. candidate in American Culture at the University of Michigan.

Rhonda Wilcox is assistant professor of English at Gordon College. She won a 1994 award from the Popular Culture Association of the South for her essay on *Northern Exposure*.

J. P. Williams teaches at Georgia Southern College and is the author of several published articles (including an essay on *Moonlighting* in *The Journal of Popular Film and Television*).

''Deny All Knowledge''

1

Introduction

GENERATION X—*THE X-FILES*
AND THE CULTURAL MOMENT

David Lavery, Angela Hague,
and Marla Cartwright

> The Cold War is absent from *The X-Files,* replaced by a more
> cosmic paranoia. The show reflects the end of the millen-
> nium, the flip side of the New Age. Beneath the soothing
> cover of incense, mantras, and Tibetan chants, rude beasts
> are awakening—Gnosticism reborn.
>
> —James Wolcott, " 'X' Factor"

> The most unsettling thing about *The X-Files* is how inviting,
> how lulling this slightly alien world looks. The curtain of
> what we accept as reality seems to have torn, allowing
> Mulder and Scully to search for meanings usually obscured.
> Week after week, this elegant twilight zone beckons like the
> land of the free and the home of the brave.
>
> —Charles Taylor, "Truth Decay: Sleuths After Reagan"

Given X . . .

Psychohistorians—those curious scholarly investigators who attempt to read (and understand) historical subjects as psychological
phenomena, motivated/driven/governed by unconscious factors—
have not paid all that much attention to popular culture. To do so,
however, might be highly productive and revealing. Why, for example,
does a successful television show "happen" when it does? Is there a
connection between the coming (and the going) of *Twin Peaks* in the

early 1990s and the Bush presidency?[1] Is *The X-Files* in some way a Clinton-era phenomenon, a product of psychohistorical factors operative in the mid-90s? Is this series—which, as Paula Vitaris has noted (17), is "akin to one of its own mutant characters, with its own eclectic genetic heritage," "part police procedural, part suspense thriller, part action adventure, part medical drama, part science fiction and part horror"[2]—a product of its cultural moment?[3]

In an insightful essay in *millennium pop*, Charles Taylor offers a discerning answer. Calling *The X-Files* "the most subversive show to hit American television since *Wiseguy*,"[4] Taylor links it to the contemporary cultural/political scene. *The X-Files* is a product of its time not because it holds a mirror to reality[5] but because it reflects the mindset of its era:

1. Because *Twin Peaks* will receive more than passing mention in the pages ahead, we should, in the interest of full disclosure, reveal our involvement with it: one of us (Lavery) edited a collection of essays on the series and two of us (Lavery and Hague) contributed essays to that volume.

2. *The X-Files*, James Wolcott observes more simply, is actually "television's first otherworldly procedural"(98).

3. Not surprisingly, Steven Daly and Nathaniel Wice's new reference book, *alt culture: An A-to-Z Guide to the '90s—Underground, Online, and Over-the-Counter* (now available on the World Wide Web at http://www.altculture.com/home/tml), offers an entry on *The X-Files*, which may serve (for uninitiates) as a basic overview of the series as a cultural phenomenon:

> Supernatural, UFO-minded detective series which debuted to little fanfare in fall 1993, then quietly built a fanatical following. Languidly paced, hazily lit, often open-ended, and dolorously soundtracked, *The X-Files* has prospered by ignoring many of TV's commonly held tenets. The protagonists, a charismatic pair of wayward FBI agents named Fox Mulder (David Duchovny) and Dana Scully (Gillian Anderson), view their paranormal beat with varying degrees of skepticism (he's open-minded, she's less so)—which provides one old TV reliable, Unresolved Sexual Tension. *The X-Files* was one of the first shows to flourish on the Internet: self-styled "X-Philes" accrue mountains of data about the show, discuss it live online, and write e-mail to the producers, who carefully note their comments (In 1995 Fox began sponsoring X-File conventions in attempts to create *Star Trek*-like longevity and fan following.) The show's progress from obscurity to cult favorite is in pointed contrast to that of 1990–91's ill-starred *Twin Peaks*.

4. "Subversive TV," Taylor notes, "doesn't announce itself. Usually, it occupies its appointed time slot, hovering on the verge of cancellation, unnoticed except for the few critics and viewers who gradually spread the word, while managing only to convey that this show is 'different.' " The genius of *Wiseguy*, Taylor continues, was its ability to realize "that, with Reagan and then Bush blurring the boundaries that separated political, criminal, and corporate life, American politics had become the stuff of genre fiction" (x).

5. "You can't say that the storylines resemble the realities of American political life," Taylor notes, and then proves his point, *reductio ad absurdum,* simply by describing

What links up the show to the zeitgeist is that Mulder and Scully are working to get out from under the most enduring legacy of the Reagan/Bush era: the way government, in the words of the Situationist philosopher Guy Debord, "[proclaims] that whatever it said was all there was." In other words, that the truth is irrelevant. *The X-Files* is about insisting on truth that runs counter to all ideas about how things are supposed to work, ideas so deeply ingrained that those in power can call them up to deny reality merely because it sounds crazy. Week after week, in the course of their investigations, Mulder and Scully find that behind their cases lies some secret government experiment or program kept from the public because it won't be able to "handle" the truth. (The Reagan years were scary because, though the facts were often out in the open, people "handled" the truth by denying it, rushing to defend Reagan as a nice guy. . . .) What makes Mulder and Scully so dangerous—and what makes them heroes—is that, having glimpsed a government that wants to rein them in, they choose to operate as if that government really worked the way it claims to. They're watching their backs as much as they're watching the skies.

If agents Fox Mulder and Dana Scully need eyes in the back as well as the top of their heads, so too do critics pondering the show's significance and seeking to read clearly its cultural and media meanings need special equipment. *The X-Files* is as complex and controversial a phenomenon as the medium of television has produced in many years; not only because the series has dared to suggest (with great seriousness) that the government of the United States is involved in a vast conspiracy with former Nazi and Japanese scientists to assist alien beings in performing experiments—including, perhaps, genetic hybridization!—on American citizens, it also has experimented—televisually, narratologically, semiotically—with the medium in innovative ways.

Writing this introduction during the third season of *The X-Files*, we have just learned the intriguing names of the next four episodes— "Avatar," "Quagmire," "Wet Wired," and "Talitha Cumi"—from Cliff

---

some episodes: "the show is about two FBI agents . . . who investigate paranormal phenomena that run to the likes of a genetic mutant serial killer who feeds on victims' livers, man-eating prehistoric insects reactivated by volcanic radiation, UFOs trying to rescue shipmates who've crash-landed behind NATO lines, a dead businessman using telekinesis from beyond the grave to expose his partner's illegal arms trading, and, in the best episode, a killer on death row . . . who claims he has the psychic ability to lead the agents to a serial killer and will do so if he's spared the gas chamber" (x).

Chen's episode guide on the Internet (http://bird.taponline.com/~cliff/). We are not certain what they portend nor how the year will end, but we assume and expect a dramatic close, something akin to the episodes that ended seasons one and two: "The Erlenmeyer Flask" (in which Mulder's mysterious ally Deep Throat was assassinated) and the cliffhanger "Anasazi" (in which Mulder was left seemingly dead in a buried and torched train car containing the bodies of aliens as well). We presume, of course, that the season finale will return to *The X-Files'* continuing "serial story" of alien abduction (including the abduction of Samantha, Mulder's sister) and government conspiracy. If *The X-Files* were canceled tomorrow (and it has, of course, already been renewed for a fourth season, the stars have been signed for five, and creator/producer Chris Carter and company regularly speak of a six-or seven-year run), there would still exist over 3,000 minutes and slightly over fifty hours of *X-Files* text—the equivalent of twenty-five feature length films[6]—for our consideration.

As we write, *The X-Files*—now about to go into syndication—has reached and perhaps passed the zenith of its popularity. It nevertheless continues to generate merchandise and to make news (assuming, that is, that media hype constitutes news), and this season it has emerged from cult status to become a mainstream hit and an "activated text" (John Fiske's term) with polysemic, intertextual relations. Topps comic book tie-ins,[7] a multitude of T-shirts (as many as twelve designs), phone cards, hats, posters, collector cards,[8] calendars, and coffee mugs are for sale. Two guidebooks to the series, Brian Lowry's *The Truth is Out There: The Official Guide to The X-Files* and N. E. Genge's *The Unofficial X-Files Companion,* both released in the fall of 1995, made it to the *USA Today* bestseller list for a time.[9] (Other guidebooks are on the way, including one focused exclusively on the third season, not to mention a reported collection of scholarly essays on the series by academics.) Not too long ago, Gillian Anderson won the Screen Actor's Guild

6. Carter and his cocreators like to think of each week's episode as being, in both complexity and quality, like a movie. See the indispensable special issue of *Cinefantastique* on the making of *The X-Files,* which includes behind-the-scenes reports (researched and written by Paula Vitaris) on everything from music to special effects to makeup to casting to post production.

7. The Topps Comics *X-Files* comic books are written by Stefan Petrucha and drawn by Charles Adlard. The first issue sold out at most comic retailers in one day.

8. From comic books, Topps branched into collectible trading cards, the first series consisting of seventy-two regular cards, ten super-premium "chase" cards, and a companion series of seventy-two chromium-etched cards. Topps touted these as "the most anticipated trading card series of the year."

9. Genge's book carries on its cover the following disclaimer: "This book is TOTALLY UNOFFICIAL and completely covert. It has not been prepared, approved, licensed, endorsed, or in any way authorized by any entity that created or produced THE X-FILES."

award for Best Actress in a Dramatic Series for her portrayal of Dana Scully. In the May 16, 1996 issue of *Rolling Stone,* Scully and Mulder appeared in fantasy-consummating photographs, partially unclothed and in bed together (including one photo in which Carter shares their bed and Scully smokes a postcoital cigarette), and Anderson and David Duchovny (the real-life Mulder), dressed in evening wear, recently graced the cover of a *TV Guide* that featured a fluffy story on "X Exposed: 20 Things You Need to Know About *The X-Files*." A CD collection of music from and inspired by the series *Songs in the Key of X,* is available, and an *X-Files* feature film is in the works (after season five). Fans flock to conventions, which have become as popular as those devoted to *Star Trek* and its various manifestations. Internet surfers are able to read about their favorite show on scores of World Wide Web pages.[10] (Interestingly, an October 1995 survey on the chaos.taylored.com usergroup identified a significant portion of fans as either students who plan within the year to enter graduate school, current graduate students, or postgraduate students in fields as diverse as bioengineering, law, literature, and physics.) At sites like alt.tv.x-files.creative, some fans offer additional and sometimes alternative fanfiction (and slash fanfiction)[11] adventures for Scully, Mulder, Assistant Director Skinner, Agent Krychek, etc.[12] Finally, an Associated Press story states that "*X-Files* [is] doing boffo in Japan," the first series since *Twin Peaks* to be a big hit in that country. (The series has been a big

---

10. At http://www cosc.brocku ca/~rw94an/x-files/expts1.html, obsessed fans can assess the seriousness of their addiction by taking Rene Weber's "X-Philic Test," which will force them to come clean on such questions as "Have you ever invited someone to watch *The X-Files* as a come-on?" "Does your login name have any mention of *The X-Files?*" and "Have you ever seen something in a store and thought to yourself, 'Mulder/Scully would like/wear/have that'?" In chapter 3 of this volume, Susan Clerc discusses in detail *The X-Files* on the Internet.

11. Slash fanfiction, in which ordinarily heterosexual (or sometimes asexual) characters are reimagined engaged in homosexual activity, first gained notoriety as a response to *Star Trek. ST* slash fanfiction regularly posits Mr. Spock and Captain Kirk as lovers. Slash fanfiction also exists for such shows as *Miami Vice, Quantum Leap,* and *Magnum P.I.* A 1992 article by Constance Penley first called attention to the phenomenon.

12. As Laura Akers has noted in an as-yet-unpublished essay entitled "Waking Up in Another Man's Bed: *The X-Files* and Slash Fanfiction," well over half of online *X-Files* fanfiction features a romantic relationship (in a variety of stages) between the two agents, while the remainder tends to describe their platonic relationship as supportive and mutually beneficial: However, *The X-Files* has generated "slash fanfiction" as well.

stories [that] contain elements which re-create, between men, the very kinds of imbalances which (according to Penley) women are trying to overcome by creating slash fanfiction. Some of these stories involve sexual partners whose disparate ranks within an organization create insurmountable obstacles to equality. *Discipline,* for example, depicts an encounter between Mulder and success in other foreign lands as well; one comprehensive WWW index of sites [http://www.tiac.net/users/bpaq/1.2/xfiles.html] lists national home pages for Finland, Switzerland, Australia, England, France, Ireland, Scotland, and Germany.)

As we write, however, *The X-Files* itself is in a stall. Over the last two months, we have had only a few new episodes to whet our appetite (since January, only eight new episodes have been broadcast, leaving us to make do with rebroadcasts of earlier episodes on many Fridays). A good time, it would seem, to reflect on the series—its origin, its nature, and its future direction.

At one level," Frank McConnell has observed, "*X-Files* has all the subtlety of those headlines in the tabloids ("Aliens Clone Hitler's Child") that you wish . . . you could peruse in full, if only the guy ahead of you had fourteen more frozen dinners to check out" (17). This tendency, too, gives the series the stamp of its cultural moment.[13]

Skinner, in which the Assistant Director paddles his subordinate to punish him for a procedural mistake. In other stories, the sexual interaction is distinctly sado-masochistic and occasionally non-consensual. In *Krychek* by Brenda Antrim, Mulder is suffering from amnesia, which allows Krychek to seduce the agent who can remember neither the nature of his true relationship nor his past sexual practices Very few stories actually involve two men constructing the kind of positive, mutually beneficial relationship which already exists between Mulder and Scully.

According to Penley, this phenomenon has a ready explanation—at least in regard to *Star Trek*—as Akers summarizes:

female fans were frustrated at the rather obvious sexism of the original *Star Trek's* otherwise quite utopian vision. These inequalities existed not only in the public contexts of the *Star Trek* universe (Uhura's inferior position within the bridge's hierarchy, the lack of any strong, permanent female characters in the series, etc.) but within the private sphere as well. The romantic relationships in the original series are marked by an almost universal imbalance of power between the two lovers being represented. Most of Kirk's women reinforce the stereotype of the helpless damsel-in-distress, embodying the kind of sexually submissive vapidness which many women in the 1960s were rebelling against in their personal and professional lives.

The appearance of *X-Files* slash fanfiction, Akers argues, forces a reexamination of Penley's thesis that such writing "is based on the female fan's desire to overcome the sexism which she perceives in the primary text. In the case of *The X-Files* . . . there is far less apparent sexism operating; indeed, from the point of view of many women who view the program, the character of Dana Scully provides a very positive role model."

13. With television rather than the check-out line in mind, Elaine Rapping has likewise noted this aspect of *The X-Files'* cultural moment; "Every night before prime

Foremost among its tabloidesque subjects, of course, is alien abduction. The phenomenon of abduction constitutes much more than simply a plot device or theme of *The X-Files*; rather, it has always been the show's very inspiration, instrumental to its genesis and perhaps the key ingredient in its growing complexity. Thus, for our purposes, abduction provides an important thread linking the show to the larger cultural/historical context.

Alien Abduction and the Zeitgeist

> "I found it fascinating to hear this," Carter said. "This man [Dr. John Mack of Harvard, author of *Abduction: Human Encounters with Aliens*] in the highest levels of academia and a scientist using rigorous scientific methods had come up with something quite astounding. So I thought that was a wonderful entry into explorations of the paranormal. And so I came up with Mulder and Scully, the FBI, and this fictional investigative unit called the X-files."
>
> —from Paula Vitaris, *"The X-Files"*

> "Roswell! Roswell!"
>
> —Blaine Faulkner, in
> "Jose Chung's *From Outer Space*"

It is certainly no accident that an image of a flying saucer begins the credits to *The X-Files*, an image that—like most purported photographs of flying disks—has a hazy, imprecise, even dreamy quality that underscores its possible unreliability. It is equally unsurprising that *The X-Files* uses the UFO abduction phenomenon as its basic serial narrative, because tales of alien abduction are unrivaled in contemporary America for their ability to combine the most terrifying aspects of paranormal experience with various cultural elements: science fiction; New Age obsessions with channeling, reincarnation, near-death experiences, and spiritual advancement; Byzantine government conspiracy stories, which include secret medical experiments upon unsuspecting citizens; and concerns with sexual abuse and genetic engineering. In the past fifteen years, public interest in UFOs has transformed itself

---

time (and lately even during prime time sometimes) we are served up a creepy mix of 'reality based' tabloids where UFOs, unnatural beings performing unnatural deeds, and other 'unexplained' phenomena are presented.... These syndicated offerings, with names like *Unsolved Mysteries* and *Believe It or Not*, feature 'dramatic reenactments' based on 'case files' of events so far beyond the pale of reason that they remain 'unsolved' and 'unexplained' by authorities" (35).

into a fascination with alien abduction, a shift in focus that intensely personalizes extraterrestrial encounters, bringing them down from the skies right into the bedroom.

Modern ufological history began on June 24, 1947, with civilian pilot Kenneth Arnold's sighting of several "flying saucers" (a term derived from his description of what he saw) while he flew his own plane near Mount Rainier. Curiously, the first alleged encounter with aliens happened only days after Arnold's experience. On July 2, 1947, a rancher named Mac Brazel found metal debris on his property in Roswell, New Mexico, and the most famous UFO/alien legend was born. Subsequently, the Roswell story has come to include the finding of a crashed disk, the recovery of dead (and one living) alien bodies, a massive governmental coverup that some believe extends until the present day, and President Truman's creation of the Majestic Twelve (MJ-12) on September 12, 1947, a top-secret group of "experts" brought together to investigate the events at Roswell.[14] In the early 1950s, a group of persons who called themselves "contactees," led by George Adamski, announced that they had been visited by benevolent aliens from Venus, "Space Brothers" who had arrived to warn earthlings about nuclear testing and to promote peace and love. However, it was the story told by Barney and Betty Hill that provided the model for the more sinister narratives that have come to dominate abduction literature. The Hills' alleged experience—being removed from their car one September night in 1961 and taken aboard a UFO, where they were subjected to a variety of medical procedures, including a gynecological examination and a sperm extraction—has become the paradigmatic UFO abduction. Both of them experienced "missing time"[15] and remembered their journey only after undergoing regression hypnosis. Many skeptics believe that John Fuller's book about the Hills' abduction, *The Interrupted Journey* (1966), and the made-for-TV film of the same name (starring James Earl Jones and Estelle Parsons) were themselves the key factors that created the images and events of a "typical" alien abduction that have become increasingly familiar to the public.

In the 1970s, New York artist Budd Hopkins began an exploration of UFO abduction cases using regression hypnosis, further refining the structure of alien abduction in *Missing Time: A Documented Study of UFO Abductions* (1981) and *Intruders: The Incredible Visitations at Copley Woods* (1987). In *Intruders*, Hopkins focuses on the genetic project of

14. The best historical treatment of UFO history is Jacobs, *The UFO Controversy in America;* a brief but pithy overview of alien contact and abduction can be found in Bader.
15. Hopkins describes "missing time" as a time lapse of approximately two hours, after which the abductee can consciously remember little or nothing of the experience.

the aliens, a project that includes the hybridizing of the human and alien species. His disciple, Temple University history professor David Jacobs, adopted Hopkins' notions about the alien genetic agenda and began to regress his own abductees. His *Secret Life: Firsthand Accounts of UFO Abductions* (1992) contains both transcriptions of these hypnosis sessions and the conclusions Jacobs has drawn from them, neatly summarized in a terse quotation from one of the abductees: "They're breeding us" (158). "We have been invaded," Jacobs portentously tells the reader. "It is not an occupation, but it is an invasion . . . a disturbing program of apparent exploitation of one species by another" (316). Women, however, are more exploited than men in Jacobs' alien scenario, for he tends to focus on the experience of female abductees, who "seem to have a larger number of more complex experiences" and whom he portrays as the "victims" of emotionless, indifferent, relentlessly efficient alien beings (15). Jacobs' aliens also have some definite sexual proclivities, including forcing humans (usually female) to become sexually aroused and to climax during the lengthy gynecological procedures carried out on board the spacecraft.

The growing tendency of abduction narratives to cast women as the victims of high-tech rapes and alien breeding programs has been reiterated by the writers of *The X-Files*, contradicting the show's usual undermining of traditional male-female stereotypes. Although there are some male abductees, among them Duane Barry in "Duane Barry" and Harold in "Jose Chung's *From Outer Space*," it is Scully and Samantha—not Mulder—who are supposedly abducted, and the eerie gathering of implanted abductees who greet Scully in "Nisei" are all women. (Female Mutual UFO Network members beware!)

The publication and popularity of Whitley Strieber's *Communion* (1987) made the alien face a household image and acquainted a much larger section of the public with alien behavior. *Communion* focuses on the bizarre and terrifying nature of the abduction experience and hints at a theme that Strieber develops at greater length in later books, the philosophical and spiritual nature of the experience.[16] In *Transformation*

16. Any serious study of the UFO/abduction phenomenon should begin with Jacques Vallee's 1969 *Passport to Magonia*. Vallee, a scientist trained in computers and astrophysics, began theorizing about the interdimensional and psychological aspects of extraterrestrial contact when UFO research was still firmly committed to a "nuts-and-bolts" approach, and his research into the correspondences between folklore and contemporary UFO narratives is the most provocative work that has been done in the field. Vallee's "alien contact trilogy" (*Dimensions* [1988], *Confrontations* [1990], and *Revelations* [1991]) provides the most knowledgeable and speculative exploration of the UFO/alien phenomenon that has yet been undertaken. Vallee's eminence as a UFO researcher became part of film history when Steven Spielberg cast him as a character in *Close Encounters of the Third Kind*, played by French film director François Truffaut.

(1988) and *Breakthrough: The Next Step* (1995), Strieber distances himself
from the Hopkins/Jacobs nuts-and-bolts approach to abduction, which
emphasizes the genetic machinations of the aliens and the physical
nature of the experience, and instead speculates about the psychical
dimension of what he renames "the visitor experience." Calling one of
his visitors "somebody from another meaning" (*Breakthrough,* 199),
Strieber describes the abduction experience as a "thoroughgoing revi-
sion of being" (280) that allows the abductee to understand "the indeterminacy that is at the core of the world" (284). "The challenge to the
worldview that is at the heart of the experience . . . is among the very
most shattering and profound assaults that a person can sustain," says
Strieber, adding that visitor contact allows the experiencer to "perceive
the world . . . in ranges and probabilities rather than definite, seemingly immutable structures" (118, 203). Thus, communion with an alien
reality is the catalyst for a soul journey, one that requires "a surrendered openness" on the part of the "experiencer" [17] (206).

Strieber's books greatly widened public interest in alien abduction,
but it was John Mack's *Abduction: Human Encounters with Aliens* (1994)
that created a highly-publicized controversy about the nature of the
abduction experience and about the treatment of abductees by thera-
pists and counselors. Mack, a professor of psychiatry at Harvard Medical School for thirty years and the 1977 Pulitzer Prize-winning author
of a biography of T. E. Lawrence, runs the Cambridge Program for
Extraordinary Experience Research (PEER) and cosponsored the 1992
Abduction Study Conference held at MIT. After being investigated for
more than a year by Harvard Medical School for allegedly "affirming
the delusions" of patients who believed themselves to be alien abductees, a special faculty committee decided that Mack could retain his
tenure and would not be censured for his conduct.[18] The publicity
surrounding Mack's problems at Harvard only increased interest in
Abduction, which Chris Carter claims to have been an important influence upon the development of *The X-Files* (see the epigraph above).
Mack, however, has little interest in the biological experiments and
government conspiracy stories that *The X-Files* has explored so
frequently; rather, he—like Strieber—is interested in the spiritual
dimension of the abduction experience. Although Mack does not deny
the work of Hopkins and Jacobs (*Abduction* is dedicated "To Budd

17. In "Jose Chung's *From Outer Space,*" Chung asks Scully whether she prefers the
term "experiencer" or "abductee."

18. For an informative summary of the Mack case, see Beam. The same issue of the
MUFON UFO Journal (Sept. 1995) also contains the General Accounting Office's official
report on the events at Roswell, New Mexico, in 1947.

Hopkins, who led the way," and Mack wrote a glowing foreword to Jacobs' *Secret Life*), he gently chides both men for having failed to come to terms with "the profound implications of the abduction phenomenon for the expansion of human consciousness, the opening of perception to realities beyond the manifest physical world and the necessity of changing our place in the cosmic order if the earth's living systems are to survive the human onslaught" (15). Mack's abductees, like those described by Strieber in *Breakthough*, undergo a transformation of consciousness that includes acquiring paranormal powers and an increased concern for planetary survival.

With John Mack, the connection between UFOs, alien abduction, and New Age spiritual and ecological awareness is made complete, a connection beautifully mocked by the "expanded consciousnesses" sported by the abductees at the conclusion of "Jose Chung's *From Outer Space.*" For Mack, the essence of the abduction experience is nothing less than an epistemological crisis in which abductees experience "ontological shock" (44) and require "another ontological paradigm" (389) after realizing the limitations of a chronological, physically-based interpretation of reality. He describes at length the changes in perception that abductees undergo and quotes patients who describe experiencing "dimensional merging" and "converging time frames" (404–5). ("Jose Chung" comically and also quite accurately depicts what UFO literature calls the "high strangeness level" of alien encounters and the bizarre discrepancies of the stories told by experiencers.) The loss of physical and psychological control described by abductees is "in some way 'designed' to bring about a kind of ego death from which spiritual growth and the expansion of consciousness may follow" (399); this new consciousness is one that perceives the falsity of the scientific/materialist worldview that is perpetuated by the intellectual and political elite of our culture. According to Mack, the UFO abduction experience radically undermines the assumptions of a culture that seeks to place human beings at the center of the universe, able to control and predict all events: "to a large degree, the scientific and government elite and the selected media that it controls . . . determine what we are to believe is real, for these monoliths are the principle beneficiaries of the dominant ideology" (410–11). The discrepancy between the message of human powerlessness that is communicated by the aliens and the pretenses to power and knowledge of governmental, academic, and media institutions makes up what Mack calls "the politics of ontology." [19] Mack's conspiracy theory, certainly more philosophically provocative and Foucauldian than the

19. See Mack's 1992 article "The Politics of Ontology."

more simplistic narratives played out in *The X-Files*, casts the U.S. government in the role of an ignorant and frightened onlooker to an alien agenda that it does not comprehend and cannot stop, a view shared by Strieber in *Breakthrough*. *The X-Files*, by contrast, with its recurrent themes of government pirating of alien technology and staging of phony UFO and abduction events, reiterates the dominant cultural ideology that privileges human power and control, reducing the entire alien phenomenon to a comical coverup of government misbehavior. Jacobs' warning that "They're breeding us" becomes (in "The Erlenmeyer Flask") "We're breeding them," a more comfortable and domesticated scenario than having aliens direct an intergalactic breeding program in which humans function as passive and mindless laboratory animals.

It is equally true, however, that *The X-Files* always refrains from passing any final judgment on the issue of alien abduction and seems to validate Mulder's state of "ontological shock" more frequently than Scully's scientific-reductionist theories. Curiously, Mulder—always the bridesmaid during abductions—undergoes the spiritual transformation that Mack describes so eloquently not during an encounter with aliens but during his near-death experience in "The Blessing Way." In fact, it seems that Chris Carter is as yet hesitant to explore the full epistemological implications that Mack says are the foundation of the abduction experience, a "reintegration of the self, an immersion or entrenchment into states and/or knowledge not previously accessible" (8) and the realization of "the total separation of the spirit and the physical world" (418). Mulder's intuitions and experiences are always open to question: did he actually witness his sister's abduction during "Little Green Men" or was she merely "taken" by human agency because her father preferred Mulder to her, as we learn in "Paper Clip"? Who abducted whom in "Jose Chung's *From Outer Space*"? By always suggesting a possible human agency behind ostensible extraterrestrial encounters and (in "Jose Chung") parodying the now-generic alien narrative, Carter leaves all his options open and avoids sending anyone into ontological shock.

This is not to say, however, that the alien abduction narrative in *The X-Files* is used to validate materialist assumptions about the nature of reality or to depict the U.S. (and world) government as an omnipotent, omniscient force. In fact, quite the opposite is true. For many viewers, their weekly encounter with the show is an unsettling, sometimes frightening experience that powerfully interrogates a consensus reality that excludes the paranormal. Mack's conclusion to *Abduction*, which speculates about the intention and effects of alien encounters, is equally applicable to *The X-Files*:

> The intelligence that appears to be at work here . . . is subtler, and its method is to invite, to remind, to permeate our culture from the bottom up as well as the top down, and to open our consciousness in a way that avoids a conclusion, that is different from the ways we traditionally require. It is an intelligence that provides enough evidence that something profoundly important is at work, but it does not offer the kinds of proof that would satisfy an exclusively empirical, rationalistic way of knowing. (421)

Like Mulder, many X-philes want to believe, but Carter refuses to provide him or them any easy answers.

Narrative Abduction: "Jose Chung's *From Outer Space*"

> Your scientists have yet to discover how neural networks create self-consciousness, let alone how the human brain processes two-dimensional retinal images into the three dimensional phenomenon known as perception. Yet you somehow brazenly declare that seeing is believing.
> —The Man in Black, in "Jose Chung's *From Outer Space*"

Judging by the reviews recorded in the *X-Files* Ratings and Reviews on the World Wide Web (http://wwwamaroq.com/x-files/3.20/review.html), the April 1996 episode "Jose Chung" was by no means a consensus hit. Michael T. MacDonell, for example, loved the episode:

> It doesn't get any better than this. My admiration for Chris Carter has increased 10-fold. There are a number of philosophies that hold that we are each three people. The person we are, the one we perceive ourselves to be, and the one perceived by others. In this story, Carter has managed to show us a kaleidoscope of the three views of all of the characters. Including the audience! At the same time, Carter has presented a story that is, in itself, most interesting and most thought provoking. Superb!

Andrea Lingenfelter, however, did not:

> This was the most disappointing *X-Files* I've ever seen. Maybe I didn't get it but it was poorly written and confusing. Even ones that I have not liked the story lines (like Gargoyles) displayed good writing and organization. What happened to this one. It was annoying to watch. I usually tape the show and watch it later. Had I been watching it on tape I would have turned it off—I've never done that to an X-Files!!!! If anyone can improve my view of this one, please let me know.

Another commentator, David Evans, noted that "Carter is walking a fine line here by spoofing his show (and its audience)," while Chuck Cruzan observed that the show "failed to involve me emotionally." Like other episodes written by Darin Morgan ("Humbug," "The War of the Coprophages," "Clyde Bruckman's Final Repose"), "Jose Chung" had a postmodern, *Twin Peaks*-ish air about it. It made some heavy demands on the viewer, the sort of demands seemingly designed for academics like ourselves, always on the lookout for television material difficult enough to present a true challenge to our encyclopedic vocabulary of allusions[20] and to our arsenal of critical methodologies (semiotic, psychoanalytical, narratological, reader/viewer-response, deconstructionist, etc.).[21]

For example, it would take a team of narratologists working overtime to unravel the complexities of the storyline of "Jose Chung."[22] After a precredit sequence depicting the abduction of two young lovers on a lonely road in Washington state, the episode proper takes place some considerable time later, as Scully tells her version of the subsequent investigation to noted author Jose Chung, who is writing a book about the abduction—a book to be entitled *From Outer Space*. Most of the remaining story unfolds within this frame tale, as Scully sits with her onscreen narratee[23] Chung, relating her take on recent events and answering his questions.

"The vast majority of television narrators," Sarah Kozloff has observed, "strive for neutrality and self-effacement, as if viewers are supposed to overlook the fact that the story is coming through a mediator and instead believe that they are looking in on reality" (83). "Jose Chung" is anything but majority television narrative. Scully's story is far from straightforward, for it incorporates numerous other "nested" narratives as well, some by highly unreliable narrators for whom she serves, within her own narrative, as an onscreen narratee. Nor is Scully herself completely honest in her narration; we know, for example, that she is acting as a censor (of Detective Manners' profane language), and

20. The allusions in "Jose Chung" range from the esoteric (Alex Trebek) to the exoteric (the name of the third alien, who interrupts the gray aliens about to abduct Chrissy and Harold in the precredit sequence, is, we later learn, "Lord Kimbote," the name of an obscure character in Vladimir Nabokov's *Pale Fire* [1962]). None of the three of us, all English professors, was able to make the latter identification, which we owe to an *X-Files* discussion group.

21. For an excellent overview of these and other approaches to television study, see the essays collected in Robert C Allen's *Channels of Discourse, Reassembled*.

22. See Kozloff (in *Channels of Discourse*) for a comprehensive examination of narratological interpretations of TV.

23. A "narratee" is anyone to whom a story is told or narrated A television anchor, for example, serves as a narratee for a reporter in the field; a talk-show host becomes a narratee for his or her guests.

thus we may wonder if she might be giving her own subjective spin to other matters as well.

Sitting in Mulder's office (the signature "I Want to Believe" poster visible in the background), Scully tells Chung of the results of their interrogation of Harold and Chrissy, the abductees. As Chrissy tells her story under hypnosis, we witness in her mindscreen her encounter on board the alien spaceship with her abductors. After Chrissy is hypnotized a second time, however, we see that her memories may have been implanted by Air Force officials to cover her real abduction by the government. Later, when utility company lineman Rocky Crickerson tells Mulder and Scully the bizarre story of the visitation of the Men in Black and his eyewitnessing of the abduction of Chrissy and Harold, he is likewise a possibly (probably) unreliable narrator. His version of the abduction and of his encounter with Lord Kimbote, though, is not the product of his mindscreen. It takes place instead in Mulder's own mindscreen as he reads Crickerson's manuscript aloud to Scully (who is narrating his reading to Chung in the episode's outermost frame). In this scene, then, Crickerson is the narrator (via his manuscript); Mulder is the primary narratee (whose slowing pace of his reading of Crickerson's account signals us that he has come to doubt its veracity); and Scully is a secondary narratee (who lets us know by her looks of disbelief—especially her rolling eyes and dubious stare—that she, too, is incredulous). The account offered by Blaine Faulkner, a young man obsessed with UFOs (who hopes to be abducted, he explains, so he won't have to look for a job), of his discovery of an alien in the woods is even more fully unreliable. This time, Blaine tells his story to Chung, who relates it, in turn, to Scully. In Blaine's eyes, the show's heroes become "men in black": Scully is suspected of being a man masquerading as a woman, and Mulder appears to be a violent and threatening "mandroid."

In subsequent scenes, the narrative becomes even more convoluted. For example, Scully relates (to Chung) Mulder's version of a conversation at a local diner with Lieutenant Schafer, the Air Force pilot of a flying saucer (and gray alien in disguise). In this account, Mulder, of course, serves as onscreen narratee to Schafer's bizarre ramblings. The latter insists that, even though he has pretended to be a (gray) alien charged with abducting individuals like Harold and Chrissy for obscure "covert intelligence operations," he is absolutely certain that he has himself been abducted. He asks Mulder, "Have you ever flown a flying saucer? Afterwards, sex seems trite." He expresses grave doubts about the existence of the food on his plate and even of Mulder himself. Finally, Schafer knows the name of Lord Kimbote, who we had earlier been led to believe was the lunatic raving of Rocky Crickerson. Chung calls this account immediately into question, however, by relating another version of the event as told to him by the cook, one in which no pilot is present.

In the episode's closing scenes, two more narrative layers are added on. Mulder arrives—presumably after Scully's departure—at Chung's to plead with him not to write his book. His appeal is futile, however, and in the epilogue Chung reads the final words of *From Outer Space* (in which Scully and Mulder have both been given fictional names) as his words come visually alive before us. In an *American Graffiti*-style "where are they now?" recapitulation, we see: Blaine Faulkner at his new job as a utility company lineman; Rocky Crickerson leading a New Age group dedicated to the belief that beings of higher consciousness exist at the earth's core; Scully and Mulder getting on with their lives (Scully is reading Chung's book; Mulder, described by Chung as "a ticking timebomb of insanity," is lying alone in bed watching a show about Bigfoot); and Chrissy at work as an environmental/peace activist, fulfilling the imperative given her during her "abduction" to help to save the planet.

It is not only the episode's complex narrative structure, however, that makes it both rich and difficult. "Jose Chung's *From Outer Space*" is a very postmodern text, ripe with what Eco has called the weight of "the already said," opulently intertextual and self-referential, studded with allusion upon illusion. An attentive, cultish watcher would take pride in noting at least the following.

• The episode's opening image is a *Star Wars* homage slow tracking shot of the underbelly of a star cruiser that turns out to be in reality the bottom of the lift basket of a utility company line repair truck.

• The equation of electric company linemen with UFOs is an allusion to *Close Encounters of the Third Kind*, in which Roy Neary (Richard Dreyfuss) experiences his Third Encounter while out on assignment during a blackout. Moreover, in the aforementioned scene in the diner between Lieutenant Schafer and Mulder, the former is eating, and playing with, his mashed potatoes, whose ultimate metaphysical reality he questions to his companion. Illusion or not, the potatoes are another direct allusion to *Close Encounters of the Third Kind*, in which, in a famous scene, Neary sculpts a replica of the Devil Tower's rendezvous site from his spuds.

• The Washington county where the abduction takes place, Klass, has the same name as a leading UFO Doubting Thomas, author Philip Klass (a.k.a. science fiction writer William Tenn).

• The appearance of Alex Trebek, the host of the popular television quiz show *Jeopardy*, constitutes an inside joke: David Duchovny (Fox Mulder) had actually appeared in a segment of "Celebrity *Jeopardy*," losing to novelist Stephen King because of his inability to supply the question "What is *Breakfast at Tiffany's?*" to a "final jeopardy" answer. Earlier in the episode, Scully is, of course, seen reading Capote's novel.

• In a scene in a local diner that may or may not be illusory, Mulder momentarily becomes Agent Cooper of *Twin Peaks*, obsessed with pie (sweet potato, though, not cherry).

• A very profane local police detective bears the same name— Manners—as one of the series' chief creative forces, writer/producer/ director Kim Manners.[24]

• A character (Blaine Faulkner) wears a *Space: Above and Beyond* T-shirt, product-placement for another Fox Network show created by former *X-Files* writers/producers Glen Morgan (brother of "Jose Chung" author Darin Morgan) and James Wong.[25]

• A videotaped autopsy (performed by Scully) on a supposed alien, bears an uncanny resemblance in its visual style to the infamous *Alien Autopsy* shown on Fox a year ago. (The host for the autopsy's screening is The Stupendous Yappi, the dubious psychic we had first met in "Clyde Bruckman's Final Repose.")

• When Scully completes her narration of the events to Jose Chung, she admits that it "probably doesn't have the sense of closure you want, but it has more than our other cases"—a very self-conscious allusion to/defense of the often-complained-about tendency of Mulder's and Scully's cases (and every *X-Files* episode) to end enigmatically and without full resolution.[26]

24. As has often been noted, television is a "producer's medium," in which executive producers/creators like Steven Bochco or David Lynch are regularly given auteurist credit for their work even long after their actual input may have declined; moreover, the usually invisible day-to-day, hands-on producers, directors, and writers often go without acknowledgment. Kim Manners epitomizes such anonymity Manners, who joined *The X-Files* in its second season, had earlier in his career played similarly key roles in such series as *Simon and Simon* and *Baywatch*, both of which would seem to have little or nothing in common with Chris Carter's creation, and yet Manners has now become a very important, trusted team player in *The X-Files*.

25. This was not the first time that *The X-Files* plugged other Fox programs; Fox produced other, "nonfiction" programs on UFOs and paranormal phenomena, for which *The X-Files* served, in effect, as a promo; prior to the telecast of Fox's first Super Bowl (in January 1996), not surprisingly the aptly named "Fox" Mulder demonstrated a great interest in football. (For this insight, we are indebted to an unpublished essay entitled "Fox and the Scene of Writing" by Joseph Milutis of the University of Wisconsin.)

26. Responding to the complaint of several others (*X-Files* Ratings and Reviews on the World Wide Web) about lack of closure in "Jose Chung" (and *The X-Files* generally), Judy Stevenson writes, "What I can't figure out is why so many people are frustrated by the lack of a neat, tidy ending after all this time. It's so you can draw your own conclusions for bleep sake." Charles Taylor likewise defends the series' perpetual absence of resolution. "What makes the show truly frightening is that it doesn't explain away any of its horror. . . . Watching each episode is like watching a photo that comes

For some Internet commentators, "Jose Chung" represents a turning point for the series. David Evans observes, "Watching *X-Files* used to make me lock the doors at night. Now it makes me chuckle at odd moments (Alex Trebeck !??!?)." And Chris Chia, while ready to praise "Chris Carter & company's willingness to spoof/parody the series and its protagonists," admits that the episode nevertheless poses a real problem: "I don't think I can ever watch another UFO-related episode with a straight face."

"David Lynch wrecked the trance of *Twin Peaks*," James Wolcott observed during *The X-Files'* first season, "when he abandoned all interest in even a quaint semblance of normality and began to strobe the screen in a fit of expressionism" (99). No doubt a few X-Philes are afraid (perhaps very afraid) that Carter et al. are about to go down the same path.[27]

Thomas Schatz has delineated a life cycle for movie genres. A genre, he shows, routinely passes through four stages:

> an *experimental* stage, during which its conventions are isolated and established, a *classic* stage, in which the conventions reach their "equilibrium" and are mutually understood by artist and audience, an age of *refinement*, during which certain formal and stylistic details embellish the form, and finally a *baroque* (or "mannerist," or "self-reflexive") stage, when the form and its establishments are accented to the point where they "themselves become the 'substance' or 'content' of the work. (37–38)

Does a television series, regardless of genre, undergo over the course of its history a similar metamorphosis? Many questions would need to be answered to establish the validity of that hypothesis. (For example, was not a series like *Twin Peaks* born "baroque"?) We present the hypothesis here only for its illustrative value in considering the progress of *X-Files* evolution. Certainly, a terribly self-conscious, cannibalistic episode like "Jose Chung" seems to indicate a move to Schatz's baroque stage. Another explanation is possible, however: Perhaps *The X-Files* is increasingly self-reflexive not out of any genre-driven or

---

up in a chemical bath and suddenly goes bad; what seemed crystal clear clouds over, leaving us to grasp at what we thought we saw."

27. Before "Jose Chung," no less an *X-Files* authority than Paula Vitaris had concluded, admiringly, that the series "plays it straight—its tone is without irony—and in so doing it has created a world where the creatures and the conspirators are truly to be feared" (17).

television programming-dictated desire/inclination to subvert itself but because the evolution of consciousness has now brought the human mind, as it grapples with increasingly alien realities, to the epistemological equivalent of Schatz's baroque stage.

After Scully finishes her narrative in "Jose Chung," the story picks up at an unspecified moment in the future. Mulder appears at Chung's office and asks to see him (he had previously been unwilling to speak with the author and therefore had not contributed firsthand to the narrative). Noting that many well-meaning individuals who seek to tell of their real UFO/abduction experiences appear to be crazy when they do so, he pleads with Chung not to publish the book.

> You'll perform a disservice to a field of inquiry that has always strug-
> gled for respectability. You're a gifted writer but no amount of talent
> could describe the events that occurred in any realistic vein because
> they deal with alternative realities that we're not yet able to compre-
> hend, and when presented in the wrong way, in the wrong context,
> the incidents and the people involved in them can appear foolish, if
> not downright psychotic.

Chung denies his request and asks Mulder himself to finally go on the record—to explain exactly what did happen. "How the hell should I know?" Mulder responds.

Though Chung's book is not uncritical (as we learn when he reads its conclusion in the episode's final scene), it is no more a disservice to our understanding of the UFO/abduction phenomenon than is "Jose Chung's *From Outer Space*" itself. Indeed, Mulder's plea not to ridicule is, in a sense, a self-referential one that could have been made (and, according to some of the talk on the Internet, should have been made) to Carter and company. At the same time, it also constitutes a metade-fense that lifts the continuing *X-Files'* serial story of abduction and conspiracy—a metastory in which "Jose Chung" stands as a vital part —to a higher, more epistemological plane. (After all, as we learn in Chrissy's second hypnotism, the government has no more idea of what happened in Klass County, Washington, than Scully, Mulder, or Chung do.) The Man in Black's admonition to Rocky (see the epigraph to this section) to recall that the UFO mystery is not the only mystery—that we are still completely in the dark about such minor matters as the nature of self-consciousness and the construction of reality in percep-tion—articulated ingeniously one of *The X-Files'* always implicit themes. In "Jose Chung," this "baroque" theme takes center stage, and it will probably shadow all future episodes as they explore "alternative realities that we're not yet able to comprehend." If this self-reflexive awareness makes *The X-Files* increasingly baroque, if it leads to the series' accentuation of its own "form and its embellishments . . . to the point where they themselves become the 'substance' or 'content' of the work," such a development should not surprise us, for philosophy, psychology, quantum physics, anthropology, cosmology, and so on are now similarly baroque. The surprise lies in our encounter with such an ultimate dilemma on Friday night on the Fox Network.[28]

Preview of Coming Attractions

The essays which follow seek to read/interpret *The X-Files* from a variety of perspectives. We offer here only a brief "tease"/gloss on each as a preliminary, umbrella guide to your perusal of the book's contents.

• In "Rewriting Popularity: The Cult *Files,*" **Jimmie L. Reeves** of Texas Tech University and **Mark C. Rodgers,** and **Michael Epstein,** each of the University of Michigan, place *The X-Files* in its proper television context, seeking to understand the development of "cult TV" generally and *The X-Files* in particular as a manifestation of a major sea change in the nature of American mass communication.

• As the *alt. culture* entry cited above notes, *The X-Files* was "one of the first shows to flourish on the Internet," and in "DDEB, GATB, MPPB, and Ratboy: *The X-Files'* Media Fandom, Online and Off," **Susan J. Clerc** of Bowling Green State University examines how and why fans of the series used this new communication medium to enhance their viewing pleasure.

• **Allison Graham** of University of Memphis finds *The X-Files* a splicing together of 1970s conspiracy films and the science fiction films of the '50s in her " 'Are You Now or Have You Ever Been?': Conspiracy Theory and *The X-Files,*" an essay which situates the series in a wide cultural, political, and psychological context. Mulder and Scully and their agency superiors are the most recent in a long line of FBI agent characters in popular culture.

• The contribution of **Michele Malach** (Fort Lewis College), " 'I Want to Believe . . . in the FBI': The Special Agent and *The X-Files,*" examines the series as part of a continuing cultural dialogue about law and order, freedom and safety, right and wrong, truth and falsity.

• Folklorist and independent scholar **Leslie Jones** offers a comprehensive examination of *The X-Files'* indebted to folkloric and mythic sources in " 'Last Week We Had an Omen': The Mythological *X-Files.*"

---

28. However, perhaps it should not surprise us. As Frank McConnell notes (with *The X-Files* in mind), "the mass-cult imagination, as history teaches us, is a much more fertile soil for art than the hydroponic gardens of 'refined' taste" (15).

- **Rhonda Wilcox** (Gordon College) and **J. P. Williams** (Georgia Southern College) carefully probe Scully and Mulder's gender roles and delineate the many ways in which the series represents a departure from television stereotypes in " 'What to You Think?' *The X-Files, Liminality, and Gender Pleasure.*"

- **Lisa Parks** of the University of Wisconsin offers a much less favorable feminist interpretation of the series, grounded in Donna Haraway's theory of the female as cyborg, in "Special Agent or Monstrosity?: Finding the Feminine in *The X-Files.*"

- In "How to Talk the Unknown into Existence: An Exercise in X-Filology," **Alec McHoul** of Murdoch University, Australia, offers a "microlinguistic" analysis of the way language is used in this series devoted to the exploration of the unknowable.

- In "The Rebirth of the Clinic: The Body as Alien in *The X-Files,*" **Linda Badley,** of Middle Tennessee State University, drawing on sources as diverse as Foucault, Haraway, Sartre, and Todorov, examines the series' culturally self-conscious, postmodern adaptation/adoption of motifs of body invasion, mutation, and vampirism from modern horror-sci-fi film.

- Utilizing Jacques Lacan's fusion of psychoanalysis and semiotic/structuralist methods, **Elizabeth B. Kubek** of Syracuse University presents a far-reaching, all-inclusive Lacanian reading of the series in " 'You Only Expose Your Father': The Imaginary, Voyeurism, and the Symbolic Order in *The X-Files.*"

Perhaps appropriately, the essays in this volume—including this one—offer no more closure than a typical *X-Files* episode. No doubt they raise as many questions as they answer. Our hope is that they nonetheless enrich your present and future experience of the series in all its complexity.

2

Rewriting Popularity

THE CULT *FILES*

Jimmie L. Reeves, Mark C. Rodgers, and Michael Epstein

> I also know that your publishing house is owned by Warden-White, Inc., a subsidiary of McDougall-Kessler, which makes me suspect a covert agenda on the behalf of the military-industrial-entertainment complex.
>
> —Mulder, in "Jose Chung's *From Outer Space*"

In our chart of the family tree of cult TV, diehard supporters of the Dallas Cowboys and rabid followers of the World Wrestling Federation are positioned as their beer-swilling uncles. Their homebound aunts organize weekday routines around the intrigues of *Days of Our Lives* or *All My Children*. Rush Limbaugh's Ditto Heads and Jerry Garcia's Dead Heads are their first cousins. Offspring of the Trekkie clan, their siblings include disciples of *Twin Peaks, Mystery Science Theater 3000,* and *Beavis and Butthead*. Because of their fondness for Fox's *The X-Files*, they call themselves "X-Philes"—and because of their high profile on the express lane of the information superhighway, they have generated a great deal of media attention, putting stars Gillian Anderson (Dana Scully) and David Duchovny (Fox Mulder) on the covers of *People, TV Guide,* and a host of other magazines that hope to cash in on the cult.

There is, indeed, a lot of cash in them thar *Files*/Philes. Directly connecting the marketing of *X-Files* paraphernalia to the *Star Trek* gold rush, *People* observes that "Like *Star Trek, X-Files* has spawned novels, comic books, T-shirts (emblazoned with the show's motto, The Truth

Is Out There), coffee mugs and Internet bulletin boards" (Gliatto and
Tomashoff, 74). Moreover, in reporting the franchising frenzy, the popular press often describes the consumers of *X-Files* merchandise in
predatory terms. For instance, *TV Guide* opens its cover story on "20
Things You Need to Know about The X-Files" with a rather unflat-
tering comparison: "Fans of *The X-Files* crave information the way
mutant flukes crave human flesh" (Nollinger, 18). In the tradition of
William Shatner's famous "get a life" renunciation of Trekkies on *Saturday Night Live*, Duchovny publicly keeps his distance from these
voracious creatures who hunger for his image, if not his flesh. As item
10 of the *TV Guide* article reports, Duchovny believes that the "Internet
enthusiasts have a tendency to sometimes get a little out of control":
"During one discussion, perplexed fans tried to figure out why Scully
never adjusts the car seat after the much taller Mulder has been driv-
ing. 'That was probably the last time I ever looked at the Internet,
because that kind of frightened me,' Duchovny says. 'I didn't want
to see myself scrutinized in such a fashion.' " However, creator and
executive producer Chris Carter is more honest—or at least more self-
conscious—about his own entanglement in promoting X-mania. In a
bit of soul-searching that appears in the liner notes of *Songs in the Key
of X*, Carter reverses the predator/prey roles assigned by *TV Guide*:
"Here I go searching for context and corollary, reason and rationale—
writer's crampons. Why an '*X-Files*' record, album, or CD? Why indeed. Have we succumbed to the swinish flu of grubbing moneymak-
ers who see dollar signs like a fever dream, an endless sea of swag
stamped with the eponymous 'X'; the spiders to the flies of the New
World Wide Web Order, for whom mammon is its own impenetrable
logic, a one-word syllogism?"
    As authors of this article, we have asked ourselves the same ques-
tion, and arrived at roughly the same "Yes, but" answer. Yes, we too
are implicated, like it or not, in exploiting the *X-Files* phenomenon;
but, like Carter, we evade feelings of guilt by thinking of ourselves as
altruistic arachnoids who are on a mission to make the snares of the
web—and their attachments to larger entrapments—visible to the
flies. Weaving our own account of cult TV's significance around Carter's acknowledgment that "mammon" is the "impenetrable logic"
underlying this peculiar programming trend, we enlist the *Star Trek*/
X-Files genealogy to explore the political and textual economies of
what Agent Mulder has described as the "military-industrial-
entertainment complex." Without endorsing Mulderesque conspiracy
theories involving ominous Men in Black or sinister chain-smoking
operatives, we want to make it clear that the current prominence of
cult TV is still no harmless freak show in the carnival of American
popular culture. Instead, it is a phenomenon that speaks powerfully of

a divisive system of taste distinctions that both supports and masks the radical inequities of the age by dividing the audience into "insiders" and "outsiders."

In spinning out the convolutions of our argument, we treat the emergence of cult TV as one of the chief manifestations of the most extreme shift the American mass communication "complex" has experienced since the 1950s (when broadcast television displaced the movies as the culture's central narrative medium). For purposes of clarity, we describe this shift as the move from TV I to TV II (terms explained in more detail below).[1] Much more than a mere reflection of socioeconomic conditions, this transformation has been an active agent in the shaping and segmenting of contemporary realities—that is, both a response to and a generative force behind a tangled set of larger economic, technological, political, artistic, and societal developments:

• The drift from the mass marketing of the "Fordist" manufacturing economy to the niche marketing of the "post-Fordist" service economy;[2]
• The diminishing role of broadcasting after the diffusion of a host of new communication technologies;
• The displacement of the cold war order by New World Disorder;
• The dismemberment of the New Deal coalition and the triumph of Reaganism's politics of division;
• The postmodern turn in everything from architecture to advertising;
• The worsening fragmentation of American society into special-interest groups, single-issue groups, and various types of racial, ethnic, sexual, generational, lifestyle, taste, fringe, and backlash formations.

In the current prominence of "cult TV," then, we see evidence of a rewriting of popularity that expresses the deterritorializations and reterritorializations of the decline of television's consensus culture and the weakening of its unifying influences.

Fordism, TV I, and *Star Trek*

Yet, as we also hope to demonstrate, *The X-Files* differs from most other cult television shows in that it represents a step back toward the inclusiveness of TV I. A shorthand term for the broadcasting system that emerged in the 1950s, triumphed in the 1960s, and was slowly displaced in the 1970s, the term "TV I" refers to what has also been

1. The term "TV II" was first used by industry analysts in the mid 1980s. See Behrens, 8–10.
2. For a discussion of Fordism and post-Fordism, see Reeves and Campbell, 84–90.

studied as "network era television." A period dominated by a three-corporation oligopoly, TV I played a central ideological role in promoting the ethic of consumption, naturalizing the nuclear family ideal, selling suburbanization, sustaining cold war paranoia, publicizing the Civil Rights movement, and managing social upheaval. Put another way, TV I was one of the chief products and producers of Fordism—a "rigid" economic order (named for Henry Ford) that drove the general prosperity of the postwar boom through an expansive manufacturing economy of assembly-line production and mass consumption.

As an expression of Fordism, television popularity during this period was defined in terms of audience size as measured in the brute numbers of ratings and shares. Consequently, the prime-time schedule was dominated by Westerns, situation comedies, and crime shows, all designed to attract the largest possible undifferentiated viewership. Of course, many have condemned programming during TV I as "mass culture" or a "vast wasteland," but, whatever its faults, the "least objectionable programming" (or more cynically, "lowest common denominator") philosophy made sense—and also astounding profits—for the three major networks. At the same time, the definition of popularity underlying this programming philosophy resulted in the prime-time schedule evolving into a nightly showcase for what David Thorburn calls "consensus narrative," stories that attempt to speak for, and to, the core values of American culture (167–68).

Star Trek, like the Super Bowl, the *Tonight Show,* and *60 Minutes,* is a relic of TV I. Unlike these other cultural institutions, however, *Star Trek* was initially considered to be an "unpopular" failure by its home network. NBC premiered *Star Trek* on September 8, 1966, and nationwide broadcasts of the original network episodes were not able to attract large (enough) audiences: in its initial run of two and one-half seasons, *Star Trek* never made it into the top twenty highest-rated shows and frequently finished last in its timeslot against ABC's and CBS's offerings (Alexander, 366). In retrospect, though, as the harbinger of a radically new type of popularity—a type of popularity that would govern television programming in the postnetwork era—*Star Trek* is significant for three related reasons: its prototype status in the history of cult TV; the fanaticism of its avid followers; and its place in the syndication of revolution of the 1970s.

What separated *Star Trek* from its peers and its predecessors and even now establishes it as classic cult TV is audience engagement. Here, we offer a corollary to Stuart Hall's theory of "preferred reading" (which identifies three broad reading strategies—dominant, negotiated, and oppositional) to help us distinguish cult TV from normal programming. According to our scheme, nearly all entertainment programs attract three different kinds of viewers who can be categorized in terms of engagement: casual viewers, devoted viewers, and avid fans.

• Casual viewers will attend to a show if they happen to be watching TV but do not experience the show as a "special event." For the casual viewer, the show is part of the flow of television and not something that requires rapt attention nor prompts adjustments in the viewer's schedule of activities in order to tune in. Because of the limited range of viewing options during TV I, casual viewing was, probably, the dominant type of engagement with prime-time programming in the 1950s and 1960s.

• Devoted viewers will make arrangements to watch every episode of their favorite show. For the devoted viewer, a favorite show is a "special event" that disrupts the flow of television and inspires more intense levels of identification and attention than typical television fare. However, though the devoted viewer may read occasional articles about the show or talk about it with their friends, their involvement with the show falls short of fanaticism. Because of the drastically expanded range of viewing options, devoted viewing is probably more common now than in the network era. In fact, it could be argued that the serialization of prime time (as exemplified by shows like *Dallas, Hill Street Blues,* and *ER*) is at least partially attributable to the heightened competition for viewer attention in the TV II era—a competition that has encouraged the networks to develop programming forms that inspire devoted rather than casual engagement.

• Avid fans will not only take special pains to watch every episode of the show but, today, will tape the episodes so that they can review them or even archive them. The show is not only a special event but also a major source of self-definition, a kind of quasi-religious experience. Avid fans enthusiastically purchase or consume ancillary texts related to the program and often join interpretive communities that have formed around the show, such as fan clubs, online discussion groups, and APAs (American Press Association). Though the availability of such groups in cyberspace has made the recruitment process somewhat easier, it is still difficult for a new show to build "cult" interpretive communities from scratch. Therefore, most new shows hoping to cultivate a cult following tend to appeal to existing interpretive communities, particularly the large umbrella of sci-fi fandom which has in place an infrastructure of fanzines, newsgroups, and conventions. In TV I, daytime serials and professional sports programming may be considered as antecedents to cult television in that they cultivated the kind of enthusiastic viewer engagement that is characteristic of the avid fan.

Virtually every TV show has some viewers in each of the three engagement categories; somewhere out there, someone has every episode of *Full House* on tape. What distinguishes cult shows from typical fare is that a relatively large percentage of the viewers are avid fans and that these fans have relatively high visibility compared to the avid fans of other shows. Still, although the proportion of avid fans in the audience of a show like *The X-Files* is much higher than for a mass hit like *Friends,* avid fans alone would represent a relatively small audience. Somewhere around 15 million households watch *The X-Files* every week; clearly, nowhere near this many people are engaging in active fandom.

Given the economics of TV I, *Star Trek* probably would not have survived its first season had it not been for the fanaticism of its viewership, a fanaticism that was virtually unknown to network executives at the time (save for the devoted followings of nonprime fare such as NFL football and daytime serials). Disenchanted by its lackluster ratings, NBC executives threatened to cancel the show after the first and second seasons, sought creative changes that would broaden the appeal of the show, and ultimately relegated the series to the Siberia of slots on the prime-time schedule, Fridays at 10 P.M. *Star Trek*'s highest-rated rivals in the 1966 and 1967 seasons, *Bonanza* and *The Andy Griffith Show,* presented nostalgic visions of the American way of life that emphasized familiarity rather than novelty. In a time when "watching TV" was a familial ritual that meant locking into the programming routines of ABC, NBC, or CBS, these hit shows promised comfort to casual and devoted viewers, relief from the stress, worries, and turmoil of the Atomic Age, and "good, wholesome entertainment." In contrast, by emphasizing novelty rather than familiarity and hailing the audience as a "bold" new experience, *Star Trek* delivered a challenging vision that embraced change and celebrated the future rather than the past. Providing meanings and pleasures not normally associated with watching television, this vision rewarded a level of audience engagement and identification that transcended casual viewing.

As early as spring 1967, before *Star Trek* had completed its first season, it was becoming clear to both cast and crew that the series had developed a fan base unlike that of other, more highly rated prime-time shows. The first indication that there was something strikingly different about the *Star Trek* audience was the volume of mail that arrived at the studio after each episode aired (Nichols, 188). The deluge —which, according to some cast members, was measured in rooms full of mail—seemed far out of proportion to the total estimated number of viewers reported by Nielsen each week (Nichols, 162; Takei, 247). In addition to the typical fan requests for photos and autographs, a sizable number of the first generation of *Star Trek* fans wrote longer letters that detailed their opinions, suggestions, complaints, and questions about a character, an episode, or the direction of the show in general.

This extraordinary audience engagement quickly caught the attention of the show's creator, Gene Roddenberry. As recently published
letters from the Roddenberry archives suggest, Roddenberry took fan
letters seriously and made a practice of responding to the more salient
comments of fans and critics alike (see e.g. Alexander, 307–8). Roddenberry was impressed by the caliber of the people who were writing
what he considered the best letters, many of whom were college students, professionals, and scientists. As NBC's pressure to cancel the
series grew more intense, Roddenberry turned to a small cadre of these
discriminating fans in order to save his brainchild. While keeping his
distance publicly, *Star Trek*'s creator carried out a covert strategy of
inviting fan leaders to the studio, underwriting some of the costs of
fan club activities, orchestrating a letter-writing campaign to the network, and even appearing incognito at fan pickets of NBC (Alexander,
301–14; Takei, 264). In the short term, the strategy resulted in the series
being renewed for a second season; in the long term, even though the
next year Roddenberry lost the battle to keep his show on the air, he
ultimately won the war by galvanizing fan demand for future incarnations of *Star Trek*.

United in their affinity for the *Star Trek* universe and buoyed by
the apparent impact they had on Roddenberry and NBC, the loyal
Trek fans of the late 1960s continued to stay active even after the series
closed production. Fan groups founded "zines" devoted to fan-
authored *Star Trek* stories, convened fan meetings that would later be
called conventions, and continued to petition the television establishment to revive the series. Active fan interest helped speed *Star Trek*
reruns into syndication within months of cancellation, notwithstand-
ing the show's short run of 79 episodes (Alexander, 377). By December
1971, *Star Trek* was airing in more than one hundred local television
markets in the United States and seventy more internationally (Beerman, 1, 69). By 1977, after eight years in syndication, *Star Trek* was
aired in 134 American markets and 131 overseas, was aired 308 times
a week, and was the number one offnetwork show for men ages 18–
49 (Alexander, 447). In daily reruns, Roddenberry's "Wagon Train of
the stars" finally got the exposure it needed to attract a huge number
of new viewers, many of whom found it easy and appealing to become
active participants in the established fan culture as "Trekkies" or
"Trekkers." The result was that *Star Trek* fandom became even more
vibrant and pervasive (see e.g. Jenkins 19–22, 185–86, 193–94). In
short, the extraordinary audience engagement generated by *Star Trek*
in the 1960s had been transformed into a full-fledged cult by the mid-
1970s—and in the process, Paramount became the preeminent syndi-
cator in the industry, completely altering the marketing of structure
for offnetwork series television and ushering in a new economics of

popularity associated with the systematic fragmentation of television's mass audience into lifestyle sectors, psychographic segments, and niche markets.

Post-Fordism, TV II, and *The X-Files*

In the 1970s, as Fordism's manufacturing economy was traumatized by the end of the Vietnam War, oil embargoes, inflation, and deindustrialization, a new economic order emerged—an order that David Harvey identifies as "flexible accumulation" (141–72) and others simply call "post-Fordism." As the name implies, flexible accumulation departs drastically from the rigidities of the Fordist order. Displacing the long-term stabilities of Fordism with the instabilities of short-term engagement, flexible accumulation promotes a fundamental shift in collective norms and beliefs toward the values of an entrepreneurial culture based on oldfashioned competitive individualism. Oriented on windfall profits, hit-and-run marketing, and "paper entrepreneurialism," these values emphasize (in Harvey's words) "the new, the fleeting, the ephemeral, the fugitive, and the contingent in modern life, rather than the more solid values implanted under Fordism" (171). On the supply side, flexible accumulation has been marked by expansions of the service sector (most notably, in the private health-care, banking, real estate, fast-food, and entertainment industries), accelerations in the pace of product innovation, reductions in turnover time, and— most significantly for this essay—explorations of highly specialized market niches. On the demand side, it has entailed what Mike Davis terms "overconsumptionism" (156). Indeed, the relationship between Fordism's classic consumerism and post-Fordism's fashionable overconsumptionism is roughly analogous to the relationship between what we have described as TV I's casual viewing and cult TV's avid fanship.

Just as TV I was one of the chief products and producers of Fordism, TV II exhibits a complicated product/producer relationship with post-Fordism. In other words, TV II's combination satellite and cable distribution system, augmented by remote controls, personal computers, and video cassette recorders, in conforming to the grand logic of flexible accumulation has also played a decisive role in naturalizing that logic and promoting the values of its overconsumptionism. Ironically, in the transformation from TV I to TV II, the three networks that dominated the first three decades of television found themselves caught in roughly the same vulnerable situation experienced by Hollywood's major studios during the chaotic years attending the arrival of broadcast TV—that is, the networks, like the major studios before them, were forced to witness the disturbing spectacle of their audiences fragmenting and dissipating before their very eyes. Where once ABC, NBC, and CBS commanded over 90 percent of the audience, today the major network audience has decreased to about 60 percent. Several developments in the 1970s prepared the way for the new television order. In sync with the syndication revolution, a new paradigm in programming strategy emerged in the early 1970s. Whereas the "lowest common denominator" philosophy had defined popularity in terms of brute ratings, the emergent philosophy reshaped popularity in terms of the quest for "quality demographics"—a giant step toward the "niche audience" strategies of the 1980s and 1990s. One of the earliest manifestations of this emergent view of popularity was CBS's "rural purge" in 1971, the cancellation of highly rated shows (most notably *Mayberry R.F.D.* and *Hee Haw*) because they did not attract segments of the population that were most valued by advertisers. According to Jane Feuer, the cancellation of the "hayseed" comedies signaled the industry's reconceptualization of the audience not as "an aggregate or mass" but as a "differentiated mass possessing identifiable demographic categories": " 'Popularity' came to mean high ratings with the eighteen- to forty-nine-year-old urban dweller, rather than popularity with the older rural audience" (152). The emergent regime of popularity, in Feuer's estimation, is largely responsible for the reinvention of the sitcom genre by Norman Lear and MTM Productions in the 1970s.

In the early 1980s, this "quality demographic" view of popularity also sponsored the narrative innovations of *Magnum, P.I.* Celebrated by Horace Newcomb as a new form of episodic storytelling, *Magnum* is a "cumulative narrative." Like the traditional series and unlike the traditional "open-ended" serial, each installment of a cumulative narrative has a distinct beginning, middle, and end; however, unlike the traditional series and like the traditional serial, one episode's events can greatly affect later episodes. As Newcomb puts it, "Each week's program is distinct, yet each is grafted onto the body of the series, its characters' pasts" (*"Magnum,"* 24). In its straddling of the series and serial forms, *Magnum* stands as an important noncult antecedent to *The X-Files.*

In addition to the refinement of cumulative narrative, the networks' pursuit of sophisticated viewers with money to burn has provided economic incentive for supporting other narrative innovations that are often labeled "postmodern." This incentive, combined with television's maturation as a storytelling medium and the parallel maturation of the "television generation," has made TV II an era when talented producers are rewarded for exploring and blurring generic boundaries. This revisioning (or blurred visioning) of the American television experience can be discerned in the hybridization of the cop show, the tabloidization of the news, and the carnivalization of the Super Bowl—but it is most clearly manifested in the current prominence of cult TV.

By the 1990s, two general types of cult television shows had emerged. The first type, in the tradition of *Star Trek,* is comprised of prime-time network programs that failed to generate large ratings numbers but succeeded in attracting substantial numbers of avid fans. *Twin Peaks* is the most outstanding recent example of this category. By contrast, shows of the second type first appear on cable or in fringe timeslots and are narrowly targeted at a niche audience. Comedy Central's *Mystery Science Theater 3000* and MTV's *Beavis & Butthead* exemplify this category of cult programming that was never intended to appeal to a mass audience.

In many ways, *The X-Files* represents a new model of cult television, due to its placement on Fox. Fox, at least at the time that *The X-Files* was introduced, was in a mediate position between the network prime-time model and the cable/fringe/syndication market. While Fox had little possibility of creating a ratings juggernaut like *Roseanne* or *Home Improvement,* it still could not afford to run a show like *Mystery Science Theater 3000* that attracted such a small (though fanatically devoted) audience. Although Fox would have been perfectly happy if *The X-Files* were a top ten show, they initially conceived of the program as a candidate for cult status, hoping that (like *Star Trek* and *Star Trek: The Next Generation*) the relatively small avid viewership of the program would gradually build to a respectably large audience. This strategy has proven successful, as *The X-Files* is now among the most popular shows on Fox and is well on its way to becoming a genuine mass hit.

Fox has also taken advantage of *The X-Files'* cult success in other ways. Active fans consume ancillary products, and so Fox has licensed a wide variety of *X-Files* merchandise, ranging from novels and comic books to coffee mugs and clothing. Fox has also used the show to promote some of its other media holdings. In Britain, first run episodes of the series appear only on Sky One, part of Rupert Murdoch's satellite network. Fox also attempted to use *The X-Files* to promote Delphi, its online service; Delphi became the official online home of *The X-Files,* and writers and producers were encouraged to frequent the discussion areas related to the show. By using the show's cult status to multiply its revenue streams, Fox has taken away some of the pressure on *The X-Files* to be a ratings hit.

Although Fox has exploited the cult success of *The X-Files* in an adroit fashion, its attempts to clone that success have failed. The network has paraded a number of unspectacular sci-fi dramas (*V.R. 5, Sliders,* and *Strange Luck*) through the 8 P.M. slot preceding *The X-Files,* only to watch each of them fail to attract even a cult audience. *Space: Above and Beyond,* which was developed by writers and producers from *The X-Files'* first two seasons, has also failed to find an audience.

Despite being on the brink of mass success, *The X-Files* still shares a number of characteristics with other cult programs, particularly in its narrative structure and audience engagement. *The X-Files* has been especially canny in courting several preexisting fan cultures. Most importantly, the show's generic migrations allow it to appeal to a variety of subgroups within sci-fi fandom. The omnipresent discussion of UFOs and aliens brings its own particular group of fans to the show, as does the incorporation of high-tech, hard science elements in the plotlines of episodes like "Roland," "Ghost in the Machine," and "Soft Light." The frequent plots dealing with serial killers and/or the supernatural draw in fans from the horror/dark fantasy fan groups that exist on the margins of sci-fi fandom. Dana Scully, clearly patterned after Agent Starling in *Silence of the Lambs,* represents in many ways the traditional scientist hero of classic sci-fi. She is an expert in one scientific area, forensic pathology, but has a mastery of the scientific method that allows her to venture outside her specialty. *The X-Files* has also aggressively courted the fans of television's most spectacular cult failure, *Twin Peaks.* Beyond the obvious connection through David Duchovny, who played the transvestite DEA agent Dennis/Denise Bryson in *Twin Peaks,* both shows have at their center a brilliant if quirky FBI agent who believes in the supernatural. A number of actors have appeared in both series: *Twin Peaks'*s Michael Horse (Deputy Hawk), Michael J. Anderson (Man from Another Place), and Kenneth Welsh (Windom Earle) appeared in the *X-Files* episodes "Shapes," "Humbug," and "Revelations," respectively. Don Davis (*Twin Peaks'*s Major Garland Briggs) appeared in "Beyond the Sea" as Scully's father, now a naval captain rather than an air force major.

Judging by the amount of carryover between the two fan communities, *The X-Files* has been at least moderately successful in courting the *Twin Peaks* audience. There are several examples of fan fiction crossovers between the two programs, the most notable being Peggy Mei-Ling Li's "Out of the Woods." The alt.tv.x-files newsgroup frequently contains rumors about possible *Twin Peaks/X-Files* crossovers, which probably represent more wishful thinking than anything else. *Wrapped in Plastic,* the premiere *Twin Peaks* fanzine, devoted an entire issue to *The X-Files* and features a regular column that reports on the show.

Of course, *The X-Files* shares some other properties of previous cult shows. It is both difficult and uncommon to be able to deal with a series in holistic fashion because of the sheer breadth of the narrative. The engagement of the fan audience with cult television, however, through re-viewing and discussion, goes far beyond the hour the program is on the air. This leads to a focus on minutia within the program between episodes. Fan fascination with *The X-Files* is generally either fixed on certain elements of the program (as exemplified by the David Duchovny Estrogen Brigade, a fan group infatuated with the male star) or on particular episodes (often the current ones, although fans will often cite earlier episodes or scenes when references are made to them in new episodes). Though the series is less quirky and quotable than *Twin Peaks,* fans of *The X-Files* do remember certain scenes (Scully eating the cricket in "Humbug") or certain lines (an archive of Mulderisms and Scullyisms exists online).

Obviously, Chris Carter and the other producers of *The X-Files* learned from the failures of *Twin Peaks,* particularly in terms of taking a different narrative strategy. Serial elements are important in a cult show because they reward regular viewers and give reasons for re-viewing earlier episodes. At the same time, programs that are continuously serial may alienate new viewers who lack knowledge of events in previous episodes. Once the initial luster of *Twin Peaks* wore off, the show began to hemorrhage viewers; because it was a continuous serial, it was difficult to recruit new viewers to replace the deserters.

The X-Files, like *Magnum,* walks an intermediate path between the episodic series and the open-ended serial, one that is for the most part episodic but in which certain ongoing plotlines carry across episodes and even seasons. Consequently, *The X-Files* qualifies as a cumulative narrative (or what Marc Dolan [34] terms a "sequential series"). *The X-Files* has dealt with the problem of recruiting new viewers by presenting self-contained installments that feature only minor references to continuous plotlines, like the appearances of Mr. X in "Soft Light" or the Lone Gunmen in "Fearful Symmetry." At the same time, the program continues to tell a serial story in the linked episodes that deal with UFOs, the government conspiracy, and the disappearance of Samantha Mulder. These episodes (the pilot, "Deep Throat," "Fallen Angel," "E.B.E.," and "The Erlenmeyer Flask" from season one; "Little Green Men," "Duane Barry"/"Ascension," "One Breath," "Colony"/ "Endgame," and "Anasazi" from season two; "The Blessing Way"/ "Paper Clip," "Nisei"/"731," and "Piper Maru"/"Apocrypha" from season three), while each somewhat self-contained, form a sort of mini-serial within the series.

By shifting gears between the serial and the episodic, *The X-Files* self-consciously rewards avid fans by drawing on the continuity of previous episodes, hence validating their diligent viewing, while at the same time welcoming new audience members since most of the plotlines don't rely on previous knowledge of the series. In fact, *The X-Files* is even able to switch gears within the same episode. In "F.

Emasculata," the mysterious Cancer Man argues with Mulder about whether the FBI should have made a public disclosure about the deadly plague carried by two ex-convicts. While fans of the show will read this exchange in light of their knowledge of the history of the interaction between Mulder and Cancer Man, the episode is constructed so the interchange is still comprehensive and not alienating to first-time viewers.

Mark Frost has claimed that in the original development of *Twin Peaks*, he hoped to devise a program that would appeal to a "coalition of viewers" (Collins, 338). However, as *Twin Peaks* played out, this coalition quickly took on a hierarchical arrangement that privileged those who were in on the postmodern joke and alienated those who were not. *The X-Files*, on the other hand, has succeeded in forging, maintaining, and expanding a viewing coalition that includes readers of supermarket tabloids, horror aficionados, New Agers, Netscapers, Twin Peakers, Trekkers, tech-heads, and just plain folks. The "cumulative narrative" form is one of the decisive factors in *The X-Files'* success.

Another factor, however, may be just as decisive: *The X-Files* is almost militantly anti-postmodern. Many of the other cult TV shows are contaminated by the tedium of postmodern irony in which cynicism passes for artistry, nihilism is "cool," sincerity "sucks," and truth is always already an illusion. In its most disturbing expressions, cult TV gives credence to Fredric Jameson's view that postmodernism is simply a manifestation of late capitalism's lust to commodify every aspect of everyday life.

After all, what *Beavis & Butthead* manages to do for MTV and *Mystery Science Theater 3000* accomplishes for Comedy Central is to commodify oppositional reading and cash in on viewer resistance to commercial culture.[3] Like commercials that sell products by making fun of commercials, *Beavis & Butthead* and *Mystery Science Theater 3000* have cleverly turned viewer resistance to commercialism into a commercial proposition. In exemplifying how expansive and all-encompassing the market has become in the age of flexible accumulation, *Mystery Science Theater 3000* and *Beavis & Butthead* seem to prove that nothing—neither profane nor sacred, passive nor active, highbrow nor lowbrow, dominant nor oppositional—is safe from commercial exploitation.

Although the generic sampling and episodic/serial straddle of *The*

---

3. We thank Timothy Shuker-Haines for offering this insight during a class discussion of *Mystery Science Theater 3000* at the University of Michigan in 1994.

X-Files could be interpreted as boundary blurring, other aspects of the program are explicitly anti-postmodern. The assertion that "The Truth Is Out There" runs counter to postmodernism's doctrine of disbelief. Together, the hermeneutics of faith practiced by Mulder and the hermeneutics of suspicion practiced by Scully provide a bifocal outlook on unexplained phenomenon that is characterized by a sincerity that stands in stark contrast to the mockeries of *Twin Peaks, Mystery Science Theater 3000*, and *Beavis & Butthead.* "Humbug," the most self-reflexive and least sincere episode of *The X-Files'* first two seasons, was justified by its airing on April Fool's Day. Otherwise, Mulder, Scully, and Carter have played it refreshingly straight. In the final analysis, *The X-Files* is worth studying not just because it is the most successful cult series of the 1990s but also because it may very well be the first truly post-postmodern television show. Hopefully, the success of *The X-Files* represents yet another rewriting of popularity—only this time, a rewriting whose inclusiveness signals a reinvigoration of consensus culture and a renunciation of the excesses and exclusions of postmodernism.

3

DDEB, GATB, MPPB, and Ratboy

THE X-FILES' MEDIA FANDOM,
ONLINE AND OFF

Susan J. Clerc

The netters hoped that *Twin Peaks* would be "full of secrets": that it would provide fodder for their speculations for years to come. For these fans, the computer had become an integral part of their experience of the series and the many fan meta-texts that circulated on alt.tv.twinpeaks were as compelling as the aired episodes themselves. The computer provided a way of linking their own, admittedly obsessive, fixation upon *Twin Peaks'* enigmas to a broader social community of others who shared similar fascinations and frustrations. Participating in this virtual community became a way of increasing the intensity and density of those speculations, of building up other fans' explorations and expanding upon their theories. Both the mode and content of this television talk originated not only within the complexities of Lynch's text but also within the traditions and interests of computer culture.

—Henry Jenkins,
" 'Do You Enjoy Making the Rest of Us Feel Stupid?' "

"Welcome to the world of high technology."
—Walter Skinner, in "Paper Clip"

Do you know who Ratboy is? Why Scully's digital clock often reads 11:21? What DDEB stands for? The meaning of GATB?[1] If you answered "yes" to any of the above, chances are you're an X-Phile, one of the thousands of *X-Files* fans who exchange information and opinions about the series online. The name "X-Philes" is the one online fans have adopted for themselves over the unwieldy "File-o-philes" suggested by series creator Chris Carter. Every day, X-Philes flood their online discussion groups with hundreds of messages about all facets of the series. They create drinking games (take one sip every time the agents use their flashlights, and take two sips if they drop them), collect lines from the series to use as .sig files or buttons ("The Truth Is Out There," "This is where you pucker up and kiss my ass"), compile detailed episode guides to the series with official titles and cast lists, review and rate the episodes, share information about the actors' other roles and appearances on talk shows, report on magazine and newspaper articles about the series, evaluate the comic books, trading cards, and other merchandise sold by commercial vendors, and speculate about the aliens and conspiracies that are running themes of the series.

The meat of fan discussion, however, is analysis and interpretation of the multilayered text. This can be as basic as determining together what precisely happened during a discrete episode. Following a summer of speculation about how Mulder would escape from the boxcar, for example, many fans were unsatisfied with the cryptic visual and narrative clues in the third-season opener. After "The Blessing Way" aired, fans posted their impressions to the online groups, countering or supporting each other's interpretations until a loose consensus was reached on the explanation that accounted for the most clues:

> I didn't get that flashback scene—did the aliens help Mulder escape?

> No, they'd dug a hole in the side of the car after the gas tank was dropped in; that's why the bodies were all piled up in that corner. They were trying to get out.

> There was a hole in the side, but I think it was already there—if you look at the right side of the screen it looks like there was already a jagged hole in the side and that's what the creatures ran for when the cyanide tank was dropped in.

1. "Ratboy" is the name X-Philes have given Agent Alex Krychek; 11:21 refers to Chris Carter's wife's birthday; "DDEB" stands for the David Duchovny Estrogen Brigade, and "GATB" for the Gillian Anderson Testosterone Brigade

Don't forget that Albert said he'd found a body (presumably
alien since the buzzards wouldn't touch it) there before (and we saw
it next to Mulder in the rocks) so at least one alien (or whatever) had
managed to tunnel out. Mulder was in the tunnel the aliens had dug
to escape.

Although some fans were disappointed that the means of escape were
not stated explicitly, others pointed out that the failure to "spoon-feed"
viewers all the answers is one of the series' charms.

Unresolved endings and hanging threads are both a source of
pleasure and a source of frustration for fans, echoing Henry Jenkins'
observation (in *Textual Peachers*) that fans in general have a mixed
attitude toward their favorite texts, one of both fascination and frustration. The frustration of not having all the threads tied together is also
a source of pleasure, though, giving rise to speculation and analysis of
the gaps in the narrative. The narrative is not restricted to individual
episodes but spans the entire breadth of the series, what Jenkins refers
to as the metatext. *The X-Files*, with its recurring characters and story
arcs, is better suited to construction of the metatext than the episodic
storytelling of series like the original *Star Trek*. Fans of that series had
to create the metatext for themselves, as a way of making emotional
sense of the characters. In real life, people are affected by the events in
their lives and the effects carry over to the next day, month, year; in
much of television, however, characters seem unaffected by previous
events and sometimes forget they even happened. With *The X-Files*
and other series that feature continuing story lines, fans do not need
to construct the metatext as much as they need to understand it—the
producers seem to have some plan in mind and the fans want to
decipher it, to put all the pieces together into a coherent picture.

With X-Philes, constructing/understanding the metatext often
takes the form of complex theories about the many conspiracies (or is
it just one?) that wind through several of the episodes. Unlike the
specific events within an episode, consensus is rarely reached on these
theories; they are the work of individual fans rather than the group.
The reason is that these theories are provisional and must be adapted
and reworked as new evidence appears in new episodes. Speculation
regarding the truth about Samantha Mulder's disappearance, for instance, has undergone many changes as viewers were first led to believe she was simply abducted by aliens, then that she had been cloned
and raised by aliens living on earth, and finally that she had been
abducted to ensure her father's silence about governmental experiments with alien DNA. But what do we really know? There are several
"black" organizations working together and at cross purposes; there
was a consortium of several of the characters, including Deep Throat,

Cancer Man, and Fox's father Bill Mulder; it all has something to do with alien DNA. Many gaps in the back story remain to be filled, however, before the whole is uncovered. Fans play with the facts and assess the credibility of some of the characters' accounts of their activities to try to fill the gaps and give themselves a coherent model of the series' universe.

Filling in the gaps extends to the psychological and emotional levels of the series as well. Here, too, theories about the characters' motivations must be provisional, although some consensus is possible. Following "The Colony" and "End Game," online discussion of the Mulder family focused on its dysfunctional nature and how Samantha's abduction would have led to the parents' divorce. Fans brought in their personal knowledge of families whose children had been killed or kidnapped as evidence that the strain would tear a family apart. Given that Fox's guilt over the abduction is a fundamental theme of the series, conversation also emphasized the relationship between him and his father and how his father's attitude supported Fox's judgment of himself; Bill seemed to blame his son just as Fox blamed himself. Earlier comments about his father that reflected emotional distance between them were recalled when discussing the scenes in the present episodes. Some fans noted that the distance between them was physically demonstrated in Fox's rebuffed attempt to embrace his father (later, fans immediately picked up on the parallel scene in "Anasazi" where Bill's attempted embrace fails). There was much speculation on how this had affected Fox's character and his inability to let down his emotional guard with Scully, and scenes from other episodes were cited to support the fact that Fox routinely blocked attempts at emotional connection with humor. Later, during the summer between the second and third seasons, there was much speculation over how his father's death would affect Mulder. Following the revelations in "The Blessing Way" and "Paper Clip," these speculations continued but adapted to include Fox's anger and the knowledge that Bill's attitude toward Fox was more problematic than it had appeared in the earlier episodes. As the series continues, scenes will be scrutinized for indications that his father's duplicity has left deep scars on Fox's psyche.

Although the motivations of and interactions between all of the significant characters are grist for fan debate, the relationship between the two lead characters generates the most interest. Discussion of whether Mulder and Scully should become lovers continues unabated in spite of Chris Carter's repeated declarations that they will not: "You'll never see Mulder and Scully romantically involved," Carter says in a *TV Guide* article (Nollinger, 24), reiterating a statement he has made at fan conventions and in print magazines and online chat sessions since the series began. Opinions among fans vary widely:

They obviously love each other and they're the only ones that each of them trusts. They belong together. Let them do it!

It's unrealistic that they should keep getting closer emotionally and not have a physical relationship. It can't go on unresolved forever and stay real.

Oh God no, don't let them go to bed! Remember what happened with *Moonlighting?* They finally get to bed and the show went downhill faster than you can say unresolved sexual tension!

In theory, I have nothing against the two of them consummating their love for each other. In practice, it's a different matter. CC [Chris Carter] has said that a relationship between S & M would detract from the real focus of the series—the investigations. I agree. I don't want *The X-Files* to turn into a soap opera.

I LIKE the fact that they are equal partners and it's platonic. What's wrong with finally having a series where men and women are FRIENDS and equals for a change?

As much faith as I have in CC and co, I really don't want to see Mulder and Scully as lovers. In real life, men and women can be lovers and remain equal, but on TV whenever sex enters the picture, the woman gets relegated to the sidelines and becomes the plot excuse for heroic action on the part of the man. I don't want to see that happen to Scully.

In online discourse about their relationship, actual or potential, we can see a definite awareness of gender politics. Fans are aware of how rare it is to see men and women partners and how unsuccessful television has been in presenting sexual couples in action-adventure series who can be both lovers and partners. Some fans speculate that it would make the male partner look "weak" if he "allowed" his lover to go into danger instead of protecting her; as long as they are partners on the job but not in their private lives, both can face danger without it reflecting negatively on the other. Fans are also aware of how gender is played out in the series and discuss both the quantity and quality of times each partner rescues the other. When it seemed as if Scully was being rescued more than Mulder during a sequence of episodes, there were complaints in the online groups. Several other fans replied with an episode-by-episode list of who had rescued whom and who had been portrayed as victim. Further discussion turned to the quality of those scenes: Was Scully shown as a victim for longer periods of time, or dealing with her attackers in a less effective manner? The quality of the equality between the two is also a debated issue. Although many fans see the two as equals, others point out that Mulder tends to give Scully orders and send her into perilous situations (often without briefing her on the dangers) and that the reverse is rarely true; Mulder gets into trouble on his own initiative; he isn't sent into it by Scully.

Gender within the series is a topic for debate among X-Philes, but it also influences who talks about what in the discussion groups themselves. Conversations about the lead characters' relationship and about gender roles on screen are conducted primarily by women, who as a group have higher stakes in these issues than their male counterparts. Women also tend to contribute more to discussions about character psychology and motivation. Following "The Blessing Way," for example, it was possible to detect a general pattern of interests. Women posters tended to focus on the character interactions: Did Scully show sufficient grief over Mulder's supposed death? Was Mulder too brusque with his mother or was she being obstructive? How would Mulder deal with his father's death when he recovered? Men, by contrast, tended to focus on why Mulder didn't grab one of the bodies for evidence while he was escaping, giving their opinions on how metal detectors work and whether the dream sequences looked "cheesy." Male Philes were also more likely than were women to refer to outside sources in an effort to clarify or dispute plot points. After the airing of "Paper Clip," many male fans posted long treatises on how DAT cartridges work and why Skinner should have been able to print from or copy the MJ-12 files. Women were more likely to accept Skinner's statement as a plot device and move on to the repercussions of Albert having the data in his head and relaying it to other Navajo. They were also interested in Skinner's new relationship to Mulder and Scully. This parallels what Jenkins found in his comparison of female *Star Trek* fans and male *Twin Peaks* fans: men used the character interactions to illuminate the plot and referred to outside information to solve narrative problems; women used the plot to illuminate aspects of the characters' internal lives and worked within the universe established by the series. When women do refer to outside sources, it tends to be to personal experience, as a means of establishing "emotional realism" ("Do You Enjoy," 60). One fan summed up the broad categories of male and female participation this way: "Men seem to like posting discussions about the plot elements almost exclusively. They also tend to dominate the collectibles threads, with endless discussions of the comic books and merchandise. Women talk more about The Relationship, in conformity with my most despised stereotype, but they also seem to dominate the literary discussion threads."

To be sure, it is important to note that no topic is the exclusive property of either gender. Men do talk about relationships and character issues; women do analyze plot elements and conspiracies. It is tempting to credit this fluidity of gender lines and topics to the series itself, because the characters of Scully and Mulder can be read as transgressive. Scully, the woman, is the skeptic and the one with the hard science background; Mulder, the man, is the one who believes in "extreme possibilities" and has the soft science background. The series occasionally plays with the gender confusion created by the characters, as in "Jose Chung's *From Outer Space*," where Mulder gives out a "girlie scream" and a clearly untrustworthy witness believes that Scully "was disguised as a woman but wasn't pulling it off." It is more likely, however, that the fluidity of gender and topics is a reflection of real life. Men and women who watch the series are attracted to it for a variety of reasons and differ in the degrees of their interest in specific aspects—men usually are more interested in the "factual," women in the "emotional"—but the line is never as rigid or clear-cut as broad generalizations make it seem.

Gender also influences how people use the medium to discuss the series. Early research in computer-mediated communication (cmc) emphasized the democratizing potential of a medium that removed all visual cues of race, gender, age, class, and attractiveness. The idealism inherent in this approach, popularized in the slogan "on the 'net no one knows you're a dog," still holds sway over many cmc users and scholars. However, as Susan Herring points out, "there is an increasing awareness among both researchers and the general public that women and men have different preferred styles in computer use, including computer-mediated communication" ("Politeness," 2). As I have discussed elsewhere, women fans tend to prefer mailing lists to newsgroups, and X-Philes are no exception. The two general-focus public online groups that receive the majority of traffic are the Usenet group, alt.tv.x-files, and the Internet mailing list, X-Files@chaos.taylored.edu. Twenty-five percent of the posts to alt.tv.x-files over an average three-day period were made by women, compared to nearly 50 percent of the posts to X-Files@chaos on those same days. The preference for mailing lists boils down to the desire to make personal connections with other people, to feel part of a community; mailing lists must be sought out and joined, they require some commitment from members ("you have to be there every day"), and the mail comes directly to subscribers rather than being stored at a remote site. Because they may not be browsed anonymously, lists also attract fewer "clueless newbies" (who have just discovered the series and want very basic information) and fewer "trolls" (people, usually adolescent males, who post inflammatory remarks in order to enjoy the uproar in anonymous safety). As a result, lists are often seen as safer, more civil places than newsgroups, to post and promote a greater sense of community. These features appeal particularly to women, as suggested by the number of small, specialized groups women have begun and belong to.

A partial list of the specialized groups that have sprouted from alt.tv.x-files and the Chaos list includes alt.tv.x-files.creative, three separate David Duchovny Estrogen Brigades (DDEB, DDEB2, DDEB3), the Mitch Pileggi Pheromone Brigade (MPPB), Smart Young X-Philes (SYX), the Gillian Anderson Testosterone Brigade (GATB), and duchovny-l. Other unpublicized private groups have also developed for consideration of specialized interests such as fan fiction or literary analysis of the series. Most of these groups draw their membership from the two main forums, but subscribers to America Online, Delphi, and other pay services may also belong to them as well as participate in *X-Files* areas and folders provided by the company. Although some of the specialized conferences are quite large (SYX currently has over 250 members, duchovny-1 somewhere around 200), most of the mailing lists seem to range between fifteen and fifty people, and even a sizable forum like AOL's primary *X-Files* folder is dwarfed by the 1500-plus membership of the Chaos list and the unrecorded thousands who can browse alt.tv.x-files without leaving a trace.

The proliferation of venues is not unique to *X-Files* fans; the first DDEB was created by a member of two similar *Star Trek* groups, the Star Fleet Ladies' Auxiliary Embroidery and Baking Society and the Patrick Stewart Estrogen Brigade (see the DDEB Frequently Asked Questions [FAQ] web page). Many other private mailing lists, not as well known as the *Star Trek* ones, have also sprung up in the last few years as the number of women fans joining the Internet has grown. Nor is the fragmentation unique to online fandom; rather, it is a reflection of offline traditions. Camille Bacon-Smith describes media-fan subculture as a set of interlocking circles, starting with large groups of between 250 and 500 people, "an optimal number of participants that provides members with a comfortable balance between variety in product and control over their social environment" (24) but one that, while "maintaining a sense of unity as a group . . . is far too large to meet the personal needs of its members for close connections" (26). For close connections, fans prefer groups of from ten to thirty people, and groups of more than twenty-five usually splinter (29). The huge growth of the Internet has also made fragmentation inevitable. The enormous amount of traffic on some newsgroups makes them impossible to follow regularly, and although fans value the multitude of voices and opinions on the large groups, they also seek out smaller circles to discuss their special interests: "In any group you get together with people who are like-minded. All the X-Philes are on alt.tv.x-files because we all like *X-Files* but we all find different things in it so you tend to splinter off into your own groups" (Paula Vitaris, interview with author, Sept. 6, 1995).

The trend toward specialized, private conferences is apparent outside of fandom as well, as some recent scholarship in computer-mediated communication has discussed (see e.g. Herring et al.). One common feature of these groups is that they are composed entirely or predominantly of women. Herring offers suggestions as to why women tend to form their own groups more often than men; citing Carol Gilligan, Herring says that "women favor an ethic of caring and interpersonal responsibility, while men favor an ethic of rights and protection from interference by others" ("Politeness," 2). She then posits two different value systems, an anarchic/agonistic male system that privileges "freedom from censorship, candor, and debate" ("Posting," 11) and a female politeness ethic marked by "expressions of support and appreciation" and presentation of opinions in hedged terms ("Posting," 4) and a general dislike of flaming. Computer-mediated discourse is permeated by the male anarchic/agonistic system "with the result that women with a politeness ethic must create and defend women-centered spaces on-line in order to carry out the kinds of discourse they value" ("Posting," 3). Herring also observes that "while the number of women-only groups on the Internet continues to grow, groups with a 'men-only' policy are virtually nonexistent" (Herring et al., 2). Herring's model is reminiscent of Deborah Tannen's categories of "report-talk," a distinctly male mode of discourse that values information and independence, and "rapport-talk," a female model of communication that stresses connections to others and avoidance of open conflict.

The specialized groups that women X-Philes have begun or joined bear out Tannen's and Herring's theories. The various Estrogen Brigades and the unnamed private mailing lists are either women-only or women-mainly and range from fifteen to fifty members. The larger duchovny-1 is reported to be "95% women and 5% gay men." The exceptions to the pattern are SYX, whose web page roster is almost evenly split between men and women, and the men-only GATB. The GATB seems to be the only functioning men-only private list on the Internet, or at least the only one whose existence is known. What the women value most about their mailing lists is the sense of being part of a close-knit, supportive community where it is safe to unwind and share personal information:

> The DDEB is my living room; the newsgroup is a public meeting hall. The DDEB is not just a drool group, not any more anyway. We moved out of that stage about a year ago. . . . These are my dearest friends,

the ones I can pour my heart out to. . . . They are more than a support group; they are a second family.

This SYX list is Soooooooooo personal! They say that the internet is an impersonal place, but I'm the first one to object. I totally feel like I "know" these people. . . . We discuss personal things, besides just *X-Files* . . . like complaining about hard days at school/work . . . getting married (as one SYXer is next year!) . . . you name it! It's really friendly, and it seems like you've known the other list members for years.

Some of comments support Herring's observations that dissatisfaction with the conflict model prevalent on the large public groups is one reason for the formation of alternative venues. The duchovny-1 FAQ web page, for example, attributes the group's origins to a distaste for flaming and gently urges members to abstain from it: "Duchovny-1 came about when several members of *The X-Files* mailing list decided that it was better to 'drool in peace' without having to be flamed by those that don't appreciate David. Remember, we're all one happy family here, and flaming isn't very nice." None of the other groups' public documents on the web have antiflaming clauses or cite flaming as a reason for their birth, but comments from members repeatedly make the point that their groups are warmer and friendlier places than alt.tv.x-files and the Chaos list and that flaming was a rare event. Quotes often link the two thoughts, showing the connection between lack of flaming and a sense of harmony/community:

I read the newsgroup sometimes. I find that it often degenerates into a screaming match much more often than the list. On the list, I have made some friends and I feel like I can talk to them. Not only about *The X-Files*, but about other things as well.

Alt.tv.X-Files is not as personal . . . they are more prone to flames and cut-downs. The SYXers are a sensitive little bunch. You do come to know people by name on A.t.x, but there's such a huge number of them, and the posts are often inane or offensive . . . so I tend to stick with SYX, and read the newsgroup with my defenses up. You can't expect a reply if you post to alt.tv.x-files, but in SYX you'll always stir conversation.

I feel I must add that this newsgroup is not nearly as much pure fun as the AOL x-boards, where I have such a good time that I have to adhere to a schedule in order to keep my bill down every month. There, I feel that I'm logging on to visit my friends, and even arguments are amicable. Here, I'm continually encountering people I'd

rather not meet—folks who are mean and impatient, folks who say
the same things over and over again mindlessly, folks who will e-mail
you just to tell you to get a life, etc.

The link between lack of temper and the sense of emotional closeness, and the difference between how men and women react to conflict
and intimacy, is clear when we compare two quotes, the first from a
member of the duchovniks and the second from a member of the
GATB:

> Another thing that is perhaps unique to this kind of woman-centered
> list is the sharing of personal problems (job troubles, anorexia, bad
> break-ups, deaths) and the outpouring of support that occurs. There
> is never judgment, and rarely know-it-all advice, merely concern and
> care. I don't think I've ever seen a flame on this list.

> This is more like a community of buddies than anything else—oh,
> we have our differences; hot buttons are pushed on a semi-regular
> basis it seems. Discussions are not limited strictly to GA, but have
> included in the past OS2/Warp?Windoze 95 (I keep out of that, I'm a
> Mac man at home; at work I use a Sun workstation), cars, the right to
> bear arms and arm bears, taxes, baseball, football. Kinda like a guy
> club, where we can shoot the shit and not have to worry about always
> having to talk about *X-Files* or GA / DD / CC and the like. . . . I
> guess I can sum it up as a male quilting bee. (Tony Perreau, personal
> correspondence with author, Sept. 7, 1995)

Aside from creating a flame-free atmosphere, the specialized lists also
establish a close-knit circle by ensuring a similar level of competency
among members, limiting the size of the group, having a moderator,
and/or the presence of a strong communal identity.

One of the primary causes for clashes is between those who are
new to the series and those who have been talking about it online for
a long time: newbies versus the old guard. For those who have been
around, Frequently Asked Questions can be extremely annoying. They
want to discuss the series, not answer basic questions that have already
been compiled and answered by dedicated fans in FAQ files posted to
the Usenet group and made available by ftp and on the World Wide
Web. To newcomers, this attitude reeks of elitism and snobbery, but
for those in specialized groups sharing a competence level serves as a
unifying factor. If all members of a group are on an even basis in terms
of knowledge about the series, the clashes between fans with different
levels of expertise are avoided. Sharing a similar competence level also
means that discussion flows more smoothly without posters having
to explain basic details; they can assume the others will understand

references and abbreviations and share the same lexicon. An equal level of expertise can be established by making membership by invitation only: "We don't publicize; you have to be invited in. If you post something intelligent, we say 'hey, let's invite so and so'" (Vitaris, interview with author). It can also be achieved by setting an arbitrary number of memberships and closing the group to new members when the number is reached. All of the DDEBs are now closed, for example, having reached a preset number. Keeping the list small allows members to reach a similar plateau of expertise without a continuous flow of newbies upsetting the balance: "We all know what David's middle name is."

Keeping a list small also makes it easier for members to adjust to each other and to get to know each other. "It's easier to get to know 40 people well than 400," one fan pointed out. A stable membership base permits trust to grow, and many groups develop from merely a place to "be silly and drool over David" into the sort of closeness described in the DDEB FAQ:

> In all honesty we talk about more than DD! We talk about our lives/ work/SO/kids/life in general—not to mention other actors we find talented (and not just in the looks department and not just male ones either). Things like how your 4 year old is having fits cuz you are taking him to daycare for the first time and cries when you leave; or how the sysadmin at your work failed to make a new back-up BE-FORE they replaced hardware and so you lost all the work you did the day before and it can not be recovered, or being supportive when one of the group finds out that they will not be getting paid for a contract job they had been working on for the previous 6 months and now they don't know what they will do for food!

Although a limited size seems to be an optimal way to ensure a sense of intimacy and community, other sources of group identity may fulfill the same purpose. Both duchovny-l and SYX have group projects that help their hundreds of subscribers bond. In addition, SYX members have a strong sense of group identity based on their age. The full name of their group is Young X-Philes Who Are Mature And Smart Enough To Understand A Great Show When They See One, an identity that both sets them apart from other members of their age cohort who aren't mature and smart enough to appreciate *The X-Files* and distinguishes them from other X-Philes who are older than they are.

The presence of a moderator is another way in which large, mixed-sex groups can foster a sense of community. Several America Online subscribers describe the general *X-Files* folder on that service as a warm and happy place, although more people are in it than in the

DDEBs and other small groups. Members attribute this to AOL's system of having hosts or moderators who monitor the conversation:

> Internet's so big it's so much more impersonal. AOL is big, too, but X Files is really friendly and familiar. It's moderated so you sort of feel like Mom and Dad are watching and you have to mind your manners and be nice. . . . It's like a great big family. (Vitaris, interview with author)

> Each board also has a host, who stands ready to mediate disputes and uncover violations. For instance, the biggest ruction I've seen so far occurred on the Spoiler board when someone claiming to be "Laura Carter, Chris Carter's daughter" started giving out "spoilers" that everybody hated. The host quickly checked her out and exposed her as an impostor, though she tried for a week to keep controversy alive by posting "objective" defenses of herself under other names. (I think she was claiming to be four different people at one time.) In an anarchic board like alt.tv.x-files such a person could linger for ages . . . interfering with everybody else's fun.

The activity of women on the Chaos list and the many specialized lists may create the impression that they are fleeing Usenet, but that is not the case. While creating and joining mailing lists that fulfill a need for community not met by newsgroups, many women continue to post to the latter. In fact, compared to newsgroups for other ongoing series that fall within the same genre matrix and are represented on Usenet, alt.tv.x-files has a high percentage of women participants. On average, 25 percent of the posts to alt.tv.x-files were from women (45 percent men, 30 percent unspecified gender) compared to 14 percent of the posters on rec.arts.startrek.current (66 percent men, 20 percent unspecified) and 16 percent on rec.arts.sf.tv.babylon5 (69 percent men, 15 percent unspecified). Although the exact percentages are in a perpetual state of flux, the patterns they imply remain intact across several newsgroups: alt.tv.x-files attracts more women posters than newsgroups for comparable series.

Why do women X-Philes manage to overcome societal attitudes regarding women's speech in public more often than women fans in other forums? The most obvious reason is that *The X-Files* may have more fans among women online than other TV series. *The X-Files* blends a number of genres, including horror and mystery, giving it a larger audience pool to draw from than series that stay within one genre, such as science fiction. The series also contains elements typified by John Fiske as part of a feminine television aesthetic: open-ended storytelling with continuing plot lines, a strong female character, room to question a central narrative voice (although the story follows one pair of investigators, there are many subsidiary characters running their own games), and an emphasis on process rather than a triumphal resolution of the problem (*Television Culture*, 179–97). Many women are also attracted by David Duchovny (as the many estrogen brigades attest), by the supernatural events investigated in the stories, and by the relationship between Mulder and Scully. All of these factors may mean that the series has more women fans online than do other series, but sheer numbers are not enough to explain why women feel more comfortable speaking out about *The X-Files* than they do about other series, especially since they cannot be sure other women are there unless those other women post.

The series itself may hold the answer to why its women fans feel more comfortable posting to Usenet. The character of Scully creates a space within the series for women to speak, and this carries over to the fans. Anyone watching the series must accept Scully as a valid character with a legitimate place within the narrative, and therefore discussion of her by her peers is valid:

> Scully is nobody's "girl." She stands on her own. She's Mulder's partner but she isn't defined by him or by her relationships with any other man.

> Nobody acts like she has to justify her being there. She's just another agent. Mulder, Skinner, all of the other guys take her presence for granted. You don't get lines like "what's a nice girl like you doing in a nasty business like this." She's just there.

> Scully is intelligent, strong, resourceful, and brave. She's no damsel in distress or some bimbo, she's good at her job and doesn't take any crap from anybody, including Mulder.

At the same time, however, Scully is involved in an ongoing platonic relationship with Mulder. The relationship at the center of the narrative provides an entree for women because women are accorded by our culture competence in discussing emotions and relationships. Having gained a foothold via the relationship, they are free to move into other areas of the series. Both Scully as a character in her own right and the relationship between her and Mulder create a space for women to enter into discourse about the text, a space that grants them authority on at least those aspects of it. Paralleling the role of Scully on the television screen are the core of regulars on the computer screen. Alt.tv.x-Files is fortunate in having a set of women regulars who are intelligent, articulate, and prolific posters. Seeing these real life women continue to post in spite of flames and trolls encourages and sets an example for other women and perhaps empowers them to speak.

In addition to having role models on the newsgroup to emulate, women fans may also have the benefit of support systems. If they belong to any of the specialized groups, they may gain confidence from their reception there and then begin posting on the public groups. Many women online are also part of the media fan community offline, and this, too, can facilitate their posting online; they are used to speaking up and being part of a community that listens to women because it is composed primarily of women. Clearly, there is a striking contrast between the current gender composition of online and offline fandom. This may eventually have a negative impact on the offline community if more women do not make their presence known online, particularly on Usenet (as it remains the most visible segment of cmc, and journalists and producers alike tend to monitor it because it demands no commitment from them and they may browse anonymously). While women X-Philes keep a high profile and continue to be active in all *X-Files* groups, other women fans may find themselves marginalized if they post only in specialized conferences and become (or remain) invisible to producers. Similar arguments might be made about fans who cannot afford or do not wish to use one of the major commercial Internet service providers, where people who work in television production often lurk and less often delurk.

Access to producers and creators of series is one of the draws of online fan venues: science fiction writers drop in on newsgroups dedicated to discussion of their work; chat sessions with actors draw large crowds on the pay services; some *Star Trek* writers are known to browse the many *Star Trek* conferences, and several of the actors have spoken about Internet fans in interviews; certainly much of the traffic on rec.arts.sf.tv.babylon5 was generated because series creator J. Michael Straczynski participated on that newsgroup. X-Philes feel a particularly strong bond to their series because they receive attention from the cast and crew. Although none of *The X-Files* writers or producers have delurked on the Chaos list, a few of them have dropped in on the America Online folders. Some of the fans who post to the Chaos list and to alt.tv.x-files do have connections to people involved in the production of the series and pass along news to other fans. Individual alt.tv.x-files regulars were acknowledged by having their names appear in the passenger list in "Little Green Men," some AOL subscribers were similarly honored in other episodes, and "Paper Clip" ended with a dedication to a fan who ran an AOL folder. Recognition by producers and the possibility that their posts are being read create a strong(er) emotional investment in the series for online fans, who feel that they are influencing the text through their voiced opinions. In the end, however, although cmc has increased the amount of contact between fans and producers, it has not changed the essence of fan activities. Analysis, interpretation, and speculation, building a community through shared texts and playfully appropriating them for their own ends—these are the defining features of fandom both online and off. Fans are fans because they engage in these practices.

4

"Are You Now or Have You Ever Been?"

CONSPIRACY THEORY AND *THE X-FILES*

Allison Graham

> Even a paranoid can have enemies.
>
> —Henry Kissinger

Sometime during the 1970s, Jane Fonda and Donald Sutherland asked political satirist Mort Sahl how he would make a movie about the Kennedy assassination. "I proceeded to tell them," he recalled,

> that the way I would have done it some years ago was definitely not the same way I would do it now, because we're somewhat separated by time from the shock of November 1963. But I told them I would make it abstract, or, at any rate, not specifically the Kennedy case. I would have a reporter, a skeptical reporter, a very cynical guy, to-gether with a girl reporter investigating the case. Neither of them would believe in conspiracy, but the conspiracy would eventually kill the girl. The man would then feel a sense of loss and would under-stand the horror of murder. (Sahl, 128–29)

Leaving aside the well-worn cliché of disposable "girl" and enlight-ened "guy," we can only wonder what Sahl must make of *The X-Files*, a cult television series premised on the very ideas that decimated his career in the 1960s. Unlike producer Chris Carter's amply-rewarded fascination with conspiracy theory, Sahl's obsession with government coverups earned him only bookings in the entertainment hinterlands for decades. Labeled a "bona fide paranoiac" by political pundits for his mockery of the Warren Commission, he would have to wait thirty years for the media declassification of paranoia. During that time, events transpired that would lead to Sahl's vindication, not the least of which was Fox Mulder's coming of age. For if Sahl was the nation's cast-out Conspirator General, Mulder became his New Age prophet, come in the guise of an FBI agent to rehabilitate the fallen reputations of those who wanted to believe.

Although Mulder may seem an unlikely inheritor of the mantle, David Duchovny's portrayal of him imbues the character with the kind of cool perceptiveness popularized by Sahl's generation of postwar cynics. Like his contemporaries Lenny Bruce and Tom Lehrer, Sahl had plumbed the depths of political hypocrisy for laughs, but unlike the obscene party crasher or the effete professor, he had been able to fashion a more marketable performance style. A California hybrid of showbiz and the G.I. Bill, the Sahl persona of the late 1950s foreshadowed the hip intellectualism of the coming Camelot years, managing (like JFK's persona as well) to connote both detachment and involvement, wit and high seriousness.

As many people who lived through those times have now forgotten, the Kennedy assassination signaled the beginning of the end of Sahl's immense popularity—and of the kind of humor he practiced. To a mainstream audience obsessed with postwar conformity, deconstructing Americana had been an act of political rebellion, a flagrant airing of the "deep background" that was invariably deleted from the national cover story. "When I made fun of Eisenhower," he later wrote, "the college audiences thought that I was making chaos out of order" (Sahl, 103). However, real-life social chaos consistently upstaged Sahl's hypothetical examples throughout the 1960s. No fictional scenario could compete with the historical spectacle, and while many comedians fled the battleground of political satire altogether, Sahl surrendered honorably to the victor. He became a student of the biggest jokemeister of them all: the U.S. government.

Moving to New Orleans to help Jim Garrison unravel the Kennedy plot, Sahl fashioned a new persona, that of the political investigator. Coolness was replaced by an ironic passion that bordered on outrage, as Sahl's performances—reading aloud from the Warren Commission report—became more like Lenny Bruce's dramatic readings from his own court cases. The team of Garrison and Sahl provided potential material for scores of aspiring comics, yet none would risk more than a quip. To do so would be to court professional disaster and public humiliation. One of Woody Allen's standard nightclub remarks of the 1960s, for example ("I was reading a great novel the other day—the Warren report"), was recycled in *Annie Hall* to demonstrate Alvy Singer's "anhedonic" paranoia. Only professional agitators could play the "conspiracy card" routinely; their careers, in fact, depended on it. The nightly news at times seemed to be the new Borscht Belt, as Abbie Hoffman and Jerry Rubin staged epic slapstick for a national audience (flooding the floor of the Stock Exchange with money, running a pig for president, attempting to levitate the Pentagon). The press loved it. The press did not love professional competition, however. Hoffman and Rubin were funny; Garrison and Sahl were not. Rogue demonstrators were televisual; rogue investigators were offscreen noise. The New Orleans duo ran out of money, and their show was assigned a permanent slot in the back pages of newspapers. Clearly, by the late 1960s, to be labeled a "communist nut" or a "hippie nut" was bad, but to be dismissed as a "conspiracy nut" was far worse.

Then came Watergate. Although upstaged again, this time by the younger and more media-savvy team of Woodward and Bernstein (and then by the televised hearings themselves), Sahl at least found public vindication. "I had to live the past ten years with the word 'paranoia,' " he said in 1976. But "all the things that caused Garrison and me to be labeled paranoids came to be true. We saw that the CIA does train local police departments. We saw that the federal government is not to be trusted. We saw that government officials do tap telephones. We saw that they do take bribes. We saw that the CIA does start wars, implicating the Army, and that the Army in turn implicates the people" (129). Suddenly in sync with the culture, Sahl now found work. If students of the 1950s thought he was "making chaos out of order," students of the 1970s—Watergate groupies feeding their addiction to one of the central cult events of the decade—asked him to "bring order to chaos" (103). His message? That post-1963 America, "presided over first by a President who succeeded because of an assassination that has never been officially admitted to; then by a President who was removed from office; and then by a President who was not elected and who has just recently been told by his Vice President (who also was not elected) that he does not care to run" (101), was a sham democracy run by secret forces. "How could it break down in fifteen years?" he asked. "Only by plan" (105). Stitching together the loose threads of postwar history—Cuban minions, CIA novelists, Mafia assassins, West Coast defense contractors—into a seamless cloak of conspiracy, Sahl became Fabricator Emeritus of a growing assembly of apprentices. Writers, academics, television preachers, and finally even comedians joined the chorus, chanting what was surely the mantra of 1970s politics: Trust no one, trust no one.

Seeming to echo the spirit of the times, Don Corleone told Sonny, "Don't ever let anyone outside the family know what you're thinking." By 1974, however, when Francis Ford Coppola made part two of the

Godfather saga, even the family had turned on itself. It was a theme repeated in most genres of the 1970s: horror *(The Exorcist, The Omen, Halloween)*, war films *(Apocalypse Now, The Deer Hunter, Twilight's Last Gleaming)*, satire *(Network, Shampoo)*, melodrama *(The Great Santini, Looking for Mr. Goodbar)*, crime thrillers and detective films *(Dirty Harry, Deliverance, Taxi Driver, The Long Goodbye, Chinatown)*, westerns *(The Missouri Breaks, McCabe and Mrs. Miller)*, and even musicals *(New York, New York; Nashville)*.

One director, however, managed to turn the paranoia of the era into a look (thanks to "Prince of Darkness" cinematographer Gordon Willis) and a genre of its own. Joining *film noir* and horror in a new "conspiracy" style, Alan Pakula directed a series of thrillers that found moral sickness insinuating itself into the deepest levels of American society: the family *(Klute)*, business *(The Parallax View)*, and, finally, government itself *(All the President's Men)*. In *Klute*, a corporate executive terrorized and murdered prostitutes when he was away from home, pinning the blame on his best employee. He even tape recorded the murders, and few critics found it strange that the criminal looked like Richard Nixon. But if Pakula's self-incriminating executive was oddly prescient (the film was released in 1971), the agents, double agents, and triple agents of *The Parallax View* (1974) appeared to be cast straight from the front pages. After the Kennedy and King assassinations of 1968, the attempted assassination of George Wallace in 1972, the Allende coup, the Pentagon Papers, the ITT scandal, the Watergate trials and impeachment proceedings, and growing allegations of CIA and FBI misconduct, Pakula's secret assassination corporation seemed plausible to many. That these professional assassins would escape detection seemed even more plausible after a decade of "lone gunman" theorizing by government investigators. Oswald, Sirhan, Ray, Bremer: how could so many antisocial misfits—"acting alone"—orchestrate a political agenda that to many pointed in only one direction (Nixon)? Pakula's film said they couldn't. It was the business of the Parallax Corporation, in fact, to maintain public belief in unconnected events; fall guys ("nobodies") could always be found to provide cover for its systematic murders. Those who dared to penetrate the mysteries of the monolithic corporation (like the reporter played by Warren Beatty) played right into its hands and became fall guys themselves. In centrally-controlled corporate America, "acting alone" was suicidal.

Pakula had to back away from this thesis the following year, however, when he agreed to direct the film version of Bob Woodward and Carl Bernstein's bestselling tribute to investigative journalism, *All the President's Men*. As America approached its Bicentennial with its government intact (despite yet another assassination attempt on a president), the saga of a crusade into—and out of—the national heart of darkness seemed tailor made for the zeitgeist. If *The Parallax View,* by its very title, acknowledged situational distortions in any point of view, *All the President's Men* placed full confidence in its investigators' intuitions; if the investigator in the former film never cracked the cover of his story (instead, *his* cover was cracked), the investigators in the latter relentlessly penetrated deep background. Watergate was, after all, a story about depth: the story seeped out through "leaks"; "plumbers" were caught trying to create or plug leaks (depending on which version of the event one believes); significant information issued from "Deep Throat," whose words were spoken only in dark parking garages (and who, in the Pakula film, appears and disappears magically after issuing guru-like admonitions to "follow the money"); hidden tape recorders caught illegal plans forming in the Oval Office; eighteen minutes were then found "missing" from the tapes; and all of it was known simply as a "coverup."

Like psychoanalysts, Woodward and Bernstein (Robert Redford and Dustin Hoffman) thrived on the tension between hypocrisy and truth, denial and confession, manifest cover and latent content. What better subject than a president who had publicly displayed his inner demons for decades, made countless Freudian slips, and, in an abysmal urge to self-destruct, documented his crimes with his own hidden tape recorders? In fact, the nation learned of the existence of Nixon's office and phone tapes almost by accident: a lower-level administration source let it "slip out" at the Watergate hearings. By the time the president was finally ordered to turn over the tapes, suspense had built to a fever pitch. Surely the "smoking gun," undeniable evidence of Nixon's direct involvement in an illegal coverup, would finally surface. The tapes, however, were all smoke—smoke, that is, swirling about an eighteen-and-a-half-minute vortex. Crucial dialogue between Nixon and his aides had "mysteriously" disappeared—mistakenly erased, he said, by his secretary during transcription of the tapes. Front-page photographs of Rosemary Woods demonstrating the contortion necessary for such a gaffe fooled no one, but that didn't matter. Nixon's secret had vanished, as it were, into thin air.

It was probably inevitable that someone would revisit that moment in history—that moment when America almost came face to face with the repressed demons of postwar politics, that moment when decisions were made to bury the monsters and "deny everything." Oliver Stone did so in 1995, with his film *Nixon;* a year earlier, however, Chris Carter not only revisited the moment but established it as the central crisis of *The X-Files,* television's fin de siècle compendium of conspiracy theories. Calling Watergate "the most formative event of my youth" (Lowry, 12), series creator Carter has not hesitated to register its reverberations in 1990s America on the psyche of his alter ego Fox Mulder, a man similarly haunted by the debacle of 1973. "The Truth Is Out There," most episodes announce in the opening credits. For agents Scully and Mulder, however, the truth usually seems to be "in there": in the alien tissue and communication devices stored in the bowels of the Pentagon, in the sewers of New Jersey, in the inner rings of ancient trees, in mushrooms grown in a New England basement, in subterranean Arctic ice cores, in trains buried in the New Mexico desert, in the intelligence community's covert "groups within groups," and most importantly of all, in the recesses of Fox Mulder's memory. The series, in fact, is premised upon the persistence of this memory. Mulder is introduced in the very first episode by the slogan "I Want to Believe" (the caption on a poster of a UFO in his office), and throughout the first season of the series he validated his obsession with the paranormal by reference to the unsolved childhood disappearance of his sister. His belief in alien abduction provided a motivation for his dedication to his work on unexplained phenomena and inspired the skeptical Scully to suspend disbelief from time to time, if only to placate her "spooky" partner. By the beginning of the second season of the series, however, the political contours of Mulder's "belief" were finally revealed.

In a flashback triggered in the parking basement of the Watergate Hotel (in "Little Green Men"), Mulder relives the evening of November 27, 1973. As a television news story relates the discovery of the missing eighteen and one-half minutes from the Nixon tapes, young Fox and his sister Samantha argue about what to watch that night; Samantha turns the channel, but Fox keeps turning it back to the Watergate news. As they squabble, the electricity goes off, and in a flash of light that nearly immobilizes Fox, Samantha "floats" out the window. The flashback abruptly cuts to Mulder's dark apartment. His front door opens, a silhouette says, "We're going to the Hill," and Mulder ends up in the office of Senator Mathison (a closet "believer" himself), where he is told that both his apartment and the Senator's office are bugged. Although the FBI has shut down the "X-Files Project" and taken Mulder and Scully off the case, Mulder (at Mathison's suggestion) leaves the country to recover tapes of extraterrestrial communication at an abandoned observatory in Puerto Rico. He even makes his own recording of an apparent "contact." When he listens to the tape back in Washington, though, it has been erased.

"Recovered memory," is, of course, a central convention of abduction narratives, and Mulder's flashback contains traditional features of such stories. The series seems to be staking out larger ground, however, implying that Mulder's visions might be collective rather than personal. As in the first season, alien abduction is linked to government crime, but now the link has become psychological as well as political. What Mulder recovers is both the memory of erasure (Nixon's) and the erasure of memory (his own). His "undeleted file" of childhood memory stands in contrast to the "deleted file" of official misconduct, but they both tell only one story: disappearance. The erasure of presidential crimes would be followed by the erasure of larger military and corporate crimes from national consciousness during the 1970s and 1980s (the "organized forgetting," or planned apathy, so painstakingly chronicled by Noam Chomsky). Just what was lost in 1973 is a question that looms over the series, a question Mulder seems "chosen" to answer by his peculiar attachment to history. *The X-Files'* mysterious Deep Throat (a 1990s version of Woodward's informant)— a player at the highest level of the government, at least until his apparent murder at the end of the first season—confesses in "E.B.E." to having participated in "some of the most insidious lies and . . . deeds that no crazed man could imagine." He was "haunted" by these acts until he found Mulder. "That's why I come to you," he says. "To atone for what I've done. And maybe sometime, through you, the truth will be known." In this transference of guilt, Mulder becomes the custodian of America's secret postwar history. He is now the haunted one, the living "memory bank" of officially denied images (which, come to think of it, may not be a bad way to describe the FBI itself).

What he shelters in his psyche is a nightmare—a "long national nightmare," to be precise. Gerald Ford claimed the nightmare was over when Nixon resigned, but Mulder (and possibly David Duchovny as well) would not agree. (Duchovny's father, after all, wrote the 1967 off-Broadway play *The Trial of Lee Harvey Oswald*.) "The Kennedy assassination, MIA's, radiation experiments on terminal patients, Watergate, Iran-Contra, Roswell, the Tuskegee experiments—where will it end?" Mulder asks Deep Throat rhetorically. Where exactly the nightmare began, however, is a question the series does not hesitate to answer: 1947. That year—the beginning of the cold war, the year Nixon first took office in Congress as the coldest of warriors and the House Un-American Activities Commission (HUAC) began "investigating" communist "infiltration" in the media, and the year of the Roswell crash —was also the year (according to the series) when the Jersey Devil first appeared, when alien tissues were first collected by the government, and when the governments of the United States, the Soviet Union, China, both Germanies, Britain, and France secretly agreed to "exterminate" any alien retrieved from a UFO crash.

If there is a ghost animating the machinery of *The X-Files*, it is most likely Richard Nixon, the icon of paranoia whose career virtually defined the golden age of American conspiracy theory. Quoting lavishly from Watergate-era films, the series makes no secret of the inspiration it draws from Nixon's political demise. *All the President's Men*, of course, is its most prominent source: Scully and Mulder are Woodward and Bernstein (with Mort Sahl's gender twist), thrown together on a project no one else wants, kept under surveillance, forced to summon Deep Throat by arcane means and to meet him in inconspicuous Washington locations. Other conspiracy films make their appearance: Deep Throat quotes the Corleones ("Keep your friends close, but keep your enemies closer"); Mulder quotes Dirty Harry and, like Harry Caul in *The Conversation*, tears up his apartment looking for surveillance devices; bodies are suspended in *Coma*-like tanks; the government attempts to assassinate Mulder the way it did the CIA worker played by Robert Redford in *Three Days of the Condor*; people are possessed in *Exorcist*-like fashion (a film which producer Carter certainly remembers was set in post-Watergate Washington). The "lone gunman" theory of political assassinations so mocked in *The Parallax View* is given short shrift here as well through Mulder's friendship with "conspiracy nuts" who publish a bulletin called *The Lone Gunman*. In case anyone thinks this all merely random pastiche, the boss who sets the whole scenario in motion in the first episode—and who brings Scully and Mulder together—is played by Charles Cioffi, the Nixon-clone murderer in *Klute*.[1] (Nixon's visage even appears in cartoon form on one of the Lone Gunmen's screensavers, complete with the bubbled caption, "I am not a crook.")

If *The X-Files* is overtly indebted to 1970s conspiracy films, however, it owes its soul to the science fiction films of the 1950s. The splicing of the two genres might seem genetically impossible, for their politics are hardly compatible, and yet one is undoubtedly the progenitor of the other. Who understands cold war xenophobia better than someone raised in the bomb shelter of 1950s paranoia? Who detects monsters in one's own government better than someone trained to suspect friends and family of "subversive leanings"? Whose sense, in other words, of an Alien Nation is more finely tuned than that of someone raised at the crossroads of movies, politics, and psychology?

"For me," Stephen King has written, "the terror—the real terror, as opposed to whatever demons and boogies which might have been living in my own mind—began on an afternoon in October of 1957. I had just turned ten. . . . I was in a movie theater" (1). In the middle of *Earth vs. The Flying Saucers*, "just as the saucers were mounting their attack on Our Nation's Capital," the projector stopped. The manager

---

1. The series quotes many other films as well: *The Silence of the Lambs*, *2001: A Space Odyssey*, *Cape Fear*, *The Lady From Shanghai*, *Freaks*, *North By Northwest*, *Star Wars*, and *Alien* are some of the most obvious.

walked onto the stage and announced to a silenced audience that the Russians had launched Sputnik. "Six years later, in 1963, I flashed on that moment when, one Friday afternoon in November, the guy who drove us home from school told us that the President had been shot in Dallas" (3).

"The real terror." A moment when mass fantasy and history conjoin. A moment when one is permanently "alienated" from social reality, haunted by political acts in which the imaginary "them" becomes the surreal "us." It was a scenario that had been playing out in the public forum since 1947. On the domestic front of the cold war, the House Un-American Activities Committee (HUAC) opened its "investigations" in Hollywood, but by the time of the Army-McCarthy hearings, communist infiltration had been "discovered" at all levels of American society and government. The central question of the era— "Are you now or have you ever been a member of the Communist Party?"—was unanswerable. Whatever one answered (or didn't answer) was proof of one's un-Americanness, one's status as the most undesirable of aliens. As the wagons circled tighter, the wilderness beyond became populated by political phantoms, people who were not then and maybe never had been who they said they were.

It was a fantastic tale, this national shape-shifting. Clearly, "we" were not alone; alter egos seemed to exist "out there" in infinite supply, at least in the movies. Martians, pod-people, and blobs invaded from the skies; giant ants, zombies, and prehistoric creatures crept up from beneath the earth. Whether the product of cosmic collectivism or scientific hubris, earthly and unearthly monsters alike operated according to one principle: infiltration. Once inside the system, takeover was nearly inevitable. Only federal agents and brilliant scientists could exterminate the brutes.

Only a few science fiction films of the era suggested otherwise. The most famous, *The Day the Earth Stood Still* (1951), allowed its audience to identify with the point of view of Klaatu, a morally and intellectually superior alien. Mingling with the people of Washington, Klaatu observed the hysteria of people who were convinced that "one of them" was among their ranks ("passing," in other words). His unspoken romance with Helen, a government secretary (and a "believer"), hinted of a possible federal-galactic liaison that could save planet Earth. Such a happy ending, however, was not to be. The government attempted to assassinate him, not knowing that his planet had discovered the secret of regeneration and immortality. Klaatu left the earth with a warning to cease its "petty squabbles" or risk the wrath of the universe. Apparently, the earth didn't heed the warning; by 1993, according to *The X-Files*, the government could no longer ignore what certainly appeared to be "the wrath."

Like the child Helen and Klaatu might have had, Fox Mulder is the most unlikely of characters—a federal worker with a cosmic consciousness. In the post-cold war FBI, Mulder is something of a double mole: an agent with often privileged access to paranormal phenomena, and a "true believer" in charge of government data collecting. In the absence of the Soviet "other," the government has resurrected the metaphorical enemy of the cold war—space invaders. However, as Mulder (and eventually even Scully) seems to intuit, the old dichotomy just doesn't work. Children of the 1970s, they were witnesses to the collapse of "us/them" thinking: the Evil Empire was not "out there," it was in the Oval Office and the Pentagon. The external enemy had moved inside—and it is still inside.

This issue is a troubling one for many *X-Files* fans, who find the series' recycling of old science fiction imagery hopelessly unenlightened. The radical step, they claim, would be a positive representation of paranormal phenomena. Within the context of the series, however, no other imagery is possible. The government, after all, has constructed the scenario and chosen the players. True, Mulder and Scully sometimes snoop too intensely or get "too close" to sensitive matters, but they are kept on. Why? To find the incriminating remnants of past "misdeeds"? This often seems the case; in the past three years, Mulder and Scully have often collected evidence that is promptly destroyed or impounded. Their job is reconnaissance, but not into "enemy" territory. The labyrinth to which they are assigned is the covert history of government crime.

When Deep Throat tells Mulder about his murder of an extraterrestrial shot down over Hanoi, his description of its "innocent and blank expression as I pulled the trigger" (a phrase remarkably similar to those used by U.S. soldiers to describe My Lai victims) leaves no doubt about the culpability of high-level "operatives" in the cold war. Innocence, however, was not an official adjective for "the enemy," just as innocent Klaatu could not survive the generic demands of cold war science fiction. The official enemy was a monstrous projection, and like most projections, it came back to haunt its creators. The horrific Other spawned in the secret chambers of the Pentagon, the CIA, and the FBI returned home after tour duty in Russia, Vietnam, and phantom flying saucers. There it waits, having outlived its usefulness—but knowing too much. Like Mulder's father, a former operative, it, too, will be terminated with extreme prejudice.

Mulder and Scully move through an underworld of their fathers' creation, Mulder's father guilty of covert crimes and possibly the disappearance of his own daughter, Scully's father a military officer who speaks after his death through the medium of a mass murderer. Is it surprising, then, that the inhabitants of this underworld so often look like the recycled "things," "pods," and "creatures" of cold war science fiction? Is it surprising that the sewage from the old Evil Empire backs up into this underworld, contaminating the northeastern water supply with Chernobyl runoff from an offshore Russian tanker? "Three species disappear from the earth everyday," Mulder tells Scully. Gazing into the polluted Potomac, he muses, "You wonder how many *new* ones are being created." A cut to a claustrophobic tracking shot into the Washington sewer system answers his question: The mutations festering in the bowels of the capital seem infinite.

Like Klaatu, Mulder is "killed" by government agents (near the birthplace of the Bomb in the New Mexico desert) and brought back to life by possibly alien means. His guides through this process are the old Navajo Code Talkers of World War II. Through the access to covert knowledge gained from Deep Throat and from the government encrypters, Mulder's understanding of that night in 1973 should deepen. However,"Little Green Men" hints that perhaps that moment—so filled with political and emotional significance—is, actually, an unfathomable abyss. The episode begins with the sounds transmitted into deep space since 1977 by *Voyager II*, and suggests that responses to the sounds have been received. Remembering that Samantha's disappearance occurred during the nation's discovery of Nixon's tape erasure, Mulder is determined to retrieve—on tape—"solid" evidence that would "prove" that what he thinks happened indeed did happen. But this tape, too, is blank. What if Nixon's eighteen and one-half minutes —traveling through space like *Voyager's* recordings—were "received"? What if, in fact, they turned out to be what they were all along—a "gap," a vacuum, a black hole? Oliver Stone imagines government secrets leaking into this void, but *The X-Files* asks us to consider a far more disturbing theory: that our central crime, in the final analysis, is "unspeakable." After all, if Mulder had not been interrupted by a phone call from Deep Throat as he watched *Journey to the Center of the Earth* on television one night, he would know that although monsters roam the depths of the planet, at the center is simply a vortex, a force which pushes its investigators right back where they started—in the laboratories where they dreamed up the idea of a center of meaning in the first place.

Mort Sahl would not be pleased.

5

``I Want to Believe . . . in the FBI''

THE SPECIAL AGENT AND *THE X-FILES*

Michele Malach

> I've taken in your All American features, your dour de-
> meanor, your unimaginative necktie design, and concluded
> that you work for the government . . . an FBI agent. But you
> see the tragedy here? I have mistakenly reduced you to a
> stereotype. A caricature. Instead of regarding you as a spe-
> cific, unique individual.
>
> —Mr. Nutt to Mulder, in "Humbug"

When *The X-Files* debuted in fall 1993, the show drew almost immediate comparisons to *Twin Peaks*. Indeed, the opening shots of the
first episode—a Pacific Northwest locale, trees in an overcast forest, a
dead young woman, apparent non sequiturs—were all visual and ver-
bal markers reminiscent of *Twin Peaks*. Although *The X-Files* moved
fairly quickly away from such overt evocation of the earlier program,
the images stuck in viewers' and critics' minds for most of the first
season. As the *Twin Peaks* fanzine *Wrapped in Plastic* so succinctly
stated, "The [*X-Files'*] writers might very well have been thinking,
'These concepts are too good just to lie around waiting for Lynch to
use again' " (Miller and Thorne, "The World Spins," 29). By the end
of its first season, however, most critics—and apparently the show's
creators—had changed their minds. While still not achieving the serial
narrative complexity, filmic production standards, or high-level writing of *Twin Peaks*, *The X-Files* had begun to establish itself as its own

show, despite the superficial similarities between the two programs. Moreover (and unlike *Twin Peaks*), when in *The X-Files'* second season the show shifted its narrative direction, it picked up audience members and cemented its cult status as well as becoming more popular in the mainstream. *The X-Files* is the most popular television series since *The FBI* (1965–74) to feature FBI agent protagonists; it is also the only one to last more than one season.

The most obvious similarity between *Twin Peaks* and *The X-Files*, however, has to be their FBI agent protagonists. In both programs, FBI agents who are supposed to be federal/cultural boundary police, who occupy positions as arbiters of normalcy, behave in ways that do not always fit with the usual idea of the special agent. According to Martha Nochimson, "Television government agents are the sine qua non of television's endless and obsessive restoration of limits, barriers that authorize only the most domesticated form of desire" ("Desire," 147). Pop-culture FBI agents typically function to police character and narrative boundaries, thereby reining in desire. Like other representations of law enforcement officials, the agent character also embodies the normal. This means that he or she represents cultural categories of correctness, acting out what it means to be normal, mainstream, not-marginalized; as Richard Dyer has observed, "power in contemporary society habitually passes itself off as embodied in the normal as opposed to the superior" (45). Special agents, representatives of power, construct for us the normal through their appearance, their actions, and their ideologies. The newest model special agent—including *Twin Peaks'* Dale Cooper as well as Agents Mulder and Scully—does not always function according to these expectations. At the same time, while Cooper, Mulder, and Scully behave in ways that may not always seem rational, as pop-culture FBI agents they still symbolize what our culture considers conventional. I have written elsewhere about Cooper's position in the pantheon of pop-culture agents and their history; this essay is devoted to Mulder and Scully, their bosses, and the villains they pursue (who are sometimes the same).

According to Richard Gid Powers, the trajectory of the image of the special agent in pop-culture history begins with the G-Man. Derived from an older, well-known and well-liked literary type—the action detective—the G-Man character did not emerge as widely popular until the 1935 film *The G-Men*. The early G-Man figured as simply a gangster with a badge, a response to the enforcement of the Production Code in 1935.[1] The enforcement itself was a response to the incredible popularity of the gangster as romantic antihero. To counter that

---

1. My information about the image of the FBI agent in popular culture until 1981 comes from Powers, unless otherwise indicated.

"inappropriate valorization," the tommy-gun toting G-Man was intro-duced in *The G-Men*. As Brick Davis, James Cagney epitomized the gangster-as-federal agent. In many ways, this characterization simply appropriated the features of the already long-popular action detective —independence, autonomy, violence, a personal code of honor, and a tendency to bring his man down rather than back—and placed the G-Man label on them. Although FBI chief J. Edgar Hoover (1895–1972) worked against this representation—real special agents did not carry machine guns, and they spent as much time in the lab analyzing data as they did on the streets bringing down thugs—the public bought it and enjoyed it thoroughly.

By the time of World War II, an obsession with espionage had taken the country by storm, and the Bureau and its popularly mediated representatives became part of the fight against Axis infiltration. The villain of the piece shifted from gangsters to Nazi spies, and the G-Man, whose jurisdiction essentially ended at our national borders, fought spies at home. This characterization presented certain dilem-mas. On the one hand, his inability to cross national borders limited the special agent character's prospects at a time of great interest in international affairs. On the other, the American fear of Nazi infiltra-tion was quite real, so the FBI agent (both real and mediated) could serve an important psychological function, helping to keep fear at bay with his reassuring presence. At the end of the war, our alliance with the Soviet Union dissolved and America resumed its concern with communism, but what had previously been concern turned to preoccu-pation, a ruling passion. The FBI became the thin, dark-suited line between god-fearing democracy and godless communism.

As politicians and press alike began to promote fear of the Red Menace creeping across our country, the popularly constructed special agent was perfectly positioned to stand and do battle. Hoover had worked diligently to create a perception of the Bureau and its agents as above the machinations of politics, unlike local and state police bureaus. To some extent the image was accurate, although not in the way Hoover intended. Hoover's vision was of an FBI whose moral order and duty transcended the petty deals and drifts of party politics. The truth was that the Bureau was protected by fear; despite drasti-cally different administrations, no president dared get rid of Hoover. Once he was entrenched, the moral order the FBI followed was Hoo-ver's. His largely unchanging vision guided the Bureau for almost fifty years (1924–72), making it a remarkably stable force, largely protected from the whims of politicians—although they were not afforded the same protection. From this lofty perch, Hoover's organization could be constructed as the upholder and defender of traditional American values within the nation's borders. The special agent could be not only an enforcer of the law but also an arbiter of national morality and values.

This resulted in another significant shift in the G-Man image, as the action detective-style hero gave way to what Powers calls "the domesticated G-Man." As personified by Jimmy Stewart in *The FBI Story* (1959), this version of the pop-culture special agent concerned himself as much with home, family, and the American way of life as he did with crimebusting. He was also a team player, using the resources of the Bureau to supplement his native intelligence, hardworking zeal, and extensive training. Not accidentally, *The FBI Story* was the film adaptation of Don Whitehead's authorized history of the organization. After years of struggle with Hollywood, the image of the special agent fell more in line with Hoover's vision of the agent as the arbiter of morality as well as legality in American life and popular culture. The domesticated agent presented a safer, more reassuring image for Americans enduring the cold war.

A necessary contradiction arose as the FBI worked to combat communism, both onscreen and off. From the late 1940s through the 1960s, the communist was the primary evil the pop-culture special agent was sworn to defeat, and thus the image of the agent was tied to the communist threat. In the movies and on television, agents of the Bureau always got their man or woman, yet the communist threat never diminished. On television's *I Led Three Lives*, Communist Party infiltrator Agent Philbrick always managed to unveil the plot and defeat the enemy without crossing the line of legality, despite juggling his triple life as average citizen, operating member of the Communist Party, and FBI agent. Philbrick's weekly "triumph was the result of American character and morality besting the deceit and general malevolence of the 'Red Underground' " (MacDonald, 104). Every week, he thwarted another devious and subversive plan by the Russians to undermine the American way of life—without ever visibly diminishing the threat to national security. Granted, television FBI agents must never run out of villains, but this situation mirrored to some extent the situation in the real world, where law enforcement's ongoing efforts to eradicate communism only served as fodder for continuing hostile rhetoric. Rather than calling into question the actual size and scope of the Red Menace, the contradiction served to reinforce the notion that commies were everywhere and that everything from illegal drugs to fluoridation were communist plots—furthering the need for domestic security and obscuring other areas in which the FBI might have been engaged.[2]

2. Organized crime is one example: Hoover's refusal to admit to the existence of the Mafia, much less commit the Bureau to fighting it, is common knowledge, and most Hoover biographies and FBI histories speculate on this seemingly bizarre strategy.

The FBI's war against communism and its agents in the United States stayed in the spotlight of popular culture throughout the 1960s. Hoover's last official venture into entertainment involved one of the most popular television programs of the 1960s, *The FBI*. Efrem Zimbalist Jr. and *The FBI* were closely related to the other "spy" shows of the decade, except for the image of the agent. On the espionage programs, the spies could leave the country and use extralegal means to stop the bad guys; by contrast, FBI agents were restricted to operating (for the most part) within national boundaries and did not fight evil by forsaking Bureau procedures, stretched as they might be by the requirements of the media. Zimbalist, square-jawed, clean cut, neatly attired, and by-the-book, signified the FBI for that generation of television viewers. He was also the epitome of what the domesticated agent had become: conventional, puritanical, and inflexible.

The death of Hoover in 1972 and the revelations of the Watergate hearings dealt an irrevocable blow to the squeaky-clean image of the Bureau. Powers enumerates several occurrences that led to the image backlash: Watergate, Nixon's resignation, the inquiry into the government abuses of civil liberties, the forced resignation of an FBI director, and a variety of indictments and convictions of top FBI officials. The Watergate hearings revealed decades-long illegalities that turned out to be standard operating procedure, and with Hoover and his clout gone, the FBI had little with which to protect itself against the slings and arrows of popular culture. To make matters worse, the special agent had for the last two decades been presented not as just any law enforcement professional but as the bulwark against the erosion of traditional American values. The FBI agent was supposed to be perfect. According to Powers, "The domesticated G-Man based his claim to popular respect on his righteousness, and so, according to the unforgiving logic of popular culture, with the first stain on his cloak of moral perfection he forfeited that claim" (254). The height of the pedestal upon which popular culture had placed the special agent gave the image further to fall—and fall it did. The picture of the agent shifted again, this time radically. Audiences were now presented with a sneaky, conniving manipulator. Breaking and entering, stealing, keeping secret files, blackmail, wiretapping, and more—all entered the public consciousness as the *modus operandi* of the Bureau and its agents.

Although the counterculture had long known about the dark side of Hoover and the Bureau, it took the widespread political disillusionment of the late 1960s and especially the public hearings of the early 1970s to bring about a mainstream change in the image of the FBI agent. The special agent was not the only political and law enforcement professional to see his image suffer, but the peculiar position of the Bureau brought about a popular backlash from which the FBI as

an organization has yet to fully recover.[3] Films like *Dog Day Afternoon*
and the six-hour television docudrama *King* presented the new images
of the agent, Hoover, and the Bureau. Deeply imbedded in the cultural
debate over values, rights, and justice, movies, television and books in
the 1970s tended to portray an insensitive, inhuman agent who valued
order over justice.

The image of the agent seemed to shift again when *Today's FBI*
made its debut on ABC during the 1981–82 television season. Although the program lasted only one season, it constructed a proto-
image for the special agent that would begin to catch on a few years
later. *Today's FBI*, from the title on down, attempted to present a new
and improved image of the Bureau and the agent as a response to the
"Me Decade." The heterogeneous group of agents on the program
focused as much on bonding with each other as on catching criminals.
When they did focus on crimefighting, the agents' every move was
careful, legal, and justified. These agents "were human beings first,
agents second" (Powers, 257), and the tension between the two roles
made up a significant portion of the drama of every episode. Approved by the Bureau, the program was marketed as an honest look at
the reality of FBI agents and their work, warts and all. In fact, it
unsuccessfully attempted to promote an image of FBI agents as a diverse group who actually did care deeply about justice and not just
order. *Today's FBI* operated on the fallacious assumption that its audience still viewed special agents as "us" rather than "them," and it
pushed this angle by having the agents on the show deal with some of
the most popular crime issues of the day: child pornography, civil
rights, hijacking, and deviant religious cults. The attempt to present
the agents as concerned and caring individuals was a logical response
to the decade and to the Bureau's image problem. The public, however,
did not buy either the image or *Today's FBI*, and the show was quickly
canceled.

By the mid-1980s, this image of a "kinder, gentler" FBI agent began
to gain acceptance, beginning with *Manhunter* (1986), Michael Mann's
film of a Thomas Harris novel. The hero of the piece is Will Graham,
the man who caught Hannibal "the Cannibal" Lector but who resigned
from the Bureau in angst over his identification with the serial killers
he hunted. Called back to help capture an especially devious and
vicious killer, Graham is haunted by his past and his fears for his
family. Like the domesticated special agent, Graham is torn between

3. This is particularly clear in some of the movies and television shows of the late
1980s and 1990s, in which the FBI is portrayed as a rigid, dogmatic, inhumane bureaucracy against which the agent/hero struggles to do the right thing. See, for example,
Point Break, Betrayed, Flashback, Thunderheart, and *The X-Files.*

his family and his obligation to duty, but unlike the earlier character, he rejects the rigidity of the institution to forge his own individual identity. Although *Manhunter* did only mediocre business at the box office, it signaled the beginning of the most recent shift in the image of the pop-culture FBI agent. This image—still prevalent through the mid-1990s—includes both male and female agents, usually but not always white, who are flawed and often angst-ridden but dedicated to truth and justice. They directly address the good/evil dichotomy, not always with the same results. Central to the characterization is the tension between the individual and the institution.

Manhunter was followed by a spate of FBI movies that continued to expand and develop the newest model agent, including *Betrayed, Mississippi Burning, Point Break, Thunderheart, Flashback, Feds, Silence of the Lambs,* and *Twin Peaks: Fire Walk With Me.* With the exception of a made-for-TV movie, however, the small-screen special agent was conspicuous by his/her absence until *Twin Peaks* premiered in 1990. With its pie-eating, coffee-swilling, dream-interpreting, rock-throwing protagonist Special Agent Dale Cooper, *Twin Peaks* presented the public with a hero who invoked the old-style agent while rewriting him in the context of the 1990s. He worked alone, like the action detective-influenced G-Man.[4] With his dark suit, slicked-back hair, and square jaw, Cooper looked every inch the domesticated agent, and his decency and loyalty to the Bureau also pointed to the 1950s-era image. Cooper's charmingly old-fashioned, straitlaced appearance soon gave way, however, to a boundary-defying, sensitive crimesolver whose techniques including dream interpretation and throwing rocks at bottles.

As an example of the newest issue special agent, Cooper negotiated the tension between his roles—but not without difficulty. In his relationship to Audrey Horne and in his collaboration with the Bookhouse Boys in solving her abduction, Cooper stepped outside his role as agent and outside the bounds of the law to do the right thing as he saw it. Carefully acting off duty, he avoided the appearance of impropriety that characterized the 1970s image of the FBI agent. His actions would have been deemed unacceptable in the 1970s, but the last decade has seen a shift in attitude toward public servants. Equally disillusioned with public servants and with the system in which they work, Americans received news of the Iran-Contra scandal with little surprise and a certain cynical acceptance. When the system does not allow for expedient "justice," the moral high ground apparently requires that it be bypassed, as the rise of civilian militia groups in the wake of Ruby Ridge and Waco attest. The separation of the pop-culture image of the FBI agent into different roles created a situation in which

4. In reality, FBI agents always work in pairs, never alone.

Cooper could act as a private citizen in ways that would not be allowed in his organizational role. Even when he is suspended during an investigation of his activities, Dale Cooper, private citizen, remains committed to the notions of justice and right that he holds so dear.

Cooper's peculiar characterization also pointed to a changing definition of the agent in terms of her or his traditional function as both literal and figurative boundary restorer, the agent who polices both state lines and the boundaries of desire. According to Nochimson, "A mass media FBI agent character ordinarily depends on our understanding of the literal job of the FBI: to intervene in criminal investigations when state or national boundaries are crossed" ("Desire," 147). As officially authorized barrier specialists, agents may renegotiate as well as reestablish cultural limits of body and mind as set forth by traditional American law enforcement ideals. These ideals—of law and (most especially) order, clearly defined right and wrong, careful mind-body separation, frailty as displaced onto the body of the other —typically set rigid boundaries. As Nochimson points out, Cooper is "a specialist in crossing boundaries, a quester capable of moving confidently and productively between the mental clarity of law and the intelligent fluidity of the body" (147). Recent portrayals of the federal agent emphasize fluidity over the earlier, more rigid boundary restoration. Thus, cultural tensions in the negotiation of law and order, good and evil, and crime and punishment (which tensions are part and parcel of the institution, negotiation, disruption, and reclamation of those boundaries) are embodied in the character of the law enforcement official and the criminal he or she pursues. This shift in characterization is particularly important to *The X-Files* as well as to *Twin Peaks*.

Like Cooper, Agents Fox Mulder and Dana Scully of *The X-Files* appear to be somewhat traditional (if remarkably well-dressed) special agents. Mulder, in particular, evokes earlier incarnations of the agent with his square-jawed good looks, his dark suits, and his short hair. Scully, whose fashion sense has apparently improved over the run of the show, also harks back to the earlier tradition, though not in such a direct way; after all, the older stereotypes of the FBI agent were all male. The inclusion of a female agent as a main character falls in line with the last decade's rewriting of the agent: despite the fact that women, African Americans, Latinos, Asian Americans, and Native Americans together still make up less than twenty percent of the Bureau's force of agents, female agents make up nearly half of film and television's special agents in their most recent incarnation. Unlike this inflation of the quantity of female agents, however, agents of color are as rare in film and television as they are in real life, and of course Mulder and Scully are white. Their appearance as ordinary FBI agents in line with traditional expectations of what agents look like reminds the viewers of a time when FBI agents were trustworthy protectors of the American way of life. Because Mulder and Scully look this way, we can trust them to tell us the truth.

The *X-Files* foregrounds Mulder and Scully's hypernormality, simultaneously evoking and subverting the earlier images of the FBI and its agents. A good example is "Humbug," the twentieth episode of the second season, which takes place in a community of sideshow freaks. Someone is killing the freaks, and nearly everyone is a suspect by virtue of their abnormalities. As the program progresses, however, the tables are comically turned. Almost every encounter between the agents and the community members makes Mulder and Scully, with their "normal" appearances and worldviews, look unusual. For example, suspicious of the sheriff after discovering his earlier identity as a dog-faced boy, the agents stake out his house and see the sheriff burying something in his backyard by the light of the full moon. As Mulder and Scully dig up the object, the sheriff catches them. It turns out that the buried object is a cut potato, a traditional folk remedy for warts. The normal agents finally solve the crimes, but the murderer disappears, eaten by another freak—a kind of internal, community justice. Once again, the normal is ultimately thwarted in its desire for closure by the not-normal, and Mr. Blockhead (Jim Rose, a body manipulator in real life) reveals the moral of the episode to Scully: "I've seen the future, and the future looks just like him [pointing at Mulder]. Imagine going through your whole life looking like that! Nature abhors normality, it can't go very long without creating a mutant. Do you know why? It's a mystery. Maybe some mysteries were never meant to be solved." In addition to articulating one of the operating premises of the series, this episode suggests that the FBI signified by Mulder's and Scully's looks represents an outdated ideology that is neither desirable nor useful in today's world.

Looks aren't everything, however, and the agents themselves act in ways that subvert the earlier traditions they invoke. Although Fox Mulder may look like Jimmy Stewart in *The FBI Story*, Mulder's whole raison d'etre—finding his sister who was abducted by aliens—seems as out of character as throwing rocks at bottles for a scientifically trained federal agent. Mulder especially subverts the boundaries that separate mind and body, so important for traditionally defined law enforcement officials. Like Cooper, Mulder relies on his hunches; psychic evidence is as important to him as the physical kind, and he relies heavily on the dreams and visions of others. Mulder himself does not often dream, however, because he is an insomniac.

This character trait also points to a boundary rupture: Mulder's angst (over his sister, the X-Files, the truth, the government) will not allow his mind or body to rest. Both his body and Scully's become an integral part of their crimesolving, as they transgress the boundaries set up by the law enforcement genre. Even the corpse, when there is one (or more), does not necessarily define difference and otherness. Connections are made between the body and mind and even go beyond; after all, spirits and aliens play an essential role in both the crimes and their solutions. Although they resist the possession that dooms other characters, Mulder's and Scully's bodies often serve as staging grounds for showdowns between paranormal forces and the forces of normalcy. In "Darkness Falls," for example, they are attacked and nearly killed by the ancient fluorescent bugs released by loggers. In "Dod Kalm," the agents are trapped in a government "time wrinkle" experiment that causes premature aging and death. Even when they can determine or at least theorize about the paranormal forces surrounding them, they cannot capture, expose, or prove them. Thus, the usual need to drag the paranormal forces kicking and screaming into the light of day for examination dissolves over the run of the show, leaving viewers to follow Mulder and Scully into a universe of mind-body connections, where the boundaries are not clearly defined and never will be. For the newest model special agent, categories of normalcy cannot be so narrowly defined. Even Scully—who by virtue of her skepticism gets constructed as the more normal of the two— continually has experiences that cause her to reevaluate her belief system. In "Beyond the Sea," an episode from the first season, Scully has visions of her recently deceased father that seem to be corroborated by a potentially psychic death row inmate, Luther Lee Boggs. In a disconcerting role reversal, Scully acts on Boggs's tips and solves the crime, while Mulder (who in this episode does not believe anything paranormal is happening) gets shot because of his doubt. This necessary flexibility, this openness to possibilities, is part and parcel of the most recent FBI agent character—and a clear break with past representations.

Because nearly every episode revolves around the paranormal, our heroes function as interpreters of the not-normal for the viewer. Their ability to cross the boundaries set up by convention makes them reliable interpreters as well as (sometimes unwilling) participants in the restoration of those boundaries. On another level, *The X-Files'* agents' conspicuous normality also points to the abnormality of nearly everyone around them, from their superiors to the victims and villains of their cases. Because they are trustworthy, "normal" protagonists, anyone who does not conform to their ideology, their worldviews, is not-normal and thus to be viewed with suspicion. This especially applies to their superiors.

While the image of the FBI agent as an individual has been recuperated, the image of the institution remains ambiguous at best. The

tension between an inflexible, secretive, hierarchical organization and
the complex, conflicted individual operating within it gets fore-
grounded in the most recent versions of the FBI story. Films like *Point
Break* and *Thunderheart* base their premises (and outcomes) on that
tension, and *The X-Files* imperils Mulder and Scully's jobs—and lives
—by accenting the conflicts between them and various government
agencies, including their own. The first season ends with the X-Files
shut down and our heroes reassigned after they find proof of government experiments with alien DNA. Near the beginning of the second
season, Scully is kidnapped and apparently injected with the alien
DNA. In other episodes, shadowy government agents step in and
thwart Mulder and Scully's efforts or use them to get information they
apparently and unbelievably cannot get themselves. The second-
season cliffhanger finale shows Mulder seemingly killed by Cancer
Man; then, in the episode that opens the third season, Scully finds a
computer chip implant in her neck—and more shadow agents attempt
to kill her. Although the necessities of a continuing program require
that the special agents lose neither their jobs nor their lives, they clearly
operate within a system that does not value their autonomy and indi-
viduality. Their superiors are as likely to hinder their mission as are
the aliens and criminals they pursue.

Mulder and Scully's superiors and antagonists within the federal
government are mainly white males, men who believe—like the 1970s
model federal agent—that they know what is best for the majority of
the people and act accordingly. The FBI, and the larger federal intelligence community, are portrayed in *The X-Files* as a kind of shadow
government operating outside the boundaries of legality and accept-
ability, willing and able to do anything to achieve their own obscure
ends. They have no concern for the rights of individuals, freedom of
information, or the "truth." Drawing on the perception of the federal
government that was popularized in the 1970s by the far left and
co-opted by the right-wing populist movement, the program gives us
"the phone tapper, the bedroom bugger, the blackmailer; the scandal
monger, the racist, the character assassin; the poisoner of the well of
intellectual and political freedom" (Powers, 255). These men value
order over law, control over freedom, and power over truth. Cancer
Man, for example, appears regularly as a constantly smoking, uniden-
tified member of the intelligence community who seems to have some
link to Mulder and Scully's work. In "One Breath," he tells Mulder
that he has sacrificed everything—friends, family, a life—for what he
does because he "believe[s] what I'm doing is right. . . . If people were
to know of the things that I know, it would all fall apart. You can kill
me now, but you'll never know the truth." Mulder, of course, cannot
kill Cancer Man—not just because Mulder will not stoop to Cancer

Man's level but also because he recognizes the futility of destroying this mysterious man. Cancer Man, as his lack of proper name indicates, represents something much larger and more significant than himself, the power of these hidden levels of government to see all, know all, and reveal only what they think others need to know.

The logistics of keeping the X-Files open and the show on the air, however, dictate that Mulder and Scully have allies within this shadow government as well. Deep Throat (first season) and Mr. X (second season) represent cracks in the system, men with power who—in the pursuit of their own obscure ends—both help and hinder Mulder's quest for the truth. Where Cancer Man is committed to maintaining existing boundaries and policing them, Deep Throat and Mr. X seem to simultaneously transgress and reclaim those boundaries as they come forward and pull back, providing Mulder with information that helps him solve cases and then manipulating him and his information for their own ends. Although Deep Throat was humanized by an explanation of his interest in Mulder and the X-Files ("E.B.E," "The Erlenmeyer Flask"), Mr. X shows no signs of affection for Mulder or his cause. While both "helper" characters clearly move through worlds to which Mulder has no access, both seem to need Mulder's unique ability to make mind-body connections to provide them with information they cannot get anywhere else.

By pairing a male and a female agent, *The X-Files* also foregrounds gender issues that have traditionally been denied or dislocated in FBI narratives. Rather than displacing difference and evil/weakness onto the body of the femme fatale or the female victim, *The X-Files* presents possibilities for rewriting gender and power relationships in this context. Much has been written about Mulder and Scully's relationship, which the show's creators insist will remain platonic and which has thus far developed into a kind of sibling relationship. Clearly, the two have closely bonded by the end of the first season, and they get to take turns risking their lives and careers for one another. In "One Breath," for example, Scully is near death and Mulder almost kills Cancer Man for his part in the crime; in "End Game," Scully saves Mulder's life. To be sure, the ratio leans in Mulder's favor when the entire series is taken into consideration: he saves Scully more often than she saves him.

In addition, the program's worldview (captured in the slogan "The Truth Is Out There") is obviously Mulder's. As a believer in paranormal phenomena, he has the advantage over his partner in most episodes. Scully, however, becomes the more flexible character over time, as her experiences seem to change her worldview more than Mulder's do him. In "Excelsis Dei," for example, Mulder is completely skeptical of the entity rape while Scully is the one who believes and wants to pursue the case. Unlike the earlier role reversal in "Beyond the Sea," this one is clearly gender related, although the issue is never articulated. After all, Scully actually believes that a rape has occurred, but Mulder insists that no crime, much less an X-File crime, has occurred; he says that the documentation on these kinds of cases is not conclusive and that he does not believe that these phenomena exist. Why would he disbelieve this particular phenomenon when he believes in most others, unless it is some kind of castration fear or something to do with his relationships with women?

Mulder's relationships with women mirror in some ways those of the earlier G-Man character, for whom women—if they exist at all—are mothers, victims, or femmes fatales. He treats Scully as the sister he lost, but he clearly dislikes her New Age sister. His own mother is virtually nonexistent as a character (although his father, murdered at the end of the second season, sometimes figures prominently), and he has no romantic entanglements. However, while women do not seem especially important in Mulder's life, neither do men; he seems to have no friends and no family except his parents and presumably his sister. Finally, neither Mulder nor Scully has a romantic life, although past relationships are indicated ("Fire," "Lazarus").

Another clear break from the traditional FBI and law enforcement narratives, a break that *The X-Files* shares with *Twin Peaks* as well as other recent FBI stories, involves the sometimes frustrating but apparently necessary inability of Mulder and Scully to "bring 'em back alive"—to resolve cases by prosecuting criminals. Even when cases are solved, the perpetrator escapes ("Genderbender," "Die Hand Die Verletzt," "Eve"), dies ("Humbug," "Lazarus," "Jersey Devil," "Miracle Man"), or apparently never existed at all (most of the episodes about aliens and alien abductions). The FBI agents sometimes manage to solve a crime ("Fearful Symmetry," "Soft Light," "Our Town," "Born Again," "Irresistible") but without a diminution of mystery. Sometimes the mystery is created by the paranormal phenomena themselves; in other episodes, the government holds responsibility for the conundrums around which the resolutions flow. Humbugs which cannot and perhaps should not be solved are a clear part of the gestalt of the series: "Maybe some mysteries were never meant to be solved." It is this continuing mystery that carries the narrative forward and without which there would be no series.

Although earlier movies and even *Twin Peaks* introduced viewers to new images of the model FBI agent, *The X-Files* narrative—with its conflicted, complex agent-protagonists, its conspiratorial, inhumane organizational structure, and its fluid boundaries—represents the epit-

ome of the newest model special agent and FBI story. These characters and stories combine elements of their predecessors, but they
filter those elements through the ideological and cultural shifts that
have occurred in the last twenty-five years to create a hero(ine) who appeals to turn-of-the-century audiences without insulting our presumed
intelligence.

6

"Last Week We Had an Omen"

THE MYTHOLOGICAL *X-FILES*

Leslie Jones

"A land that has no more legends," says the poet, "is condemned to die of cold." This may well be true. But a people
without myths is already dead. The function of that class
of legends known as myths is to express dramatically the
ideology under which a society lives; not only to hold out to
its conscience the values it recognizes and the ideals it pursues from generation to generation, but above all to express
its very being and structure, the elements, the connections,
the balances, the tensions which constitute it; to justify the
rules and traditional practices without which everything
within a society would disintegrate.... Some [myths] are
drawn from authentic events and actions in a more or less
stylized fashion, embellished, and set forth as examples to
imitate; others are literary fictions incarnating important
concepts of the ideology in certain personages and translat-
ing these concepts into the connections between various
figures.

—George Dumézil, *The Destiny of the Warrior*

In the episode "Beyond the Sea," Dana Scully, shaken by a vision of
her father at the moment of his death, sneaks into the office to look
at files behind Mulder's back. She pulls out a folder labeled "X-167512:
Visionary Encounters with the Dead." "Ah hah," the watching folklor-

ist thinks to herself. "That looks just like a motif number."[1] However, as those familiar with Stith Thompson's magisterial *Motif Index to Folk Literature* (6 vols., 1932–36) are aware, folk tale motifs beginning with X belong to the category of "Jokes, Tall Tales, and Lies." This certainly puts an unexpected spin on dictum that "The Truth Is Out There." If all Reticulans are liars . . .

There is more to folklore and mythology in *The X-Files*, however, than merely uncovering the traditional tale types and motifs that pop up in the scripts, or even cataloging the wart cures, the traditional measures of warding off evil, the items of folk belief that flash before our eyes as Mulder and Scully seek the Truth. In many ways, the X-Files themselves—those cabinets lined up against the wall behind Mulder's desk and under the window—constitute a motif index to contemporary legend. In fact, I would go so far as to argue that the series itself operates mythically, that is, as a series of narratives that serve to explain why the world is the way it is; in George Dumézil's words, "myth is . . . no more than the transposition into a typical and unique narrative (presented as a fable, or lent verisimilitude according to the taste of the narrator) of a regular mechanism of behavior of a particular society" (*Mitra-Varuna*, 110). If myth is, as some Jungians have argued, the collective dream of a society (Progoff, 251), then *The X-Files* may well be the nightmare of the fin de siècle. As with other mythologies, *The X-Files* conveys its message through metaphor and symbolism, repetitions of narratives, and variations upon themes; through overdetermination and juxtaposition rather than logical exposition, as Freud (311–74) revealed in the workings of dreams; and through the mediation of binary oppositions, as Lévi-Strauss showed in the operations of myth ("Structural Study," 81–106). The core of *The X-Files* is the encounter with the Other, that elusive—if not illusive—figure who has come to pervade the pages of literary criticism, anthropology, and psychoanalysis through the works of Jacques Lacan and his followers. For Mulder, at least, this is literally an Other Presumed to Know, his quest truly a "desire of the Other" (Lacan, cited in Bowie, 82–84). Although "aliens" form the most consistent class of dangers encountered by our heroes, taken as a whole this spectrum of horrors convincingly replicates perversions or distortions of the three "functions" or social categories—sovereignty, force, and fecundity—that

1. Unfortunately, it is not really a motif number. Motifs beginning X1600 cover "Lies about the weather and climate." More relevant motifs might be E327 "Dead father's friendly return," E361.1 "Return from dead to give consoling message," E364 "Dead returns to say farewell" (perhaps more appropriate for Scully's vision of her father in "One Breath"), or E586.0 1 "Ghost returns before burial." Interestingly, I cannot find a single motif for "vision of relative at moment of death," which is such a common event in personal experience narratives of the paranormal.

Dumézil and his followers have discerned underlying the whole corpus of Indo-European mythology (*Destiny*, ix-xv), a mythology in
which American culture takes part.

In arguing for a mythological reading of *The X-Files*, I am going
against the trend of most popular commentary on the series and on
television narrative in general. Discussion of *The X-Files* on the Internet
and on services such as America Online conforms to the pattern of
insistence on a reading for "emotional realism" that Henry Jenkins
(*Textual Poachers*, 116–17) has explored in his work on television fandom (for a more detailed analysis of this online discussion, see my
"The Truth Is in Here"). Mytho-logic packs an emotional wallop, to be
sure, but it rarely conforms to the kind of emotional realism that produces characters who react and relate to the world in a "realistic" way.
Indeed, it is the very nonrealism of mythic narratives that challenges
us to investigate them: if this narrative is not realistic, then why are
these people behaving like this? What deeper truth underlies their
actions? Rather than looking at cruxes and quirks in the plots of *The
X-Files* as opportunities to nitpick ("Why does Mulder keep sending
Scully off without any back-up? FBI agents would never do that!"), I
view these disjunctions as the cracks in the narrative facade that reveal
the underlying structure of the tale; or, to shift metaphors, these are
the clues that lead us ever deeper into the labyrinth of meaning.

''They Were Raised on Stories'': Lore and Legend in *The X-Files*

Film and television have long drawn on the demons of popular lore
as material for their stories. Dracula, the Wolfman, and Frankenstein's
monster all have their antecedents in the Old World legends of vampires, werewolves, and golems brought to North America by European
immigrants. As a general rule, however, Hollywood has taken over
little more than the *notion* of a particular type of monster; not only
does Count Dracula bear little physical resemblance to the revenants
of eastern European belief (see Barber), the sexual psychodynamic
underlying nearly all vampire films—from Murnau's *Nosferatu* (1922)
to Coppola's *Bram Stoker's Dracula* (1993)—owes more to Freud than
to folklore.

Hollywood also has a typical mode of representing not only the
creatures and events of folklore and myth but also those who investigate them. I have elsewhere dubbed the results of this mode
"The Bad Anthropology Film Festival," a genre of film and television
in which the character of an anthropologist, folklorist, or other social
scientist exists merely to deliver a small lecturette on the history
and lore of the phenomenon under investigation, then to conclude
that "There's nothing to be worried about; it's only folklorrrr-

AAAAAGGGHHHHH!!!!" and to die a horrible death in the clutches
of the Beast. Those lucky souls who survive the plot do so through a
combination of large contracts, good agents, and most importantly (in
the cinematic universe, at least) a belief in the literal reality of lore
and the efficacy of traditional remedies against the supernatural.[2] Bad
Anthropology is generally an antibourgeois genre: the working classes
already know how to ward off evil by reason of their bad education,
their attachment to "superstition" and other modes of "faulty reasoning," and their general closeness to the seamy side of life whether on
the mean streets or the manure-strewn farmyard; the upper classes, for
their part, by reason of their innate aristocracy, their complete disregard of the fruits of their expensive educations, and their blood connections to the land, were born for the express purpose of ridding that
land of horrors. It is the middle classes, with their shopkeeper mentality and their willingness to risk their lives for sordid cash, who really
get it in the neck, and their progeny—who make the mistake of taking
their education seriously and humorlessly, who think they know it all
and insist on telling it to everyone within earshot, who inhabit that
fabled Ivory Tower so far removed from everything useful in life—
provide the monster with its tastiest morsels.

The X-Files occasionally dances around the edges of Bad Anthropology (Mulder's synopsis of current thought about vampires in "3"
would have spelled instant doom for a lesser man), yet in one important way the series inverts the assumptions of the Bad Anthropology narrative. Whereas belief in the supernatural offers a means for
warding off evil in Bad Anthropology, it is Mulder's belief in everything from aliens to ectoplasm that makes him vulnerable in his own
X-iverse. "Kill Mulder, he believes," says the Son in "3"; "If Mulder
knows, that will make the sacrifice all the more meaningful," suggests
a Satanist in "Die Hand die Verletzt"; "But you must be careful—he
knows you," warns the head of the Calusari. Ultimately, Bad Anthropology pretends, for the audience's titillation, that the supernatural
world is more real than the natural world and that those who ignore
its rules do so at their own risk. In contrast, The X-Files offers a vision of
competing, parallel, but equally real worlds; which world you inhabit,
which rules you are subject to, is determined by your beliefs. The
scientists, doctors, and cops who fall victim to the supernatural in The

2. A few of the gems of the Bad Anthropology Film Festival include The Lair of the
White Worm (1988), The Serpent and the Rainbow (1988), Nomads (1986), The Wickerman
(1973), and, oddly enough, Beach Party (1963)—Frankie and Annette as Other. I also
include Kalifornia (1993), which, although it contains no anthropologists, is certainly an
object lesson in the dangers of undertaking fieldwork.

X-Files seem to do so not because they believe solely in science and rationality (as Bad Anthropologists do) but because they start to suspect that science and rationality may not hold all the answers.

The X-Files has been viewed primarily as a series that deals with aliens, monsters, and governmental conspiracies (but are these really separate categories anyway?). In terms of the explicit use of folklore, of the forty-nine episodes aired in the first two seasons, 14 (29 percent) deal with material that folklorists study, of which 7 deal with aspects of folk religion, 4 with traditional monsters, and 3 with other types of folklore, mostly the stuff of legend and rumor. This is a surprisingly high percentage—nearly a third of all episodes. In comparison, 17 episodes (35 percent) deal with aliens, and the remaining 18 (36 percent) deal with more generic pop-culture weirdness. So, in general, the writers of the series are drawing equally from the stuff of folklore, UFO belief, and journalism for their storylines.[3]

To consider *The X-Files* as myth, however, it is more useful to categorize the episodes from a different perspective. Interestingly enough, this categorization also breaks down into three more or less equal categories (although some episodes must be assigned to two or even all three categories, according to their complexity). I call these categories "There's Something in the Woods," "There's Something in the House," and "There's Something in the Government," depending

3. The episodes that I consider "folkloric" are "Jersey Devil," "Genderbender," "Miracle Man," "Shapes," and "The Erlenmeyer Flask" from the first season, and "The Host," "3," "Excelsis Dei," "Die Hand Die Verletzt," "Fresh Bones," "Dod Kalm," "The Calusari," "Our Town," and "Anasazi" in the second season. Most of these are self-explanatory. I include "The Erlenmeyer Flask" because of Chris Carter's drawing upon the 1993 incident in Riverside, California, where a woman allegedly emitted toxic fumes when brought into a hospital emergency room. At the time this story hit the papers, a number of people who subscribe to the Folklore BBS on the Internet jumped to the conclusion that this was an example of an urban legend that had made it into the media, an event that has occurred a number of times in the past. (One of the more recent examples concerned a story about an exploding toilet in Israel, which was picked up and reported on national network news until a few alert folklorists pointed out that this story was a widely-known urban legend: upon checking the sources, the news media were forced to acknowledge that this incident had, in fact, not occurred. Similarly, my father tells a story of being sent out by his editor to investigate a story about a woman selling an incredibly cheap sports car—a version of "the Philanderer's Porsche" (Brunvand, 22–24)—when he worked on the *Milwaukee Sentinel* in 1960). However, in the Riverside incident, the would-be legend-spotters were quickly set straight by folklorists in the L.A. area, who confirmed the veracity of the story. Nonetheless, the story *did* have all the earmarks of a good urban legend, and Carter's use of it in "The Erlenmeyer Flask" (and the subsequent incorporation of the motif of toxic blood as a marker of "alienation" into episodes of the second season) seems to me an example of how real events are turned into folklore.

on the location of that week's mystery.[4] The first two categories reflect
the swing between center and periphery that pervades *The X-Files:* is
what Mulder (in "The Calusari") calls "the howling heart of Evil"
located Out There, in the woods, at or beyond the boundaries of civili-
zation, or is it right here, lurking in the sewers, in the house next door,
in the bodies of our children and (ex-)lovers? The third category is the
category of governmental conspiracy, locating evil in the bowels of the
Pentagon, in the persons of Mr. X, Cancer Man, and their cohorts, at
home in the center but reaching its tentacles out into the periphery
and beyond—the mediating category that collapses center and periphery into one vast conspiracy of dread and denial. The image echoes
Yeats in "The Second Coming":

> Things fall apart; the center cannot hold;
> Mere anarchy is loosed upon the world,
> The blood-dimmed tide is loosed, and everywhere
> The ceremony of innocence is drowned.

This balance of subject matter and location, the equal time given
to all three categories, produces an interesting effect. On the level of
explicit content, "folklore" material, with its roots in the Old World if
not in the primordial human past, has equal weight with the postwar

4. There's Something in the Woods: the pilot, "Conduit," "Jersey Devil," "Ice,"
"Genderbender," "E.B.E.," "Miracle Man," "Shapes," and "Darkness Falls" from the
first season; "Little Green Men," "Ascension," "Firewalker," "Red Museum," "Die Hand
Die Verletzt," "Fresh Bones," "End Game," "Fearful Symmetry," "Dod Kalm," "Our
Town," and "Anasazi" from the second.

There's Something in the House: "Squeeze," "Shadows," "Ghost in the Machine,"
"Fire," "Beyond the Sea," "Lazarus," "Tooms," "Born Again," and "Roland" from the
first season; "The Host," "3," "Excelsis Dei," "Aubrey," "Irresistible," "The Colony,"
"Humbug," "The Calusari," and "Anasazi" from the second.

There's Something in the Government: "Deep Throat," "Space," "Fallen Angel,"
"Eve," "Young at Heart," "E.B.E.," and "The Erlenmeyer Flask" from the first season;
"Little Green Men," "Blood," "Sleepless," "Duane Barry," "Ascension," "One Breath,"
"Red Museum," "The Colony," "End Game," "F. Emasculata," "Soft Light," and "Ana-
sazi" from the second.

It is probably significant that the episodes most closely involved with Mulder and
Scully's own involvement with the supernatural—the arcs of "Duane Barry" "Ascension" "3" "One Breath" and "Colony"/"End Game"—cross the most categorical boundaries. The first arc, concerning Scully's abduction and return, begins at "home" with
Duane Barry's takeover of the travel agency, then moves out into "the woods" when he
takes Scully to the abduction site. Mulder's despair at Scully's disappearance sends him
truly out into the fiery Wasteland in "3," while Scully's serene coma vision of the
rowboat in "One Breath" recalls the plight of the Fisher King in medieval Grail ro-
mances; their reunion, when Scully regains consciousness, brings them both back
"home" again. The two-parter of "The Colony" and "End Game" also traces this swing
between center and periphery, home and wilderness (frozen this time).

rumors and legends of UFOs and space aliens,[5] and both have equal
weight with the monstrous creations of modern, rational science and
technology. The juxtaposition and equal weight of ancient legend and
modern science replicates the assumptions of Frazerian anthropology,[6]
but at the same time the line that divides these categories can be
crossed in the other direction—science begins to seem much less objective when its products bear such strong resemblance to the monsters
of myth and nightmare. Likewise, the juxtaposition of ancient legend
and modern UFO belief reinforces and emphasizes the mythological
axis of the alien stories.[7] The equal weight given to each category
creates a kind of narrative osmosis, as characteristics of one category
seep into another and all narrative traits become interchangeable. We
find monsters of myth, space, and conspiracy equally out in the wilderness, at home in the sewers, and bagged, tagged, and filed for reference
in the warehouses of the Pentagon. We cannot say that the Other is
only Out There, but at the same time we cannot locate the Other solely
In Here—the Other is *everywhere*. We have met the enemy and he is
us, but *we* are not who we are.

Bugs from the Dawn of Time: Paradigms

As I have already noted, *The X-Files* is mythological not only in terms
of its explicit content but more importantly in terms of its form. One
characteristic of folktale, legend, myth, and other oral forms of narrative is that every "story" exists in multiple versions and variants. This
variability works in different ways in different genres of narrative. In
folktale, a single underlying paradigm can generate a seemingly infi-

5. It seems a pity that academic folklorists are not doing more to study beliefs in
aliens and UFOs, material which, whatever its absolute reality status (*pace* Mack, Jacobs,
Hopkins, et al.), is transmitted and perpetuated in a classically folkloric manner: infor-
mally, unofficially, in "face-to-face communication in small groups" (as Dan Ben-Amos
has defined the very term "folklore" 12).

6. "Magic . . . is a false science" (Frazer, 13) while "myth [stands] to magic in the
relation of theory to practice" (770). However, most critics of Frazer have overlooked his
conclusion to *The Golden Bough*, which seems increasingly relevant in an era where the
verities of science are coming into greater question: "In the last analysis, magic, religion,
and science are nothing but theories of thought; and as science has supplanted its predecessors, so it may hereafter be itself superseded by some more perfect hypothesis" (825–26).

7. This permeability of categories is most clear in the numerous episodes in which
Mulder instantly categorizes a phenomenon as a manifestation of folklore or popular
belief only to discover that the real cause is science or aliens—or vice versa. One good
example of this is "Eve," where he instantly suspects alien involvement in the deaths of
the girls' fathers, but ultimately uncovers a governmental conspiracy of another sort.
Another is "Our Town," where Mulder initially seems to have been spending his sleepless nights reading the collected works of the Ozark folklorist Vance Randolph, yet again
ends up by uncovering a small-town governmental conspiracy.

nite number of versions; what stays the same is a core set of actions and the relationships of core characters to each other.[8] Thus, folktale analysis takes as its basic unit of investigation the plot of the narrative; action is the ultimate source of the narrative. Mythological analysis has a different take on the relationship between uniqueness and variation in narrative: myths are generally assumed to grow out of the need to express ideas *through* action, and it is the ideas rather than the actions that stay "the same." The plot of the mythological narrative is a metaphor expressing the deeper underlying structure that frames all cultural activity, both in and out of the narrative. Folktale *is* narrative; myth operates *through* narrative.[9] Because myth is not necessarily tied

8. The tale type index compiled by Antti Aarne, translated and enlarged by Thompson as *The Types of the Folktale* (1928), provides a numbered list of basic European folktale plots, so that, for instance, versions of the tale known as "The Dragon Slayer" (considered by many folklore scholars to be the archetypal fairy tale) will be referred to as "AT 300". However, the collected versions of AT 300 can bear seemingly little superficial resemblance to each other. The names of the characters change, the locales change, some versions have more or different subplot elements than others, and even the endings and outcomes can differ. The notion of underlying tale types allows folklorists to talk about stories collected over the course of 500 years from Chinese, French, and Native American storytellers as all being versions of Cinderella. In fact, during the first half of the twentieth century, much folktale scholarship depended on the historic-geographic method of identifying tale types and tracing the spread of their variants over space and through time. The underlying assumption of this type of analysis is that there is a single, spatially and temporally locatable original tale (the *Ur-Form*), which has grown, spread, and varied over time, but all versions of which still bear the same genetic makeup—a model based on the notion that stories, like the people who tell them, have family trees, that stories, like all living beings, mutate. ("Nature," says Dr. Blockhead in "Humbug"—who does *not* hold a doctorate—"abhors normality; you just can't go very long without creating a mutant.") One drawback of this type of folktale analysis is that it becomes reductionist: people begin to assume that once they have identified and analyzed an *Ur-Form* they have uncovered the meaning of the entire corpus of tales. More recent scholarship, drawing in part from Carl von Sydow's notion of *oikotypification* (the idea that stories are adapted by their tellers to the narrative "ecology" of their environment), is beginning to consider that the *way* in which stories vary in specific places and times may be as significant as their narrative genealogy (see my "The Function of the Otherworld," 5–33).

9. As an example of mythic functioning, the underlying ideology of the relationship between the rightful king and the land he rules is expressed in Celtic mythology in what is called the myth of Sovereignty. (Most of my mythological comparisons will be to Celtic myth, but equally valid comparisons can be found in all branches of Indo-European myth.) However, this myth manifests in narrative in ways that have no "genetic" relationship to each other, in the way that we can see genetic relationships between versions of a folktale. Versions of the myth of Sovereignty include the Irish adventure of Cormac mac Airt, whose wife and children were abducted from him; when he found them held hostage in the Otherworld, he was shown a goblet containing red ale poured out by a beautiful woman; the goblet shattered when a lie was uttered in its presence, and the pieces rejoined when a truth was uttered. The woman was revealed to be the Sovereignty of Ireland, and Cormac was given the goblet (and his wife and

to any specific genre of narrative—or indeed, to narrative at all, since it can be found in ritual, in the visual arts, in the very way that people build their houses or lay out their cities and towns—myth can be found in any genre, including folktales. And television series. With this in mind, let us consider a set of *X-Files* episodes: "Ice," "Darkness Falls," and "Firewalker." All three are stories of Something in the Woods, although the wildernesses vary from the frozen arctic to the old growth forests of the Pacific Northwest to an active volcano, and the threats faced by Mulder, Scully, and their companions emanate from the elements of water, air, and fire. In each case, something goes amiss at an isolated outpost: an arctic research station, a logging camp, a geological expedition. Man's irresponsible search for profit and knowledge (two motives fatally intertwined, in that governmental and academic research are inevitably expected to have a practical, profitable application) has awakened some dormant parasite, which then threatens the existence of humankind: a worm that turns people homicidal, a bug that sucks all fluids from humans, a silicon-based fungus that breeds in the lungs and destroys the respiratory system. In each case, the parasite has been safely encased in a natural prison, frozen in the arctic core, wrapped within the growth rings of ancient timber,

---

children back as well) "for discerning between truth and falsehood" (Cross and Slover, 503–7). In another Sovereignty myth, a young man named Niall was the only one of his five brothers willing to kiss an ugly old woman in return for a drink of water. When he made love to her, the woman became young and beautiful, and she told him that he would become the king of all Ireland and his descendants would occupy the high kingship for generations to come, while his brothers, who refused her, would never have the kingship at all (Cross and Slover, 508–13). This young man was Niall of the Nine Hostages, the founder of the Ui Neill dynasty who ruled much of early medieval Ireland until the Norman conquest. The Ulster cycles of tales, especially the *Táin Bó, Cuailgne* feature Queen Medb of Connacht, who is clearly not only a fictional character but also a representation of Sovereignty herself. Her very name means "intoxicating" (cognate with Welsh *meddw* 'drunk' and English *mead*)(Rees and Rees, 73–76). "I asked a harder wedding gift than any woman ever asked before in Ireland," she says, "the absence of meanness and jealousy and fear . . . I never had one man without another standing in his shadow" (Kinsella, 53).

These narratives cannot be said to be the same "story" in any way, yet a set of themes and motifs bundle together in a consistent way: there is a beautiful woman and a man destined to be king, a drink is offered and accepted, and there is an implicit or explicit sexual relationship between the man and the woman. Or, as the Reeses put it, "Sovereignty is a bride, the server of a powerful drink, and the drink itself" (76). These narratives connect with other, nonnarrative aspects of Irish kingship: the king's inauguration, for instance, is called a *banfeis rigi,* a royal wedding, and he is referred to as being "married" to the land he rules. Just as sexual sterility was a reason for divorce in medieval Irish society, so was it a reason to depose a king, for if he was sterile, his "wife," the land, would be unfruitful, bringing famine and war to his people.

buried in the bowels of a volcano. However, although science has called forth these monsters, it is Scully's scientific and medical background that enables the two agents to identify the source of threat and ultimately avoid, eliminate, or neutralize it.[10] And in each case, someone ends up in quarantine and the source of the contamination is ruthlessly eradicated by anonymous governmental forces.

More importantly, each of these episodes revolves around questions of Mulder and Scully's trust in each other—and others' trust in them. In "Ice," the two agents are still newly partnered, and the events at the research station force Scully to decide whether she believes (and believes in) Mulder, despite the urgings of the others that he is infected and that he has killed someone. Mulder and Scully as partners are contrasted with Hodge and Da Silva; significantly, while in the set of FBI agents it is the woman, Scully, who is forced to question and then affirm her trust in her partner, in the set of doctors it turns out to be the woman who is in fact the infected one, the murderer. Hodge and Da Silva arrive united and suspicious; Hodge insists on checking everyone's I.D. to be sure that "we are who we say we are." However, it is the one he assumes he knows who turns out to be "not who she is"; both his unquestioning suspicion and his unquestioning trust turn out to be misplaced. These two pairs of partners are revealed by the end of the episode to be mirror images of each other. And Mulder proves to be trustworthy.

By the time of "Darkness Falls," the trust between Mulder and Scully has been more or less established: barring massive evidence to the contrary, Scully is willing to give Mulder the benefit of the doubt. Naturally, Mulder immediately screws up, impulsively placing *his* trust in the ecoterrorist whose booby traps have placed them in jeopardy in the first place. Although Mulder's trust in the man himself turns out not to have been misplaced—Spinney does come back for them—Spinney's monkeywrenching activities still resurface to sabotage the escape, with nearly fatal consequences. Mulder's "nice trip to the forest" puts himself and Scully in quarantine.[11]

"Firewalker" explicitly echoes Mulder's romantic vision of a nice trip to the forest when Jessie comments that Trepkos "promised me that this would be an adventure, that it would change my life."

10. This is, of course, Scully's role in many other episodes as well. "It was science that saved Mulder," she muses at the end of "End Game." Scully saves Mulder through science, whereas Mulder saves Scully through faith, as she also acknowledges at the end of "One Breath": "I had the strength of your beliefs."
11. It is interesting that Mulder and Scully so often end up quarantined: isolated and contained, monitored for infection; this is what Cancer Man and his minions would like to do to them philosophically but the government can only do to them physically. Of course, they always turn out to be "clean."

Trepkos and Jessie again offer an inversion of and a comment upon the partnership between Mulder and Scully. This episode represents Scully's first case since her abduction and return, and she repeatedly reassures Mulder that she is all right, that she can take care of herself. Where "Ice" and "Darkness Falls" mostly explored Mulder's trustworthiness, this episode uses the by-now-established paradigm to question and reaffirm Scully's reliability—not so much her moral integrity as her physical and emotional stamina. Trepkos and Mulder are both portrayed by their colleagues as brilliant eccentrics, but where Mulder is merely odd, Trepkos suffers from a diagnosable (and "treatable") bipolar disorder. Trepkos' sexual relationship with Jessie oversteps the bounds of their social roles as professor and student, creating a relationship marked by an excess of intimacy, whereas Mulder and Scully's relationship is explicitly marked by its lack of sexual intimacy. Both Mulder and Trepkos have, in their different ways, seduced a younger woman into accompanying them on their own special quest for knowledge, dragged her off to the limits of the world and the wastelands in pursuit of Truth.[12] However, we had just seen (the previous week) that no matter how unconsciously complicit Mulder may have been in Scully's abduction, no matter how much guilt he feels, her involvement in his quest has not proved fatal (not yet, at any rate). Jessie's involvement in Trepkos' search indeed proves fatal for her; just in case we were missing the point, when she tries to take Scully with her, Scully illustrates just how much she's "back, and [she's] not going anywhere" by hoisting Jessie over her shoulder and slamming her into a containment chamber before the spores can explode.

With increasing insistence, these three episodes show just how remarkable it is that Mulder and Scully always manage somehow to survive, by showing what could have happened. The two of them so easily could be Trepkos and Jessie or Hodge and Da Silva. Sarah Caudwell, in her mystery *The Sirens Sang of Murder,* cogently expressed this dilemma when her character Cantripp muses, "The trouble with real life is that you don't know whether you're the hero or just some nice chap who gets bumped off in chapter five to show what a rotter the villain is without anyone minding too much" (171). Once a character has been established as a main protagonist, it becomes increasingly difficult to arouse real suspense as to whether he or she will survive the episode or not. The focus of interest usually becomes how close the shave will be, in what manner they will escape, etc.; the focus shifts from the result to the process. However, it is also a convention of mystery and horror stories that whatever the reason for the heroes'

12. Can it be a coincidence that this episode, which reveals the discovery of that "Holy Grail of science," a silicon-based life form, takes place on "Mount Avalon"?

survival (assuming they do survive), there are a number of secondary
characters who do not survive, pointing up the strength, cunning,
divine election, or dumb luck that attends the heroes. *The X-Files* often
uses this convention in this very specific way, offering up doubles and
mirror images of Mulder and Scully as burnt sacrifices who illustrate
just how close our heroes have come to disaster. But by making it so
clear that "There but for the grace of God go Mulder and Scully," the
use of these inverted couples forces us eventually to ask, What exactly
is this grace? [13]

Mulder and Scully become defined by their difference, from each
other and from other sets of partners. Unlike Trepkos and Jessie,
Hodge and Da Silva, they are specialists in different fields, although
they are united as FBI agents. Scully specializes in the physical world,
reconstructing past events from the traces they have left in the present.
As she comments in "Irresistible," "A body has a story to tell . . . it
may be an irony only understood by those who conduct these examinations that death, like life itself, is a drama with a beginning, a middle, and end." [14] Mulder specializes in the mental world, constructing
profiles of serial killers and other criminals that predict what that
person will do in the future, so that the villain may be caught. However, while the two complement each other in one way professionally,
they complement each other in a different way emotionally. In the
conventional paradigm of men as rational and scientific and women
as intuitive and emotional, Scully—as a doctor, an officer of the law,
and a skeptic—is a "masculine" woman, and Mulder—with his obsessions with the occult, the bizarre, and the alien—is a "feminine" man.
In "Aubrey," however, we see that when presented with a tangled
situation, Scully intuits the aftermath of love and connections (she
immediately realizes that B.J. is having an affair with her boss and that
B.J. is pregnant) whereas Mulder intuits the aftermath of violence and
tragedy (he is the one who realizes that Mrs. Thibideaux was raped by
Cokely and conceived a child). Each of them labels their own mode
of reasoning "rational," the mode of their partner "intuitive." [15] The
difference in Mulder and Scully is not that they conform to *or* invert
traditional gender roles, but that they conform to *and* invert traditional

13. This is evidently a question that worries the characters themselves. At the end
of "Paper Clip," Mulder is forced to the conclusion that they have no choice about
whether they survive or not: it must be Fate.

14. Mulder certainly appreciates how Scully's knowledge supplements his own—
at times it seems that he presents bodies to her for autopsy with all the generous glee of
a cat dropping a dead mouse at her person's feet.

15. Scully: "I seem to recall you having some pretty extreme hunches." Mulder: "I
never have!"

roles, crossing boundaries in all directions while always maintaining a productive complementarity.

One thing that should be clear by now is that, while a tale type is consistent in terms of its action, and while individual tale types may tend to cluster around certain thematic concerns, there is no inherent value that can be automatically correlated with a tale type or motif. Once narrative value enters the picture, we begin to enter the arena of myth. The story-teller—whether an Irish *shennachie* or an American scriptwriter—takes the skeleton of plot from "tradition" and reworks it to his or her own ends, in his or her own style. The three episodes I've been discussing were written by four different writers: "Ice" by Glen Morgan and James Wong, "Darkness Falls" by Chris Carter, and "Fire Walker" by Howard Gordon, offering a set of versions of the tale type comparable to the versions of Cinderella we may find told by different storytellers in the oral tradition. They're all "Cinderella," but they're on their way to very different balls. "Ice," with its leitmotif of "we are not who we are," follows a trend that often surfaces in Morgan and Wong's scripts, one of questioning the very nature of personality and raising issues of aberrant behavior and dual identity: the meek animal-control inspector who is a mutant shape-shifter with a taste for human liver, the hapless residents of rural Pennsylvania driven mad by a combination of insecticides and electronic equipment, the upright, uptight PTA run by practicing Satanists. "Darkness Falls" is pervaded by the imagery of alien beings coming down from the sky to carry away their victims, the swarm of insects paralleling the "mass" quality of faceless aliens, the bugs' green glow the same phosphorescence we come to associate with alien blood, all echoes that make this episode resonate with the themes of abduction and alienation found in Carter's other scripts (where they are often focused more closely on Mulder's family saga). Finally, "Fire Walker," laying the blame for the situation as much on Trepkos' failures in interpersonal relations as on the presence of hostile natural forces, is consonant with Gordon's general tendency to write scripts in which preexistent character traits are as likely to provoke crisis as some supernatural intervention in the mundane world.[16]

''Did You Really Think You Could Call Up the Devil and Ask Him to Behave?'': The Cosmology of the X-iverse

Myth, as a system of meaning, can only be discerned by comparison. The mythic axis of a narrative is only revealed when it is seen as part

---

16. A good example of this is in "Sleepless": Preacher does not commit murders just because he has the ability to do so; rather, his religious beliefs, which he had before the operations on his brain, drive him to use the abilities he has developed to achieve

of a set with other narratives and that set of narratives seen in its relationship to the culture that generated it. *The X-Files* is a product of late-twentieth-century American culture, but American culture was not born yesterday—or even in 1776—and American culture is not confined to the boundaries of the United States. As a culture whose main roots originate in Europe, America taps into the wellspring of Indo-European mythology, the system of meaning that underlies narratives from the *Rg Veda* to the *Taín Bó Cuailgne,* the *Shah Nameh* to *Beowulf.* Dumézil proposes that one of the purposes of Indo-European mythology is to work out, in narrative form, the proper relationship among three "functions" of society: sovereignty, which is concerned with the regulation of the universe both in terms of magic/religion and law/justice; force, concerned with the regulation of aggression; and fecundity, concerned with the regulation of fertility, prosperity, and the production of material goods. Sovereignty is represented by the magician-king[17] and the judge-priest, force by the warrior, and fecundity by women and farmers or craftsmen (see Nagy, 200–204). Their respective spheres of action are the court, the battle-field, and the material world. In this context, we can see that the sources of mystery that confront Mulder and Scully each week can be described as perversions or mutations of the three functions: truth gone bad, science gone bad, and bodies gone bad. (Science, in *The X-Files,* is invariably the handmaiden of the military.)

Perversions of fecundity are the easiest to spot, for they are literally mutations: Eugene Tooms ("Squeeze," "Tooms"), the Jersey Devil ("The Jersey Devil"), the Eves ("Eve"), Cecil L'ively ("Fire"), the Kin-

---

retribution and absolution for the sins he and his comrades committed. Likewise, in "Lazarus," Dupre's already established love for Lula drives him to take advantage of the opportunities offered by inhabiting Willis' body. Contrast this with, say, Morgan and Wong's "Blood," in which people are forced by external manipulation to act contrary to their normal behavior; "Beyond the Sea," in which external personalities can enter Boggs' body and override his own personality; or even "Little Green Men," where institutionally-imposed exile from the X-Files causes Mulder to question his whole world view, even to the extent of wondering if his sister was really abducted

17. It is important to remember that although the king is a ruler, the first function is concerned with governance but not necessarily with political power. In other words, the first function is in charge of making sure that the affairs of man are in concordance with the universal Truth that is believed to model the mortal world, through the operation of good judgment and proper ritual; first function kings are sacred kings. Historically, in Western Europe and in North America, actual political power came to be vested in warrior kings, whose political power derives from the second function. Warrior kings eventually were replaced by elected officials whose power nonetheless retains a military edge—thus, the president of the United States is commander-in-chief of the armed forces.

dred ("Genderbender"), John Barnett ("Young at Heart"), the manitou ("Shapes"), the Flukeman ("The Host"), B.J. ("Aubrey"), and of course the entire cast of "Humbug." In many of these cases, not only are the "monsters" themselves literally twisted individuals but the problems they cause for the "straight" world derive from their own reproductive drives: the Jersey Devil attacks the homeless in an attempt to feed her child, the Kindred kill as a side effect of sex, the Eves are a fertility experiment run amok, and B.J.'s genetic predisposition to murder is activated by her own pregnancy. Like the Flukeman, the parasites of "Ice" and "Firewalker" are also fecundity monsters, killing their host as a byproduct of their reproductive cycle. Creation and procreation are the paramount domain of fecundity. In most of these episodes, the task faced by Mulder and Scully is simply to eradicate the mutation, to prevent it from reproducing. However, the episode invariably ends with the question hanging—Cecil still wants a smoke, how many more Eves are there (and what about the Adams), what if someone goes back down into the volcano, did Joe Goodensnake bite someone we don't know about, what *else* is breeding in the bowels of those Russian freighters?

Sovereignty episodes have tended to revolve around questions of religion and the afterlife. "Shadows," "Beyond the Sea," "Roland," "Lazarus," "Born Again," and "Excelsis Dei" all propose that the spirit survives death and can carry out its mortal agenda from beyond the grave. Indeed, these episodes illustrate that if the spirit is willing when the flesh is weak, then the hell with the flesh—the spirit can take care of business by itself. Non-mainstream religion has also been explored, in "Miracle Man," "3," "Die Hand die Verletzt," "Fresh Bones," "The Calusari," and "Our Town." All of these episodes demonstrate the power of faith to overturn the pedestrian verities of science: a holy man *can* heal just with his touch, the blood and the flesh *are* the life, the Devil *does* come when you call. Fecundity episodes create monsters that are all flesh, uninformed by intelligence or spirit; sovereignty terrors are concentrations of incorporeal venom, taking revenge on the flesh they have abandoned.[18]

I think it is significant that these episodes deal with the magico-religious side of sovereignty to the exclusion of the judicial and governmental aspects. This is a particularly late-twentieth-century American take on the role of sovereignty; indeed, Dumézil, in his study

---

18. It should be remembered that one of the most pervasive "superstitions" the world over is the belief that the spirits of the dead are envious of the living and therefore measures must be taken to prevent them from coming back to cause trouble for the loved ones they have left behind. This nearly universal truth forms the basis for the episode "The Calusari."

of sovereignty in Vedic mythology, saw the function divided between magical kingship on one hand and judicial priesthood on the other (see *Mitra-Varuna*), whereas here we are presented with overtly magical "priesthoods" and a repressed judicial rulership. *The X-Files* presents a picture of the world in which the military has co-opted and corrupted all notions of judicial fairness and of governmental honesty. The monsters and terrors of fecundity and sovereignty are essentially "natural": unplanned mutations, spirits innate in man and in the natural world. They wreak havoc on the world of man almost casually, a side effect of doing what comes naturally. The threat of force, however, is cultural: it comes from deliberate intent, by means of manipulation and active intervention on the part of man.

It is also significant that nearly all of the episodes dealing with alien visitation to Earth can be viewed as force episodes. This is because of two elements in these stories. First, the "visitation" is presented as an invasion, the abductions as acts of hostility, (indeed, the abduction of Samantha, which provides the motivation for Mulder's own quest for the Truth, is starting to look like not so much a kidnapping as an exchange of hostages between warring parties). Second, the more deeply Mulder and Scully delve into instances of alien presence on the earth, the more they discover the involvement of the military in covering up, eradicating, and denying that presence. The military is stretching out its tentacles into many other areas of life, as well: taking by force the knowledge that Dr. Chester Banton has acquired in "Soft Light," participating in the coverup of a pharmaceutical test gone awry in "F. Emasculata," sponsoring experimentation on human guinea pigs in "Sleepless." Even when specifically military presence is not implied, the abuse of physical force is invariably associated with conspiracy, as in the mysterious electronic commands that cause people to run amok in "Blood," or the involvement of Crew-Cut Man in the alien DNA experiments in "Red Museum." [19]

Analyzing the content of *The X-Files* in terms of Dumézilian functions illustrates how the series, as an artifact of American culture, fits into the framework of broader Indo-European mythology. The tendency for force to seep out, to overwhelm sovereignty and fecundity —which *The X-Files* seems to present as a byproduct of late modernity —has also been noted in the Indo-European mythologies of late antiquity, particularly those of the Roman, Celtic, and Germanic peoples

---

19. There is something ironic in the persistent association of conspiracy—a relationship that is inherently built upon silence, upon the semblance of "nothing going on" —with the violent acts that the conspiracies are shown to produce: the rapes and murders induced by conspiratorial experimentation, the executions of Men Who Know Too Much such as Deep Throat, Bill Mulder, and The Thinker.

(see Dumézil, *Destiny*, 40–45 and *passim;* Puhvel, 144–221, 241–55). Like these ancient mythologies, *The X-Files* uses mythic narrative to explore the implications of this seepage, specifically to question the role of physical force in relation to sovereignty and fecundity, and more broadly to consider what happens when any of the functions becomes "monstrous."

This analysis also shows, however, that Dumézil's three Indo-European functions can be regularly associated with the kind of binary oppositions that Lévi-Strauss sees underlying the operations of all mythology, particularly the primal opposition of nature and culture.[20] According to Lévi-Strauss, myths exist to provide solutions for insoluble eternal questions: where do we come from, where do we go when we die, how can we avoid dying at all, how can men and women get along? The myth provides solutions to these intractable problems by positing an initial pair of binary oppositions such as life and death, nature and culture. The initially irreconcilable opposition is mediated by the introduction of a third term, which in some way partially partakes of the nature of each opposed term. This third term, however, invokes its own opposed term, but this new binary opposition is not as completely intractable as the first. The process repeats, each new opposition being a little closer together than the previous one, until a set of oppositions that can provide some kind of cultural modus vivendi is reached. Thus, the opposition of nature and culture is mediated by being turned into an opposition between the raw and the cooked, whereby the raw product of nature is culturally processed through cooking. Within the mythic narrative, the association of individual characters with nature and with culture may be denoted by the rawness or cookedness of the food they eat. In many Celtic tales that deal with the relationship between mortals and the inhabitants of the Otherworld, a young man first tries to woo a fairy woman by offering her fully baked bread; when that doesn't work, he offers her raw

---

20. It should be noted that one of the main criticisms of Dumézil's theories is that these three "Indo-European" functions can be found operating in mythologies that are definitely *non*-Indo-European. In particular, the three functions have been analyzed in Japanese mythology by Atsuhiko Yoshida and his students (Littleton, 204–7, 258–60). This raises some interesting questions. Are the functions found because the people looking for them are themselves from Indo-European cultures or are (in the case of the Japanese) trained as Indo-Europeanists, or are the functions innately present no matter who is looking at them? Or are we forced to make the assumption that an Altaic band containing a few Indo-European speakers not only made their way to Japan but also had an influence on Japanese mythology out of all proportion to their numbers? If a tree falls in the forest with no one to hear it, does it still have Indo-European roots? In my opinion, although the jury may be out on whether this tripartite functionality is solely Indo-European, it is still a productive tool for understanding the generating structures of the mythologies that I, at least, deal with.

bread dough. She refuses both but is finally won when he offers her half-baked bread, the liminal nature of the bread—neither raw nor cooked—reflecting her own liminal relationship to the world of mortals (Rhys, 1–74).

As noted above, in *The X-Files* sovereignty and fecundity are associated with nature (although in different ways), while force is associated with culture. Fecundity is concerned with purely physical nature, the level at which people are not differentiated from other animals, or from trees, leaves, and liver flukes for that matter. This is an association that produces an episode like "Fearful Symmetry," in which animals are subjected to the same abductions and experiments as human abductees and in which the opposition between "human" and "animal" is mediated by Sophie, the gorilla whose name means "wisdom" and who can communicate through sign language. Sovereignty is concerned with the super-natural—literally, the nature above nature—which transcends the physical for the realm of pure spirit. Susan Lepselter has pointed out that in the myths analyzed by Lévi-Strauss, the ultimate result of mythological mediation is to associate man with culture and animals with nature. The stories of alien abduction, however, which provide the source of so many X-Files, express a new belief, perhaps a new fear: through the aliens' unemotional experimentation on forcibly acquired human bodies, man is shown to belong to nature, while the aliens are the ones who inhabit a kind of super-culture.

Sovereignty is also the function that is concerned with Truth. Sovereignty cannot function in the presence of lies: remember the story of Cormac, in which the goblet that is Sovereignty breaks into pieces when a lie is told but magically repairs itself when a truth is spoken. The one thing that unites Mulder and Scully, despite their differing opinions on the source and nature of the events they investigate, is that they both believe in a Truth that exists and that must be nurtured and protected.[21] Force, as the function which operates in the sphere of human activity and intentionality, is the function that within *The X-Files* is associated with culture. In this way, it mediates between the two "natural" functions, which either place man in too large a sphere, as just another lump of flesh, or in too narrow a sphere, in which only the incorporeal, spiritual part of man can exist.[22] Force comes to

21. It seems to me that where Cancer Man and his cohorts initially misjudged Scully is when they assumed that her scientific skepticism would blind her to their own distortions of the Truth. From the pilot episode onwards, it is the evidence of conspiracy and coverup that causes Scully to back Mulder, *despite* her skepticism about aliens and other monsters.

22. Returning to the notion of the Bad Anthropology Film Festival, it is interesting to compare this X-ish vision of the three functions in relation to the class structure of

encompass the entire realm of human activity, and this is seen as a dangerous thing.

In myth in general, the strongest characters are those who can function successfully in the most environments, those who can mediate between nature and culture, periphery and center, countryside and city, woman and man, and so on. As partners, Mulder and Scully can operate in the realms of all three functions: Mulder, as a psychologist who specializes in disturbances of the spirit, is largely a sovereignty character; Scully, as a doctor who spends much of her time cutting up dead flesh in autopsies, commands fecundity; both of them, as agents of the FBI, are employed by force. Their primary allegiance, however, as officers of the Law, is to sovereignty, to the Truth that is "out there."

I commented above on the notable repression or absence of the juridical aspect of sovereignty, the aspect concerned with truth rather than faith, in the explicit plot content of *The X-Files*. This would appear to be because the central problem posed by the series, its mythic core, is a conflict between sovereignty and force over the control of Truth. The simpler episodes of the series, mostly ones that deal with perversions of sovereignty and fecundity, present threats that arise from within the function: something that is normal mutates into something abnormal more or less spontaneously (like Tooms), or the spirit world reaches into the mortal realm through doors carelessly left open through disregard of proper ritual ("The Calusari"). The threat posed by force is that it is reaching out into the arenas of the other two functions, tinkering with children's DNA ("Red Museum"), appropriating the "very building blocks of reality" ("Soft Light"), denying everything. More basically, however, the lies told by the representatives of force are distortions, mutations, or perversions of sovereignty's Truth. Where most premodern Indo-European myths of force explore the consequences of the inevitable guilt incurred by the warrior in carrying out his function and the warrior's acceptance of his inevitable doom for the good of society as a whole, the postmodern mythology of *The X-Files* explores the consequences of force's refusal to accept its guilt, to deny that the guilt even exists. As a result of "denying everything," the price of that guilt must be paid by others, by the innocent, by sisters.

---

the classic Bad Anthropology narrative. In the latter, sovereignty and fecundity (the aristocracy, hereditarily assigned the duty of maintaining Sovereignty, and the working classes, those who produce goods) are given positive value, while force is invariably the victim of the Beast. Again, sovereignty and fecundity are represented as "natural," but this naturalness is seen as the proper and protected sphere for human activity; the solely cultural middle classes, by reason of their divorce from the natural world, are vulnerable.

So far, I have analyzed *The X-Files* by assigning the episodes to categories; in one system of categorization, a single episode may form a group with one set of other episodes, while in another system that episode may be grouped with a different set. For instance, when looked at from a Dumézilian standpoint, aliens invariably wind up in force episodes, but when looked at from a locational standpoint, aliens are in the woods, in the house, *and* in the government. This is an inherent characteristic of mythological analysis: myths, like dreams, are overdetermined in the Freudian sense, and so no single reading can provide a complete account of every possible reading of the myth. (This may be the quality that separates "myth" from "literature." Or then again, it may not be.) The best that can be achieved is a kind of kaleidoscopic view, ever-refracted, constantly changing, but always composed of the same pieces.

One failing of this type of analysis is that it tends to look at a set of narratives in a state of temporal stasis. Each narrative exists at the same point in time; plot elements, character traits, whispers and gestures are pulled out of their contexts and compared for a moment before being replaced in a narratological glass case for permanent display. However, in order to really understand the mythological import of *The X-Files,* especially as it is an artifact of late-twentieth-century America, it is necessary to consider the series as it unfolds along its temporal axis.

In the process of all of the categorizing I undertook for this essay, it began to be clear that the earlier episodes were much easier to assign simply to one class or another and that as the series has evolved, the categories have begun to collapse into each other. One of the first instances of this was "Genderbender," an episode that introduced a religious sect (sovereignty) whose sexual practices proved fatal to humans (fecundity) and that ultimately was revealed to be an extraterrestrial colony (force). As the notion of "conspiracy" has escalated, previously isolated events have begun to reveal unexpected correspondences. The pilot episode presented a small-town conspiracy to cover up a series of murders committed by (as it turned out) aliens, with the assistance of a comatose abductee. The impetus for the conspiracy was a father's natural concern for his son. By the end of the first season, the conspiracy is found to extend throughout the United States government; by the end of the second season, the conspiracy is seen to involve former Axis powers working within the U.N. However, what propels Mulder and Scully in their search for the Truth still emerges from the family. In fact, as the series has progressed, the two agents have come to mirror each other's lives: father dead, sister taken in his or her place, each having gone through death and rebirth, now alienated and exiled from "normal" life, increasingly reliant only on each other. By the third-season episode "Paper Clip," Mulder and Scully's negotiation over how or whether to turn over the MJ-12 files had come to eerily echo (and, we hope, invert) the kind of negotiation Mr. and Mrs. Mulder must have endured when deciding which child would be "taken," and the decision regarding files that must expose an international conspiracy finally rests on the need of a woman to see her sister in the hospital.

White Mythology

This essay can only begin to scratch the surface of the folkloric and mythological axis of *The X-Files*. An episode such as "The Calusari" is worthy of an entire paper in and of itself, just to chart its representation of superstition, folk religion, spiritual belief, and the ethnic and immigrant experience in the United States; "Fresh Bones" and "Die Hand die Verletzt" could be compared for their differing takes on magic and folk religion; the shamanisms of "Excelsis Dei" and "The Blessing Way"/"Paper Clip" could be further explored, as could the Arthurian quest that seems to underlie Mulder's dark night of the soul while Scully is abducted and returned in "Duane Barry," "Ascension," "3," and "One Breath."

However, the third season of *The X-Files* has opened with a set of episodes that address the central "myth" of postmodern, postindustrial Western culture: the myth of the written word. Jacques Derrida speaks of "metaphysics—the white mythology which reassembles and reflects the culture of the West: the white man takes his own mythology, Indo-European mythology, his own *logos*, that is, the *mythos* of his idiom, for the universal form that he must still wish to call reason" (Derrida, 213). More simply, Western culture denies that it has a myth by insisting that that myth is merely natural reality. One of the chief tenets of Derrida's deconstructionist philosophy is that Western culture ostensibly privileges the spoken word over the written word, that the written word wants to pretend to *be* a spoken word because the spoken word is "natural" where the written word is "cultural." The truth, however, is that for the Establishments of Western culture, oral communication isn't worth the paper it's written on; that is why Mulder doubts his quest, and that is why he finds himself (in "Little Green Men") facing the situation of "Again, nothing but facts. And again, no facts at all." There is nothing tangible in Mulder and Scully's quest.

So how ironic it is that in "Anasazi," Mulder finally gets his hands on documents, on the tangible proof of the conspiracy that he has so long suspected exists; and yet again, how ironic that what allows Skinner to get Mulder and Scully back to the FBI, his ace in the hole against

Cancer Man and his cohorts, is the oral tradition of the Navajo. Albert Hosteen and his fellow Code-Talkers turned the documents into written words in the first place, but the process of inscribing those words in the ephemeral, intangible medium of the computer tape has burned them irradicably into the oral tradition and has given them the privileged status of the spoken word. Throughout Indo-European mythology, the power of the word is in its being spoken; Truth *is* a spoken word. As J. E. Caerwyn Williams has noted of the ancient poets of the Greek, Celtic, and Germanic cultures, praise to the gods and the aristocracy did not just reflect their nobility, it caused it to exist in the first place: "Lords of the Word in a world in which words had not yet lost their magic power," speaking those words created reality (10). When the facts of government involvement with aliens are just written words in the government's hands, it is "white mythology," a palimpsest that cannot be seen; when these words enter the oral tradition of the red man, their speaking becomes the cosmic Act of Truth. Free at last, free at last, thank God Almighty, free at last—the Truth is finally Out There.

And now that we have the Truth, as Scully points out, all we need is the answer.[23]

---

23. This paper has profited greatly from discussions both electronic and oral with Paula Vitaris, Elizabeth Kubek, Paul Rabwin, Heather Joseph, Susan Scheiberg, all the Diggers, and everyone on the AOL X-Files Forum. As always, my Dumézilian tendencies must be blamed on Professors Patrick K. Ford and Joseph F. Nagy, who little realized what a monster *they* were creating.

7

"What Do You Think?"

THE X-FILES, LIMINALITY,
AND GENDER PLEASURE

Rhonda Wilcox and J. P. Williams

Scully: "What do you think?"
Mulder: "I think I want to see what's in that cellar."
—from "Squeeze"

This exchange between the protagonists of *The X-Files* can be read as a metaphor for the series' relation to issues of gender, visual pleasure, and rationality. The connection among these seemingly disparate subjects becomes evident as Fox Mulder and Dana Scully examine and question each other's values and beliefs, in a vigorous mental relationship that incorporates a sublimated sexuality. On its most basic level, the program appears to advocate an ideology in which Mulder and Scully are free to invert traditional male/female characterizations: Scully represents the rationalistic worldview usually associated with men, while Mulder regularly advocates supernatural explanations and a reliance on intuition traditionally connected with women. She applies scientific explanations and logic; he uses instinct and intuition. The two characters are presented as gender-liminal, moving back and forth across the border of traditionally accepted gender patterns.

Ironically, their frequent sex role reversals result in Scully's investigative gaze being disempowered. Time and again, Mulder sees evidence of the supernatural that Scully, by the structure of the episode, is disallowed from seeing. Despite these visual limitations, neither character is presented as merely a visual object for the other; rather, they share reciprocal looks as subjects, as I/eyes in the course of their investigations. In fact, issues of viewing pleasure and gender liminality are central to the appeal of *The X-Files*. Scully and Mulder's gender liminality combines with their sublimated sexuality to provide both male and female audiences a viewing experience of special pleasure—pleasure that, while imperfect, still challenges the position of critics (such as Laura Mulvey) who would maintain that female desire and subjectivity cannot exist within mainstream popular culture. Furthermore, as the series progresses, Scully and Mulder begin to share a position that is liminal in terms of patriarchal order as well as gender because of their ways of thinking about and seeing their world and each other. In this essay, we wish to briefly outline some of the major issues within feminist film theory as they apply to *The X-Files*, discuss antecedents of the series that help determine its approach to gender and cognition, and analyze several key episodes that illuminate the manner in which the program simultaneously negates and reinforces patriarchal concepts of male and female subjectivity.

Male and Female Gazes

> Seeing is not enough. I learned that from you.
> —Mulder to Scully, in "Little Green Men"

The 1975 publication of Laura Mulvey's "Visual Pleasure and Narrative Cinema" opened the debate concerning the operation and ideological importance of the cinematic gaze. The debate contains such a variety of theoretical positions that a complete discussion is beyond the scope of this essay. However, a few points are central to the argument we wish to pursue with regard to *The X-Files* and need summarizing here.

Mulvey's original conception of Hollywood film as constructing a passive female/active male dichotomy revolves around the assumption that one gender is empowered by its ability to look at the other. Men, according to this theory, have the power to gaze unfettered at women, "who are simultaneously looked at and displayed, with their appearance coded for strong visual and erotic impact so that they can be said to connote *to-be-looked-at-ness*" (*Visual and Other Pleasures*, 62). Male characters and spectators are granted the power to express desire, controlling women through the gaze. Such power as women possess is the power to conceptualize themselves as spectacle, serving as focus for male desire. Mulvey further posits the cinematic gaze as consisting of three parts: the gaze of the camera, the gaze of the male characters in the film, and the gaze of the film's male spectator.

Mulvey's work has led to a number of important questions, the most obvious being "What happens when the spectator is female?" Although feminist critics have taken different theoretical positions regarding that question,[1] many concede that a very different power dynamic comes into play "When the Woman Looks" (the title of a famous essay by Linda Williams). While each of these theoretical positions illuminates our understanding of the nature of female spectatorship in some way, we have chosen an approach that maintains that the gaze is somewhat more malleable than some scholars have suggested. In other words, we assume here that male and female subject positions can be alternated, with men sometimes being the passive, "to-be-looked-at" characters and women representing a more active investigating gaze. Male and female characters who can switch traditional positions at will, we contend, exist on television and help to answer the questions Jackie Stacey asks in regard to Mulvey's original argument: "How might the male body on the screen be the source of erotic pleasure?" and "Where is the place of the feminine subject?" (24).

It is important to note that Mulvey's original argument was made with regard solely to classical Hollywood cinema. Although it was not her intention to discuss other forms of mass media, scholars who have followed her have been sufficiently intrigued with the concept of the gaze to apply it to other visual media, notably television. Such studies, although sporadic, have been inevitable because television is a medium in which large blocks of programming have been conceived with the express purpose of attracting a female audience that can then be delivered to advertisers. These studies have usually focused on the soap opera format (see for example Nochimson, *No End to Her*), assuming that women tend not to be interested in the action/adventure or science fiction genres.[2] However, both demographic information supplied by the ratings services and the observations of scholars studying television fandom (Bacon-Smith, Jenkins) demonstrate that such is not the case. Women are, in fact, very much a part of the audience for genres traditionally considered male. In the case of *The X-Files*, for example, a substantial female audience has emerged via various computer bulletin board services.

However, several commentators have suggested that Mulvey's concept of the gaze cannot be applied to television studies. E. Ann Kaplan, for instance, raises the issue as to whether "theories about the 'male gaze' apply to watching television, when usually there is no

1. For an introduction to the range and breadth of this critical debate, see the special issue on female spectatorship in *Camera Obscura* 20/21 (1989).
2. Exceptions to this rule might include studies of the female detectives of *Cagney and Lacey* (e.g. D'Acci). Also, Camille Bacon-Smith's *Enterprising Women* provides a detailed study of how female fans of science fiction series interpret camera techniques.

darkened room, where there is a small screen, and where viewing is interrupted by commercials, by people moving about, or by the viewer switching channels" (230). Such a position, however, privileges the filmic over the televisual text. It assumes that the film spectator is a more attentive audience than the television viewer and subtly implies that film is more worthy of critical attention than is television. In addition, such a position fails to take into account the circumstances of contemporary television viewing. Viewers, especially fans of cult series such as *The X-Files*, are likely to tape favorite programs, watch them repeatedly (often on larger screens), and study key scenes at length. As Camille Bacon-Smith has noted, female science fiction fans in fact pay close attention to the programs they follow and are quite sophisticated in their understanding of the visual techniques used in television production.

A related problem confronting the scholar who deals with the gaze in television has been stated by Stacey:

> Since the early 1980s, cultural studies work on television audiences has been developing rapidly, and in recent years "audience studies" have become a definite "boom area." Indeed, audience studies have become *so* popular that Charlotte Brunsdon has felt it necessary to appeal for the retention of "the notion of text as an analytical category" (Brunsdon 120). Unlike film theory, then, in which the text has typically tended to be privileged over context, television studies have tended to privilege the context over the text. (35)

It is our contention that the interaction of text and audience cannot be overlooked. The nature of the gender-related pleasure that audiences derive from a series such as *The X-Files* is, to a great extent, influenced by the visual and aural clues provided in the text. For that reason, we concentrate on the text itself rather than on the empirical audience or the viewing context.

Antecedents: Rationality and Intuition as Investigative Strategies

> "The brain doesn't work like that, Mulder . . ."
> "Then you explain it to me."
> —from "Deep Throat"

Like many television series, *The X-Files* references existing texts both as inspiration and as cultural shorthand. The character of Dana Scully, for example, recalls in many ways the character of Clarice Starling as portrayed by Jodie Foster in the 1991 film *Silence of the Lambs*. Both Foster and Gillian Anderson are unusually petite to be playing the sort of heroic roles that traditionally go to more statuesque actresses such as Sigourney Weaver; moreover, especially in early episodes, Anderson is dressed and made up to resemble Foster as much as possible. Parallels can also be drawn between Starling's and Scully's uneasy positions as relatively inexperienced FBI operatives and their survival in the male-dominated environment. Shots of both characters surrounded by taller, older, physically imposing men indicate their fragile position within the patriarchal bureaucracy. Further, both are characterized in relation to the need to prove themselves to absent fathers. Starling's father, a West Virginia state trooper killed in the line of duty, influences her choice of career; Scully initially states that her parents view her FBI career as an act of rebellion and later (in "Beyond the Sea") becomes obsessed with the question of whether her father, a naval officer, was proud of her.[3]

In many ways, *Silence of the Lambs* can be read as a female coming-of-age film, "depicting the process which creates the internally disciplined professional" (Donald, 348). As Adrienne Donald points out, Starling is manipulated by her immediate superior, who fails to tell her why she has been sent to interview an imprisoned serial killer. The film depicts Starling's discovery that her quest for knowledge is going to be much harder than she expected. What she had thought would protect her—that is, the impersonality of her aspiring professionalism —reveals its own dangers in the world that she has entered (351).

In early *X-Files* episodes, Scully must choose between her professional ambitions and her dedication to the truth (and, by extension, to Mulder). At the beginning of "Squeeze," for example, she registers discomfort when a colleague addresses her as "Mrs. Spooky" (a reference to the derisive name given Mulder by others in the FBI) and bristles when it is suggested that her job is to have "close encounters of the third kind." She cites the X-Files' "conviction or case solution of seventy-five percent . . . well above the current Bureau standard" ("Tooms") as proof of the legitimacy of what she and Mulder are doing.

Eventually, however, her dedication to the truth as a doctor and investigator conflicts with her chance of professional advancement in a climate where the motto is "Deny Everything." As early as the pilot, Scully keeps a crucial piece of evidence from being destroyed; in "Squeeze," she rejects an opportunity to work with the Violent Crimes Section because she agrees with Mulder's admittedly bizarre theory. In *Silence of the Lambs,* as Donald notes, professionalism initially oper-

3. In addition to the shared theme of the woman's reconciliation with her father's memory, the scenes in "Beyond the Sea" between Scully and a possibly clairvoyant serial killer recall the Starling/Lector scenes in *Silence of the Lambs.*

ates as a "mode of self-protection" (352) for Starling. For Scully as well, the self-protection of professionalism is inadequate. Following her abduction in the second season, she consults a psychiatrist about a feeling of vulnerability that makes it difficult for her to do her job. In a scene in which the camera moves in tighter on Scully, in shots which examine her face from a variety of angles, she states, "In medical school you develop a clinical detachment to death. In your FBI training you are confronted with cases—the most violent and terrible cases. You think you can look into the face of pure evil, and then you find yourself paralyzed by it" ("Irresistible").[4]

A parallel similar to that of Starling and Scully can be found between the characters of Fox Mulder and Dale Cooper of *Twin Peaks*. Both series focus on an eccentric but brilliant detective who moves outside accepted patterns of rational, linear, patriarchal investigation and opens himself up to insights traditionally connected with the feminine. Agent Cooper has established himself as an outstanding investigator in the traditional, male-dominated world of the FBI; as early as the third episode of *Twin Peaks*, however, he displays his difference. He explains to local law enforcement that in a dream he was informed of a method of investigation that allows him access to his subconscious —the Tibetan Method, he calls it, after the exiled Dalai Lama (whom he reveres). Critic after critic has commented on Cooper's direct grappling with the occult,[5] such as the murderous spirit BOB; Vincent Ostria calls Cooper a *"mage inspiré par le ciel,"* a magus inspired by heaven (75). As Carol J. Clover points out, the man who is open to the occult is also open to the feminine in his nature and to nature at large.[6] Martha Nochimson ("Desire") discusses at length Cooper's openness to what are traditionally considered female aspects of experience both in terms of mind (nonrational, nonlinear thought) and body (openness, vulnerability).[7]

The ground-breaking *Twin Peaks'* Cooper is Mulder's direct predecessor. Scully, his newly assigned partner, has been asked to give "the proper scientific analysis" of the work of a man who has been called "the best analyst in the Violent Crimes Section" and yet is also condescendingly nicknamed "Spooky" (pilot). Mulder confronts her with his theories on such phenomena as UFOs ("logically . . . not possible," says Scully [pilot]; psychokinesis ("You mean how Carrie got even at

4. The serial killer in this episode, with his psychotic attachment to the funereal display of women's bodies, is almost a caricature of the fetishist Mulvey describes as a model of the male spectator.

5. Ledwon, Hirschman, Hampton, and Wilcox discuss these supernatural elements in some detail.

6. See especially Clover's chapter "Opening Up."

7. See also Hague on Cooper's nonrational detection.

the prom?'' asks Scully [''Shadows'']; time loss (''A universal invari-
ant!'' protests Scully [pilot]); silicon-based life forms (''Science fiction,''
says Scully [''Firewalker'']; pheromone-exuding gender-shifters (resulting in a profile of a killer of ''indeterminate height, weight, and
sex; unarmed, but extremely attractive,'' Scully points out [''Genderbender'']). Not surprisingly, Scully and Mulder's disagreements regarding the paranormal are a regular feature of the series; however, as he
says after being mocked by other agents, ''You [Scully] may not always
agree with me, but at least you respect the journey'' (''Squeeze''). In
spite of their different thought patterns, Mulder and Scully work in
consultation; ''What do you think?'' is a question asked on *The X-Files*
perhaps more than on any other series in television history.

Holmes/Mulder, Watson/Scully: Counterbalancing Gender Crossings

> ''It is no ordinary case.''
> ''None of those which come to me are.''
> —from *The Adventures of Sherlock Holmes*

The X-Files highlights a brilliant, eccentric detective and his more conservative medical colleague. In many ways, the structure of the series
draws on the pattern of the great master of masculine ratiocinative
investigation, Sherlock Holmes, and his partner, Dr. Watson. As
Holmes is the ''consulting detective'' to whom especially difficult problems are brought, so the *X-Files* by their nature are constituted of those
cases especially difficult to solve. While Mulder often takes on cases of
his own volition, cases are also brought to him specifically in request
of his special talents (''Shadows,'' ''Born Again''). When a Scotland
Yard investigator (and former lover) asks for Mulder's advice, she
refers to her case as a ''three-pipe problem,'' a direct reference to
Holmes (which Mulder elucidates for Scully and the audience of
''Fire'').[8] As Holmes has his violin, Mulder has his sunflower seeds to
munch in contemplation; as Holmes has his index of crimes and criminals, Mulder has the *X-Files* case histories for reference; and as Dr.
Watson records Holmes' adventures, Scully makes her reports on her
laptop computer.[9] This Holmes/Watson pattern suggests that Mulder
is the dominant member of the team.

Perhaps most important in the pattern is the establishment of

8. In fact, the former lover notes that she and Mulder committed a ''youthful
indiscretion'' on the grave of Arthur Conan Doyle—a resonant image for Mulder.
9. Another parallel can be drawn between Holmes' addiction to cocaine and Mulder's predilection for pornography (the latter being alluded to rather than displayed).

Mulder's ratiocinative credentials. As an FBI friend—a rarity for the Holmesian loner Mulder, and naturally destined for death before the episode ends [10]—reminds him, in Mulder's early career in the Violent Crimes Section, "You were always three jumps ahead. It was scary, Mulder—everybody said so" ("Young at Heart"). (John Cawelti points out that the classical detective's superior skill is displayed early in the narrative [82].) When Mulder, to Scully's mystification, gets out of the car and uses a paint can to draw an X on the highway to mark a spot of electromagnetic interference, his actions recall Holmes' unexplained measurings and mutterings, which baffle Watson (pilot; cf. Doyle, 1:112).[11] When Mulder notes that a spot on the carpet indicates that a victim must have been looking through his peephole, he is the only one who sees the need to check for fingerprints outside—where the victim was looking ("Soft Light"). When Mulder finds a fingerprint everyone else has missed, the well-known part of the blind, sneering, stolid, everyday policeman is played by an FBI classmate of Scully's with whom Mulder toys in Holmesian fashion ("Squeeze").

Just as Holmes' ideas are considered "theoretical" and "fantastic" (Doyle, 1:186), so are Mulder's. No one else has recognized the fingerprint because of its odd placement and its elongation; it is from the hand of a mutant and so represents one of those "extreme possibilities" to which Mulder so often refers, echoing Holmes: "When you have eliminated the impossible, whatever remains, however improbable, must be the truth" (Doyle, 1:111). While Agent Dale Cooper uses nonrational techniques, Mulder applies traditional ratiocinative techniques to paranormal events, theories, and evidence. In sum, Mulder is more than capable of masculine ratiocination, but he chooses difference in his ways of knowing, chooses ideas considered nonrational and Other/feminine.

As for Scully, she is far from the bumbling Nigel Bruce film version of Watson; rather, she is closer to Doyle's original Watson, brave and competent. She is Watson's parallel in that she is a representative of received truth. She is distinct from him, however, in many ways, perhaps most notably in her own ratiocinative brilliance. Scully wrote her physics thesis on "Einstein's Twin Paradox: A New Interpretation"; as Mulder notes in the pilot, "Now that's a credential—rewriting Einstein." Her frequent work in autopsies—often displayed on screen—places her in the traditionally masculine role of the penetrating investigator (cf. Griffin, 29; Nochimson, "Desire," 144–50). While women on

10. Holmes says to Watson, "Except yourself, I have none [no friends]" (Doyle, 1:218).
11. As the series progresses, however, less and less often does Mulder act without explaining himself to Scully.

screen often passively represent the body, Scully actively examines it. Nonetheless, it is no simple object to her: "A body has a story to tell," she says in "Irresistible." Indeed, her medical knowledge is often crucial to a case ("Ice," "The Host"). In short, while Scully plays Watson to Mulder's Holmes, she has more "masculine" power than Watson does; in Peni R. Griffin's words, she is "a walking gender issue" (30). Like Mulder, she is gender-liminal, and although the basic Holmes/Watson trope works against the equality of the partners, Scully and Mulder's gender crossing mutes the inequality.

Mulder in Crisis, Scully in Trouble

> [These films] have as their business to reimagine gender.
> —Carol Clover, *Men, Women, and Chain Saws*

Clover points out that "the conflict between White Science and Black Magic is a deeply gendered one, constitutive of a conflict between male and female . . . 'masculine' and 'feminine' " (98). In contradiction to the usual pattern, *The X-Files* associates Scully with science and Mulder with magic. Mulder, like Cooper, is an example of the "New Man," open to solutions not accepted by rational, linear, Western patriarchy (Clover, 106; cf. Nochimson, "Desire," 144–59). In episodes such as "Shapes" and "Anasazi," he is granted approval by Native American characters (themselves marginal in the Western patriarchal system): "I sense you are different, FBI. You're more open to Native American beliefs than some Native Americans. You even have an Indian name—Fox" ("Shapes").

Mulder also fits Clover's pattern in that he is the "male-in-crisis" (107), obsessed with the apparent abduction of his sister by aliens when he was twelve and she was eight. The crisis is still very alive for him, as episodes such as "Conduit," "Miracle Man," "Colony," and "End Game" demonstrate. Thus he is open—and vulnerable—in a pattern typically gendered as female. Samantha Mulder's abduction provides one of the overarching dilemmas to be resolved within the text.

Mulder first recounts the story of Samantha's abduction in the pilot; other, slightly different accounts are given in "Conduit" and "Little Green Men." Each representation of Samantha's disappearance, however, highlights Mulder's feelings of paralysis and helplessness, as well as his conviction that paranormal forces are responsible for his sister's abduction. When Mulder tells Scully the story of Samantha's abduction for the first time, it is one of their most physically as well as emotionally intimate moments. Following a power outage, Scully reclines on the bed in Mulder's candlelit hotel room. As Mulder explains the connection between Samantha's abduction and his obsession with the X-Files, his words become faster and more intense. Finally, he rises up from his sitting position on the floor to take Scully by the shoulders, thus establishing a connection between Samantha's abduction and Mulder's relationship with Scully. By "End Game," Mulder's quest to recover his missing sister has become such an obsession that he has literally traveled to the ends of the earth to answer one question: "Is she [Samantha] alive?"

Mulvey maintains that woman functions in cinema as "bearer of the bleeding wound," symbol of a male fear of castration and loss of phallic power. In *The X-Files*, however, the loss of the younger sister represents something quite different to the feminized Mulder. Loss of Samantha (and later his fear of losing Scully) is associated with fear of the loss of the feminine side of himself. Unable to connect in any but the most cursory ways to anyone but Scully, Mulder most often uses sarcasm or anger to distance himself from others. His behavior seems learned from—and a reaction to—the models provided by his father, Bill Mulder, and by father figures such as Deep Throat and Cancer Man. Each of these "fathers," in effect, obscures his motives and actions behind ambiguous language and veils of smoke;[12] they appear emotionally crippled at best, conscienceless at worst. Mulder must eventually choose between the emotionally hollow rule of the patriarchs and the feminine realm represented by the memory of Samantha and by Scully's family.

The widely admired episode "One Breath" shows Mulder's gender-liminality, his openness to experience traditionally coded as feminine. This episode begins with Scully's mother remembering aloud, in Mulder's presence, an incident in her daughter's youth. This event, involving a snake and the loss of innocence, reverses the standard Garden of Eden pattern:[13] the young Scully, who had "always been a tomboy," participates in the snake's destruction, shooting at it in the woods (read garden) with her brothers, though such killing has been forbidden by her father (read The Father). "Although deathly afraid of snakes, Dana held the animal"; the future doctor fruitlessly willed the creature to live, her mother reports as she selects Scully's tombstone. This introductory representation both condemns masculine gun-toting violence and perhaps, by putting the snake in the unusual position of victim, suggests that the object of the violence has been perceived as

---

12. Mulder's father, who (it is later suggested) worked with Cancer Man, is significantly first shown smoking in the dark, physically separated from his "daughter" and ex-wife ("The Colony").

13. Scully, incidentally, has been raised Catholic; the crucifix she wears around her neck becomes a recurrent visual symbol within the series. See, for example, "Ascension."

phallic threat. Tomboy Dana Scully reaches past her fear to attempt to heal. A parallel experience awaits Mulder.

In the weeks leading up to "One Breath," viewers had seen Mulder desperately attempting to retrieve an abducted Scully, almost to the point of obsession ("I don't sleep any more," he says in "3," the immediately preceding episode).[14] However, Scully simply reappears in a hospital, through no agency of his. She is in a coma, expected to die. The furious Mulder wants revenge, but in two instances, he is offered the opportunity for—the temptation to—revenge, and twice he resists. His superior, FBI Assistant Director Skinner, secretly passes to Mulder the location of Cancer Man, the mysterious controlling figure who so often hides away the truths Mulder and Scully discover in their investigations. Though Cancer Man hints at his complicity in Scully's abduction, he refuses to explain how or why Scully was kidnapped. As Mulder holds a gun to the older man's head, Cancer Man says Mulder is "becoming a player"; Mulder, however, refuses to become one of Them, a shadow reflection of Cancer Man. He represses the desire to kill, to claim a false control. The emotional cost, however, is such that Mulder tenders his resignation (which Skinner refuses). Already, Mulder says, "I hate what I've become."

Mulder's second trial and resultant redemption occur in conjunction with his secret source, the emotionally and physically violent Mr. X—another shadow self, who earlier in the episode has told Mulder, "I used to be you—but you're not me." [15] Mr. X sets up the men who harmed Scully, arranging for them to burglarize Mulder's apartment at a precise time so that Mulder may "defend" himself by killing them. However, Scully's sister Melissa arrives just before the scheduled time of the burglary with the news that Scully is very near death. "Why is it so much easier for you to run around trying to get even than just expressing the way you feel?" she asks. Though she leaves him sitting with his gun in his darkened apartment, the next scene finds him in

14. It should be noted that in *The X-Files*, there is no overriding pattern of Scully as the damsel in distress. Sometimes Scully rescues Mulder ("Jersey Devil," "The Erlenmeyer Flask"); sometimes Mulder rescues Scully ("Shapes," "Genderbender"); sometimes they manage to survive together ("Ice"); sometimes neither is successful and they survive by luck or by the help of an outside agency ("Darkness Falls," "Die Hand Die Verletzt," "Dod Kalm"). It should also be noted that the first partner to do the saving is Scully in "Deep Throat," the second episode of the series. Gillian Anderson remarks that Scully and Mulder "are getting closer; I mean they've saved each other's lives numerous times" (Sexton, 6).

15. Miller and Thorne ("*X-Files* Second Season") note Mr. X and the New Age sister Melissa Scully as variant reflections of Mulder, "a Mulder-without-scruples" and a "Mulder-without-science," respectively. They also cite Skinner as "a Mulder-without-faith" (13). Mulder rejects all of these shadow selves in their exaggerated forms.

the hospital with Scully. With his hand on hers, he tells the comatose
Scully, "I feel, Scully, that you believe you're not ready to go—and
you've always had the strength of your beliefs. I don't know if my
being here will help bring you back, but I'm here." Still in the dark, he
returns to find his apartment ravaged; he sinks to the floor weeping,
hands held up helplessly, knowing that he has lost his chance for
revenge and not knowing whether Scully will live.

In this episode, Mulder must choose between traditionally masculine ratiocinative control mechanisms—gun, revenge, death—and the
feminine strength of communicated emotion and self-in-relation.[16]
When Mulder returns to his apartment, his home has been invaded,
penetrated, in effect raped; by choosing to go to Scully, he has left
himself both physically and emotionally vulnerable (cf. Clover, 85–90).
Craig Miller and John Thorne point out the oddity that Scully's brothers are not at the scene of her expected death ("X-Files Second Season,"
14). However, their absence is appropriate for the subtext of the episode: in the penultimate scene, when Scully emerges from her coma,
Mulder enters a place of women—Scully, her mother, and her sister.
Moreover, when Scully says to him, "I had the strength of your
beliefs,"[17] it is clear that his presence—his choice of the nonrational
hope of communication over the desire for fruitless, phallic revenge—
has helped save her. Mulder very quickly leaves the hospital room,
that woman's place, recuperating something of his masculine status
with the humorous gift of a videotape of NFL highlights. ("I knew
there was a reason to live," says Scully.)

The presentation of Scully as comatose victim—a beautiful body,
pure object, unable to recount her perspective and experiences—is
highly unusual for The X-Files.[18] More often, with regard to the body,
Scully is an active subject—not only in the obvious manner, in the
number of shots featuring the diminutive Scully running, climbing, or

16. Mulder seems to be given a choice between what Carol Gilligan has termed the
male and the female voices of moral reasoning. Whereas the male voice speaks in terms
of rights, responsibilities, and justice (represented here by Mulder's desire to punish
those guilty for Scully's abduction), the female voice is concerned with caring, connection, and relationship (represented by Mulder's need to offer Scully what comfort he
can, even when logic dictates that she cannot survive).

17. Note the shifted pronoun reference that links the partners: the antecedent for
"your" is first Scully, then Mulder. Cf. "Fearful Symmetry," in which an ape using sign
language refers to Scully and Mulder as a single entity, "man-woman."

18. On a practical level, this presentation was necessitated by Gillian Anderson's
physical requirements following the birth of her daughter. Anderson's pregnancy is
incorporated into the text in "Ascension" when Mulder visualizes Scully's belly displayed, swollen, and threatened.

wielding a gun,[19] but in Scully's relation to the body as such. As a doctor, she is the one relating those stories the body has to tell. She literally takes the body apart and gets it to divulge its secrets. The stories she discovers she then relates to Mulder, often forcing him to revise and refine his theories. However, Scully's professional role leads to moments in which she feels vulnerable precisely because of her identification with the physical body. In the pilot and in "Darkness Falls," Scully seems unusually vulnerable in moments where her body's integrity is threatened. The mosquito bites that resemble the markings of UFO abductees (pilot) and the threat of bodily attack from prehistoric bugs ("Darkness Falls") threaten her in a manner that ingesting digitalis-laced soft drinks ("Eve") or barbecue sauce that may have been contaminated with alien DNA ("Red Museum") fails to do. Dr. Scully, whose job requires her to take bodies apart, fears the dissolution of her own physical self.

It is not surprising, then, that "Irresistible" marks the most pronounced breakdown of Scully's professional demeanor. From Scully's identification with the necrophiliac Donny's mutilated victims to her fear of becoming one of those victims, danger in this episode is represented as a threat to physical integrity even after death. Such fear seems to strike at something that Scully, both as physician and as FBI agent, is powerless to prevent. As in the earlier story of the young Dana's trying to restore the snake's life, these instances indicate an identification between patient and physician, an awareness of self as body.

Private Spaces and Sexual Tension

> "Who knows what's breeding behind the walls or in the substructure?"
> —Scully to Mulder, in "Excelsis Dei"

Just as most Sherlock Holmes stories start at Holmes and Watson's shared domicile of 221B Baker Street, so most X-Files episodes start at Scully and Mulder's shared office in the basement of FBI headquarters. Cawelti speaks of the intrusion into the detective's "retreat" (82–83); when the X-Files are temporarily closed, the sense of loss is acute. Scully and Mulder's eccentrically cluttered, shared, walled-off space is contrasted to the desks exposed to common traffic, to one of which

---

19. Although Scully is often shown drawing her gun, she is much less likely than Mulder to shoot someone (exceptions are "Lazarus" and "Anasazi"). We are indebted to Sandy Pintaric for calling this to our attention.

Mulder is assigned in disgrace. The shared domicile marks the quasi-marital relationship of Holmes and Watson,[20] and the same pattern extends to Scully and Mulder.

On the road, the office is replaced by a series of anonymous motels and rental cars. Scully and Mulder are not shown sharing rooms, but on innumerable occasions they are shown casually visiting each other's rooms. A curious intimacy is implied in these scenes. Often one partner enters the other's rooms without knocking. Their posture and behavior in one another's physical space (Scully at least has a key to Mulder's apartment and, as demonstrated in "Little Green Men" and "End Game," moves about there freely when he is gone) suggest a lowering of boundaries and limits, a freedom rare in an environment where the motto is "Trust No One." Far from being presented as sexual encounters, however, these scenes are filled with dialogue relating to their work on the case at hand. Scully and Mulder's debates on interpretations of the case echo the disagreements of a married couple. They look into each other's eyes and argue ideas, rather than gazing at each other's bodies.

The distinction between the standard Scully-Mulder reciprocal look and the objectifying gaze is clearly marked in the episode "Humbug." In separate scenes, Scully and Mulder each are used to highlight and, in effect, to deconstruct such a gaze. "Humbug" focuses (with humor) on difference, sex, and looking—misguidance through image, mistaken seeing. It is set in a town largely populated by circus freaks. One of these, Lenny, exists with a very small brother attached, Siamese fashion, to his chest. When Lenny is sent to awaken Scully one morning, the two stand in her trailer doorway looking at each other's protuberances—Scully at Lenny's partially uncovered brother, Lenny at Scully's partially uncovered breasts—until they both realize what they have been doing and simultaneously adjust their robes to cover themselves.[21] The man's gaze at the woman's difference is obviously connected with the woman's gaze at the "monster's" difference.[22] However, in this case the two recognize what they are doing and thus force the audience's recognition as well. Staring at a woman's breasts is just as unacceptable as staring at a person's "deformity"; each gaze involves the objectification of difference.

20. The quasi-marital elements of the Holmes-Watson relationship have been acknowledged from Rex Stout's "Watson Was a Woman" to modern slash (i.e., homosexual relationship) zines.

21. Making this more obvious is the fact that Scully's body is rarely objectified in such a manner. The sort of shots of breasts or legs common on other detective series (for example, *Moonlighting*) are practically nonexistent in *The X-Files*.

22. Such a strategy recalls Williams' discussion (in "When the Woman Looks") of the connection between woman and monster in classical Hollywood horror films.

Later in the episode, another member of the freak community, Dr. Blockhead, discusses his fear that the human race will attempt to genetically eliminate the sort of difference represented in their town. To illustrate, he points to Mulder; as the camera obligingly focuses on the FBI agent in the middle distance, standing head held high, arms akimbo, long, elegant trench coat perfectly draped, Blockhead says, "I've seen the future, and the future looks just like him"—like a men's cologne ad. The male as visual object is just as ridiculous, just as mistaken. The sophisticated mockery of the Mulveyan gaze in this episode only underlines the fact that Mulder and Scully do not enact such ocular manipulation of each other. Rather, they visually engage each other as partners.

Such engagement frequently leads those around them to perceive Mulder and Scully as a couple in a domestic or erotic sense. Time and again peripheral characters presume the two have a marital or sexual relationship ("Excelsis Dei," "Eve"). In "Red Museum," the thug-like son of the local sheriff tells Mulder (whom he does not know is an FBI agent), "Why don't you run along with the little wife. However, as Scully moves closer and her jacket flaps open, the boy's girlfriend blurts out, "She's got a gun!" Indeed, this "little wife" has a gun; Scully can, when she chooses, wield phallic power, just as Mulder can choose feminine ways of knowing. Gender liminality does not, in this series, preclude sexuality but rather sublimates it.

X-Files creator Chris Carter has repeatedly asserted that he has no intentions for Mulder and Scully to become romantically involved with each other. Just as determined, however, is the interest of many X-Philes in the potential sexual relationship between the two characters—the "UST" (unresolved sexual tension) many fans of the series insist exists between the characters (Sexton, 5–6). The comments above suggest ways that the relationship can be interpreted as quasi-marital; the examination of a particular episode may help justify the perception of sublimated sexual interest.

Work and Life, Job and Love

> Get a life!
>
>   —A friend to Scully, in "Jersey Devil"

The subtext of the episode "Jersey Devil" is important in clarifying, early in the series, the Mulder-Scully relationship. Mulder has dragged Scully to Atlantic City to investigate a case to which they have not been assigned. He asks her if she wants to "grab a hotel, take in a floor show . . . do a little digging on this case . . . Okay, we can skip the floor show."[23] However, Scully insists she must return to Washington because she has social plans; she is going to her godson's birthday party. The party itself serves the dual purpose of establishing the natural savagery of males, as little boys rampage through the house in ape masks (the Atlantic City case involves the sighting of a primitive man), and establishing Mulder as inaccessible in Scully's view. When her friend advises Scully to "get a life"—i.e., sexual, social, and familial connections—the friend brings up Mulder, whom Scully characterizes as attractive but "obsessed with his work."

Scully subsequently exchanges glances with a divorced father of a boy at the party. When Mulder next tries to get Scully to give him extra time for the Atlantic City case, she pleads more social plans. "Another birthday party?" he asks. "No, I have a date," she replies.[24] When Mulder asks her to cancel the date, she says, "Unlike you, Mulder, I would like to have a life." He replies, "I have a life," and she laughs at the idea. The phrase by this point has been marked in the episode and will reappear.

In the course of "Jersey Devil," a curious sexual displacement occurs. Scully endures one of television's time-honored "comparative date" scenes, in which the divorced father is seen as a poor substitute for her partner. In striking contrast to her normal businesslike attire, she is shown on her date with her hair up, wearing a white lace blouse. Her date finds it hard to come up with a subject of conversation other than his child and the "finer points of estate planning." When Mulder interrupts the date with a phone request for her help, Scully seems relieved; he is the person with whom she wants to be, and she will take him in place of the traditional date.

Mulder's parallel relationship is more curious: after the work-obsessed, intellectual Mulder has been lectured by an anthropologist on "our dual natures" and has philosophized over the question of whether we are "just beasts with big brains," he comes face to face and body to body with a beast woman whom he describes as "beautiful." The beast woman has attacked him, though Mulder argues that her territorial fear is understandable. Just as, two episodes earlier, Mulder rescued Scully from Eugene Tooms mounted dangerously over her, so now Scully rescues Mulder when the Jersey Devil mounts him. Dr. Scully's ministering arms replace the beast woman's, as Mulder

23. Mulder's attempts to spend time alone with Scully are often framed in the guise of cases or pseudo-cases. In "Irresistible," for example, he takes her to investigate a crime he is sure is not an X-File so she will attend a football game with him.

24. At this point, Rhonda's seven-year-old-son, rewatching the scene, stated, "He's gonna give her a look"—which Mulder indeed does, in a rare Mulveyan moment. (Scully is slow to look back at him.)

replaced the failed date earlier. Later, as the episode closes, Scully urges Mulder to take time off, but he has "an appointment with an ethnobiologist at the Smithsonian." As Mulder leaves their private office to request a vehicle, Scully receives a phone invitation to another date. We next see her with Mulder in the outer room, where the following conversation ensues:

> MULDER: Who was that on the phone?
> SCULLY: A guy.
> MULDER: A guy? Same guy as you had dinner with the other night?
> SCULLY: Same guy.
> MULDER: Gonna have dinner with him again?
> SCULLY: I don't think so.
> MULDER: No interest?
> SCULLY: Not at this time. *(She follows him to the door.)*
> MULDER: What are you doing?
> SCULLY: Going with you to the Smithsonian.
> MULDER: Don't you have a life?
> SCULLY: Keep that up, Mulder, and I'll hurt you like that beast woman.

The "life," the sexual-social connection, that Scully and Mulder have is with each other and with their work.[25]

Thus, these two gender-liminal characters are not denied sexuality; rather, they sublimate it.[26] Of Mulder's quest for the truth (and for his sister), he tells Scully in the pilot: "Nothing else matters to me." In "Jersey Devil," Scully seems to place professional over private life as well. But the parallel male-female pairings and the conversational cues suggest that their professional lives *are* their private lives. As Scully says, "I love this job" ("Beyond the Sea"). The Mulveyan gaze, too, is sublimated: throughout the series, Mulder and Scully look into each other's eyes in their quest for the truth of the case rather than in prelude to sexual activity. "What do you think?" are the words they

25. Indeed, the only other man to show an overtly sexual interest in Scully is the nerdish Lone Gunman Frohike, who describes her to Mulder as "hot," leading Mulder to tease Scully later that "I think it's remotely possible that someone might find you hot." As for Mulder, his romantic choices consist of his amoral former girlfriend Phoebe in "Fire" and an aspiring vampire in "3." The former occurs early in the series, the latter when Scully is missing and Mulder thinks he may have lost her forever.

26. In Robert Masello's "Romance Writers Pick TV's Hottest Moments," the first listed is the "One Breath" hospital scene, about which romance writer Catherine Coulter says, "The expression on his face just says it all: 'This is the person who means more to me than anything. I will not be whole without this person.' I'm not sure the relationship should ever change because it might not work if they actually became lovers. There's already all the emotion you'd ever want" (22). In sum, the romance is sublimated.

perhaps most often address to each other, and it seems they really want to know.

It is within this arena that audience pleasure would seem to reside. For audiences (especially female viewers) drawn to *The X-Files*, pleasure is not a matter of objectification. Certainly, moments exist in which Mulder's body is displayed: standing in his male model, *GQ* pose ("Humbug") or emerging from a swimming pool in a pair of Speedos ("Duane Barry").[27] Just as certainly, there are many women in the audience who enjoy the view. However, these rare moments are not enough, by themselves, to explain the pleasure female audiences derive from *The X-Files*. That pleasure seems to reside more firmly in the depiction of a male-female relationship in which two people trust and respect one another, where they value their partnership as one of equals, and where each is in a position to educate and occasionally rescue the other.[28] The eroticism of Scully and Mulder is not in the display of their bodies to the gaze of one another or of the viewer; rather, it is in the sharing of equal looks, in the hints of a sensuality that exists beneath the surface of their relationship, and in a respect for one another that allows each a space to explore his/her liminality.

The recurring themes of trust and paranoia combine in the episode "Ice" to explicate the more deeply buried issue of sensuality. Mulder and Scully are members of a rapidly dwindling group investigating the deaths of an Arctic expedition team. Aware of the original team's ominous final words "We are not who we are" and of the discovery of parasitic worms that cause violent behavior in their hosts, Mulder and Scully become wary both of the other members of the team and of each other. Mulder has been isolated as a suspect, and Scully has taken the traditionally masculine course of insisting on a rational examination before extending her trust.

"I want to trust you," Mulder urgently whispers to Scully before presenting his unguarded back to her. She feels for the parasites but finds only Mulder; they make brief, relieved eye contact. However, as Scully turns to leave, Mulder pulls her toward him. She gasps, but he places his hand gently against the side of her head; then, he in turn

27. At first glance, a parallel might seem to exist between the image of Mulder in his Speedos and that of Scully in her underwear when she displays what she fears are marks of victimization (pilot). However, Mulder does not look at Scully as sexual object in the pilot; instead, he reacts by reassuring her. Her willingness to share her vulnerability leads to his willingness to share with her his emotional history. In contrast, Scully is not even present in the Speedo scene, which seems provided largely for the viewer's pleasure.

28. Evidence of this can be seen in the criticisms female fans on the computer bulletin boards level at the series when they perceive Scully as falling beneath her usual level of competence. This was especially evident with "F. Emasculata."

pulls the back of her shirt down. The scene ends with Mulder placing the palm of his hand against Scully's neck. They emerge in the next scene once more a team, united against the others. "The intensity of Mulder and Scully's examination of each other's upper spine hints at a submerged sensuality—and it is all the more powerful *because* it is so understated" (Miller and Thorne, "*X-Files* Episode Guide," 13).

Disempowerment and the Failure of the Gaze

> Mulder, what happened? There was a light!
> —Scully, in the pilot

In both gender relationships and sexual relationships, then, it seems that Scully and Mulder are presented as equal. In one area, however, that equality fails: while Scully and Mulder in various senses look at each other as equals, Scully's gaze is disempowered by the text. As the exponent of conservative, logical thought, Scully is seemingly more aligned with traditional masculine power than is Mulder. However, the television episodes regularly deny Scully the vision of the paranormal that they provide the viewer. In the standard pattern of most episodes, an introduction displays an apparently paranormal event— not to the detectives but to the viewers. The most straightforward interpretation would suggest that we *are* seeing alien abduction ("Duane Barry") or we *are* seeing body-morphing ("Genderbender"). Next in the standard episode pattern (after the theme and opening credits) comes a scene in which Mulder, in their office, displays evidence for Scully. He shows her slides, stills, a video, or some other visual evidence.[29]

Each agent offers potential interpretations—Mulder's paranormal, Scully's traditionally scientific. However, Mulder is the visual guide, and the audience is aware that Mulder's interpretation is more likely the correct one. Similarly, as they investigate the scene, Mulder often comes face to face with visual evidence—often, indeed, with the monster itself—which Scully just misses seeing. In "Shadows," for instance, a vengeful ghost holds a man in mid-air before Mulder's stunned view, only to drop him one or two seconds before Scully dashes into the room. In "Excelsis Dei," a woman is flung against the wall by an invisible hand; again, Mulder gets there in time to see, but

---

29. Cases in which Scully begins the episode by showing Mulder slides, etc., do exist but are rare. A significant one, occurs in "Excelsis Dei"; dismayingly, the paranormal rape is one that Mulder does not at first cz.e to investigate. Griffin (30) discusses the "gender politics" of "Excelsis Dei" in the context of Mulder's psychology and "Scully's recent abduction."

Scully just misses it and has the door slammed in her face. Even her own abduction is something she cannot remember, cannot see in her mind. Thus, Mulder's vision is privileged, from the audience's viewpoint, in spite of his nontraditional "views."

Mulder's position as nontraditional male fits the visual pattern in another way, however. Linda Williams' "When the Woman Looks" explains a horror movie paradigm in which the woman sees the monster with a special horror because she recognizes their shared difference from the males of the established power structures. In *The X-Files*, Mulder, as noted above, is the one who most often directly confronts the monster; and "Spooky" Mulder is identified with the monster in his difference, as even his nickname indicates. His insistence on the reality of beings and experiences not acknowledged by patriarchy marks him as Other to many of patriarchy's representatives, thus aligning him with woman.

''Trying to Survive in the Boys' Club'': Patriarchal Liminality

During *The X-Files'* second season, changes occur in the patterns of sight and of Scully's relation to patriarchy. In "Little Green Men," Scully has been assigned as a teacher at the FBI training center. Her philosophizing over a Quantico corpse leads her FBI students to say she "sounded a little spooky." Scully the autopsy specialist, the woman who knows the body, has (in the middle of her directions on how to slice into a brain cavity) delivered a peroration on "what this man imagined—his dreams, who he loved . . . " Mulder, for his part, has connected mind to body; as he tells Scully, "Seeing is not enough. I should have something to hold onto, some solid evidence. I learned that from you." Thus, each of the partners has learned from, and begun to take on characteristics of, the other.

Several times in the second season, Mulder takes Scully's place in voiceover as recorder of events; his is now occasionally the voice of communication. At the same time, the text more and more allows Scully to see what Mulder sees. Particularly in cases that might be termed science fiction rather than occult, Scully is likely to see the paranormal:[30] at the end of the first season, in "The Erlenmeyer Flask," she retrieves what may be an alien fetus; in "End Game," she sees an alien body dissolve. While in the latter episode she soliloquizes on her

---

30. "Beyond the Sea" and "The Calusari" might seem occult exceptions. However, in "Beyond the Sea," Scully refuses to pursue the occult even though it might mean communication with her dead father; in "The Calusari," during which she witnesses apparently occult phenomena near the end of the episode, her interpretation is not given.

faith in science, the possibility of extraterrestrial life is something that science can stretch to include, and Agent Scully is stretching. She has also seen evidence of conspiratorial elements in the government that she once would have considered fabrications of paranoia. However, in "Little Green Men," she rescues Mulder from such a conspiratorial force.

The first postintroduction scene in the pilot presents Scully at a meeting, the object of the inquisitorial gaze of a set of grim men who (except for her interrogator) remain visually and verbally distant. Nonetheless, she is deployed as their eyes—a "spy," Mulder tells her, even as he enters into a reciprocal look (once he has turned away from the slides he is examining). At the end of the pilot, Scully and Mulder share an intense look through a one-way mirror, he on the side with the young witness reporting alien abduction, she on the side of the invisible, observing "suits" of patriarchy. Despite these differing locations, Scully and Mulder are visually and intellectually engaged with each other through the glass barrier. By the last episode of the second season, Scully is again across the table from the representatives of patriarchy, telling them that her reports validate Mulder's work. She, like Mulder, is threatened with dismissal from a position sponsored by that patriarchy, a position that has enabled the two agents to pursue their investigations more effectively.

The episode "Soft Light" clarifies Scully and Mulder's new positioning by use of a Scully parallel: one of her former students, Kelly Ryan, has asked for their advice on her mystifying first case. As Scully says, like herself, Ryan is "a woman trying to survive in the boys' club"; with her businesslike clothes and manner, Ryan has worked to align herself with the patriarchal power structure.[31] When her police superiors exclude Scully and Mulder for territorial reasons, she fails to back up the FBI agents, even though Mulder has warned that the suspect is endangering lives in ways that standard police procedures will not safeguard against. Although Scully regularly challenges Mulder's view based on her own interpretation of events, Ryan is afraid of a confrontation's effect on her job. As Mulder says to Scully, "The difference is you never put yourself ahead of your work." Ryan decides to ignore Mulder's theories despite their resulting in the perpetrator's capture. When the man escapes and she goes after him with her gun, she is killed—physically evacuated by contact with dark matter. Scully and Mulder go to the funeral, but the message is clear: on *The X-Files*, a woman who is co-opted by the patriarchal order gets turned into a puddle of goo.

31. Kate Twa, the actress who plays Kelly Ryan, was cast earlier (in "Gender-bender") as a character who could become either male or female.

Scully and Mulder walk a heroic path along the border, each engaging the other in struggles with masculine and feminine, rational and nonrational, mind and body. Their looks acknowledge each other as subjects rather than fetishizing or denying the other person. Their sublimated sexuality and gender liminality suggest hidden potency and a restraint associated with higher purpose rather than loss or lack. In sum, they are not required to be sexless in order to enjoy the freedom of gender liminality. Clover points out the importance to gender studies of such border-crossers in the example of the "portal" characters in horror. The opening sequence of every *X-Files* episode shows the two protagonists entering through a door, Mulder a step ahead of Scully. The image, taken from "Squeeze," precedes a scene in which Scully steps ahead of Mulder down the opening to the cellar below. The first of the two images is more visually striking and thus more appropriate for the series' opening; however, with its picture of Mulder moving first, it is perhaps indicative of the partners' slight inequality overall. Nonetheless, both of the partners do cross the portal; Scully and Mulder both walk through that doorway into darkness.

8

Special Agent or Monstrosity?

FINDING THE FEMININE IN *THE X-FILES*

Lisa Parks

> Inhabiting these pages are odd boundary creatures—simi-
> ans, cyborgs, and women—all of which have had a destabi-
> lizing place in the great Western evolutionary, technological,
> and biological narratives. These boundary creatures are, lit-
> erally, *monsters*, a word that shares more than its root with
> the word, to *demonstrate*. Monsters signify.
>
> —Donna Haraway, *Simians, Cyborgs, and Women*

A recent *X-Files* Internet newsgroup discussion entitled "I want to be like Scully when I grow up" featured comments from women who praised the program for its portrayal of a strong female scientist. One scientist who contributed confessed that she thought about Agent Scully for inspiration during her doctoral exams. Another woman wrote: "Scully is the real strong character; the one who doesn't gag at blood or bodies, who wants to do her job as well as she can, who is ambitious without being self-centered, who has her feet planted on the ground." Fans genuinely appreciate the power underlying Scully's scientific subjectivity, but what is perhaps most radical about the show is that Scully is a scientific object as well.

In their critique of masculinist scientific approaches, feminist sci-entists Donna Haraway, Evelyn Fox Keller, and others have envisioned a relational model of science—one that pictures the scientific object "as an actor and agent, not a screen or a ground or a resource, never finally

121

as a slave to the master that closes off the dialectic in his unique agency and authorship of 'objective' knowledge" (Haraway, *Simians,* 198). This granting of agency to the object allows for a scientific practice "that privileges contestation, deconstruction, passionate construction, webbed connections, and hope for transformation of systems of knowledge and ways of seeing" (191). Dana Scully is a figure who embodies this type of relational science. More specifically, in this essay I will analyze the scientific and legal practices through which Scully negotiates her relationship to the monstrous.

Before moving into this discussion, I would like to trace the gendered power dynamics that construct Agent Scully's scientific and legal practices. Here I want to pose the question, What does Dana Scully's identity as a "special agent" amount to? Or, put another way, how is Scully's agency "special"? Judith Butler suggests that gender is produced through the reiteration or repetition of regulatory norms established by dominant heterosexuality; the possibility of agency arises when there is a variation on that repetition (*Gender,* 145). Indeed, Scully reiterates the dominant norms of heterosexual femininity and is culturally intelligible as a "woman" precisely because she dons tailored suits, makeup, and styled hair. At the same time that Scully reiterates the visible norms of femininity, however, she cites historically masculinized discourses as well. That is, Scully's feminized body becomes the site through which scientific rational, technological, and legal discourses are articulated and negotiated. This convergence of masculinized discourse at the site of the feminized body is made monstrous because it produces an excess of power that the dominant norms of heterosexual femininity cannot accommodate. Scully's agency is "special," then, because it incorporates an excess of masculinized power, which is transformed into monstrosity as it engages with the feminine.

Drawing on the theories of feminist scientists—specifically those who propose a relational model of science—I want to suggest that Agent Scully negotiates her relationship to the monstrous in a way that empowers her. She uses scientific and legal practices to interrogate and to expose the limits of their masculinized traditions. Moreover, when Scully's own body becomes the object of alien invasion, she can no longer be a scientist or law enforcer in the same way. A "monster" herself, she is unable to exercise the "distance" necessary to be classified as a scientific rationalist. Indeed, Scully's fascination with and eventual bodily assimilation of the monstrous lead her to challenge and to subvert the masculinized scientific and legal discourses that constitute her power within the FBI.

Thus, Scully represents more the discursive struggle between the scientific rational, the law, and the monstrous than she does an unconflicted legal and scientific agent. With this in mind, I would like first to examine the discourses through which Scully's "special agency" is constituted and mobilized—scientific rationalism and law enforcement—while demonstrating their engagement with the monstrous. Then, I will turn my attention toward feminized monsters in *The X-Files* and discuss their relationship to Scully's scientific and legal power.

Scully's Science

Dana Scully's scientific rationalism is established at the outset of the *X-Files* pilot episode as the proud FBI agent marches through a labyrinth of hallways into the Director's office, where she is to receive her new assignment. During the interview we discover that Scully was recruited out of medical school and decided to join the FBI because, as she puts it, "I saw the FBI as a place where I could distinguish myself." With a cynical grin the Director informs Scully that she will begin preparing "proper scientific analyses" on some cases that are "out of the Bureau mainstream." These cases, he explains, are known as the X-Files, and are supervised by the reputable but maverick Agent Fox Mulder. Right away, the program takes on an interesting reversal with respect to the gendering of science and nature: while Scully is initially aligned with the scientific rational, Mulder is linked to the paranormal. Scully's scientific rationality is mobilized by the FBI to discipline Mulder, whose fascination with the paranormal is both feminized (especially as it is articulated through his relationship to his sister) and at the same time turned into a masculine investigatory adventure. Scully, on the other hand, is masculinized through her connection to science yet feminized by her subordination in the FBI's chain of command and by her placement "out of the Bureau mainstream."

As a scientist, Scully embodies forms of knowledge/power linked to a historically masculinized scientific tradition. She demonstrates a strong loyalty to scientific rational principles such as method, proof, and truth and is knowledgeable in a range of disciplines including pathology, forensics, psychology, and criminology. During the program's first season, Scully argues against Mulder's "ludicrous explanations," insisting that there are rational or logical approaches to the scientific questions they set out to resolve. Looking at a decayed, allegedly alien body on an autopsy table, she mutters to Mulder, "You don't honestly believe this is some kind of an extraterrestrial! I'm here to solve this case, Mulder. I want the truth." In such scenes, Scully articulates the kind of scientific rationalism that has historically worked to classify and control feminized bodies through the production of knowledge. As Keller writes, "To both scientists and their public, scientific thought is male thought" (76). This mode of scientific practice positions scientific objects as passive, there to be conquered and mastered rather than to be recognized as having agencies of their own. When Scully's own body becomes the subject of an alien impregnation, however, we see a shift in her scientific practice. After physically experiencing a monstrous invasion of her own body and after having worked closely with an avid believer in extraterrestrial life, Scully grows skeptical of scientific rational explanations. Such skepticism coincides with the feminist claim that science must be understood as a relational process rather than an objective, masculine ideal. According to Keller, relational science provides feminists with a position from which to define and struggle over the agendas of scientific knowledge (237). Historically, women's bodies have been positioned as passive objects for masculine scientific scrutiny. Within a relational model of science, however, women can redefine and reinvent the position of scientific objectivity as one of active agency rather than as one for the inscription of scientific knowledge and truth. Indeed, Scully becomes amenable to such reinvention because her own bodily experiences of abduction and impregnation begin to inform her scientific practice.

Although initially assigned to "debunk" the X-Files, Scully becomes increasingly sympathetic to Mulder's position. Over time, she displaces her allegiance to scientific rationality and joins Mulder in his struggle to define "the truth." This shift in Scully's character becomes particularly acute in an episode called "Humbug." After positing the somewhat outrageous theory that a man's detachable, malformed conjoined twin committed a series of murders, Scully receives strange looks from local officials and Mulder quips, "Now you know how I feel." Increasingly, Scully's scientific practice is based more on the dialogism between scientific rationality and the monstrous than it is on a compulsion to test and prove the validity of a singular truth. This dialogic model of science is a self-reflexive, relational science that respects the power of the scientific object rather than insisting on the scientific subject's absolute control over and resolution of it.

Scully's position as a scientist is precarious, however, because *The X-Files* uses Mulder to challenge scientific methods and principles, suggesting that there is always something "out there" that scientific rationality cannot resolve. In one sense, then, Scully's scientific rationalism is introduced during the first season as the program's sitting duck—that which it is out to challenge and dislocate. Scientific rationalism, then, is open to interrogation and critique only when it is articulated through the feminized body.

The X-Files' critique of scientific rationality is concurrent with the general rise of tabloidism within television culture. One characteristic of tabloidism is its circulation of popular knowledges that question the truths of scientific rationalism (see Glynn). John Fiske in *Power Works, Power Plays* links tabloidism to the "knowledge of the as if," which he argues "can exist only by destroying that official boundary between the true and the not true, the real and the unreal" (Fiske, 184). Reality-based programs such as *Encounters* and *Sightings* exploit popular skepticism and cynicism and compare ordinary people's "encounters" with the paranormal or the monstrous to the scientific establishment's refusal to take them seriously.

Like many tabloid TV shows, *The X-Files* relies heavily on the "knowledge of the as if." An episode called "The Host" self-consciously incorporates tabloidism as Scully, after analyzing on a computer the complex physiology of a parasitic flukeworm, discovers a tabloid newspaper with the secret to the case slipped under her office door. After flipping to a story entitled "MONSTER ON BOARD!? Bizarre accident on Russian cargo ship has officials suspicious" in *The National Comet*, Scully turns to her computer to compare the tabloid report to an encyclopedic image of the monstrous flukeworm on her computer screen. During the show's first season, Scully would have dismissed the tabloid as sensationalistic fiction. Here, she assimilates tabloidized knowledge into her scientific practice and uses it as key evidence on which to base the resolution of the case. It is Scully's repeated physical contact with monstrous objects that prompts her to incorporate "nonscientific" knowledges into her practice.

Scully's scientific practice not only absorbs tabloidism but also involves bodily relations between the scientific subject and object. This female scientist often appears in an autopsy lab either dissecting dead corpses, scrutinizing flesh samples from a monstrous body, or testing the toxicity of gooey, green alien blood. The program's emphasis on physicality becomes absurd in one episode when Scully crawls into the belly of a dead, alien-impregnated elephant to perform an autopsy. A bird's eye view shot places Scully and another female scientist in the belly of the dissected, monstrous elephant as they clear organs from its abdominal cavity. After the autopsy, Scully examines the animal's uterine tissue under a microscope. We see extreme closeup images of the mother elephant's extracted reproductive organ cross-cut with extreme closeups of Scully's pale blue eyes. The mise-en-scène of this segment structures a dialogic relationship between the scientific subject and object by framing them each within the circular, blue-lit edge of the microscope, placing both Scully and the monstrous elephant under the lens of the scientific instrument.

In conventional scientific rational fashion, Scully adduces her physical findings to support her claims; however, this practice undergoes a shift during the show's first season. Scully's tactility with the scientific object intensifies her relationship to the monstrous. Feminist scientist Barbara McClintock argues that "discovery is facilitated by becoming 'part of the system,' rather than remaining outside; one must have a 'feeling for the organism' " (cited in Keller, 243). Indeed, Scully develops a feeling for the organism simply by virtue of her own body's regular proximity to it. This embodied scientific practice results in the slow erosion of a more cerebral scientific rationalism. Monstrous bodies of evidence, then, become the discursive site through which Scully negotiates her relationship to the scientific object.

Scully's bodily connection to the monstrous is constructed quite explicitly in "Humbug," which features Lenny, the man with a murderous detachable conjoined twin. In one scene, Lenny arrives at Scully's mobile home motel to inform her about the discovery of another murder victim. Scully opens the door in her bathrobe and her eyes fixate on Lenny's deformed, bulbous stomach. A tilt up to his face shows him glancing at Scully's half-exposed breast. A parallel tilt reveals Scully's eyes peering down once again at the man's grotesque belly. After this uncomfortable exchange of looks, Lenny and Scully self-consciously adjust their robes and cover their nude protrusions. This scene structures a visual comparison between Scully's body and the monster's, implying that the body of the scientist is not so different from the monstrosity she sets out to resolve. Ironically, Gillian Anderson had just delivered her baby before the shooting of this episode, and by this point in the season's narrative arc, Scully had been impregnated by a metallic alien implant. Thus, the scene raises the questions Which of these bodies is pregnant? and Which of these bodies is monstrous? The body of the female scientist becomes monstrous through alien invasion. The male body is made monstrous and feminized with its contorted, impregnated belly. Ironically, the pregnant body of Gillian Anderson, the celebrity, is monstrous in that it can only be brought into full view when it is not pregnant. The *X-Files* producers' decision to hide Anderson behind the computer while she was pregnant, combined with the high-tech and invisible impregnation of Agent Scully —the working woman—reflects anxieties about reproduction, professionalism, and celebrity. These monstrous articulations, then, are symptomatic of social and cultural anxieties about the pregnant professional female, the pregnant celebrity body, or in the case of Lenny, the pregnant male body.

The agency Scully forms through her scientific practice is not based purely on scientific rationalism but rather on her ability to move through the continuum of scientific rationality/monstrosity. Rather than using physical evidence to explain monsters away, Scully develops increasing sympathy for them. Donna Haraway suggests that simians, cyborgs, and women are all monsters, "odd boundary creatures

... that have had a destabilizing place in the Great Western evolutionary, technological and biological narratives" (*Simians*, 2). Indeed, both Scully and the monsters she investigates are situated on the edge of scientific knowledge and as such are always testing the limits of science.

Cyborg Cop

At the same time that Scully cultivates a "feeling for the organism" within her scientific practice, she is also a "part of the system"—the Federal Bureau of Investigation. As her scientific practice becomes more embodied and more engaged with monstrous scientific objects, her power as a law enforcer is threatened. In other words, the more she strays away from scientific rationality the more tenuous becomes her position as a law enforcer. This is, in part, because the law relies on scientific rational knowledge for its efficient operation. Here, I would like to explore Scully's agency as a law enforcer, paying particular attention to the way that gendered power relations are brought to bear on her position within the FBI.

Although Scully manages to challenge some of the precepts of scientific rationality, her legal power is limited by narrative and institutional structures that work to contain her agency and desire. *The X-Files'* gendering of Mulder's and Scully's law enforcement practices is rather conventional. Scully carries a gun but rarely uses it. She accompanies Mulder on dangerous, adventurous missions (in an abandoned ship, an underground cave, a serial killer's house), but she is often discouraged from going with him. In an episode called "Irresistible," Scully ventures out on her own to track down evidence, and a mad fetishist killer runs her off the highway and kidnaps her. After being gagged and tied, she struggles to get away, only to have Mulder and an FBI SWAT team barge through the door to rescue her. (To be fair, in a more recent episode ["Clyde Bruckman's Final Repose"] Scully blasts a savage psychic as he holds Mulder at knifepoint.)

Scully's law enforcement power is constructed more through her connection to information technologies than through her resilience to violence. Rather than being a cop on the go like Mulder, Scully is a cyborg detective who works at the computer interface. As a federal employee, she has immediate and widespread access to an array of communication gadgets including cellular telephones, computers, dictation equipment, and fax machines. When she is not carving into a body, she appears in her dimly-lit office typing field reports on a computer as her voiceover narrates her findings. Scully's diligent face absorbs the blue glow of the computer screen, and the reflections of words from her own reports or technologized evidence of the monster

are mapped onto her eyeglasses. Such mise-en-scéne not only concret-
izes the cyborg metaphor but also highlights the self-reflexivity of
Scully's scientific practice, creating a discursive relationship between
Scully and the monstrosities she seeks to resolve.

This strange mixture of femininity, technology, and monstrosity
resonates with Haraway's call for an interrogation of the situated
knowledges that underpin scientific constructions. Haraway describes
cyborgs and women as "peculiar boundary creatures ... monsters, a
word that shares more than its root with the verb *to demonstrate*. Monsters signify. We need to interrogate the multifaceted biopolitical, bio-
technological, and feminist theoretical stories of the situated
knowledges by and about these promising and noninnocent monsters"
(*Simians,* 21–22). *The X-Files* draws on and creates scientific narratives
that involve monsters, cyborgs, and women, and thus becomes a key
site for the kind of interrogation Haraway demands.

Although Scully is visually constructed as a cyborg, her position
is more dystopian than Haraway might imagine, because her technologized body and skills typically serve the interests of the state or of
Mulder rather than any overtly feminist political agenda. Further,
Scully and Mulder are so marginalized within the FBI that they have
no office staff; consequently, Scully assumes the responsibilities of
scribing and documenting their investigations and provides information to Mulder via telephone, often while he is on the run. In some
respects, then, *The X-Files* positions Scully as a clerical worker as much
as an FBI agent with an M.D. Haraway provides us with a productive
model within which to reconsider feminine technologized agency, but
we must also situate that agency. In *The X-Files,* Scully's cyborgian
agency is often subordinated to the narrative aims of both Mulder and
the FBI.

As Scully becomes more amenable to Mulder's paranormal mean-
derings, her law enforcement function within the narrative shifts from
one designed to discipline Mulder with scientific rational discourse to
one that disciplines the state. Put another way, Scully relinquishes her
purely scientific rational position in order to help Mulder explain the
unexplainable. In *The X-Files,* the unexplainable is often linked to state
conspiracy and coverup; as Scully's scientific practice becomes more
relational, then, her legal position shifts as well. She becomes "paralegal"—located on the periphery or even outside of the legal system
she represents (as is made explicit in her abduction and temporary
suspension). In this capacity, she tests the validity and salience of
the state's pursuits rather than blindly exercising its power against
monstrosities that threaten the social order. By inverting these power
dynamics, Scully redefines the ways in which scientific and legal prac-

tices are put to use, and in the process, she challenges their historically masculine mobilization.

Scully's move to a more relational science and a "paralegal" position ultimately produces ambiguous effects. Is Scully a clerical worker stationed within the office? Or is she a skilled computer technician with seemingly unlimited access to information and therefore to power? Does Scully mobilize a scientific knowledge to assert her power over Mulder and over the scientific object? Or does she also use it to document and control the activities of the scientific and legal subject, in this case the state, which has conducted top secret, "covered up" scientific experiments on the bodies of its citizens? Whatever the answers to these questions, Scully's scientific and legal practices always interact with the monstrous. But how is the monstrous configured? And how does Scully's regular engagement with monsters work to soften or feminize the masculine power of scientific and legal discourses that constitute Scully's "special agency"?

Monsters

In some respects, the most powerful positions within *X-Files* narratives are occupied by monstrosities that neither Scully, Mulder, nor the FBI can resolve: a sewer-inhabiting flukeworm, killer girl clones, or the devil in disguise, for instance. Haraway's discussion of nature's objective agency corresponds well with the power of *X-Files* monsters. She links nature (the scientific object) to the coyote metaphor and describes it as "the world's witty agent and actor with whom we must learn to converse" (*Simians*, 201). "This potent trickster," Haraway writes, "can show us that historically specific human relations with 'nature' must somehow—linguistically, scientifically, ethically, politically, technologically, and epistemologically—be imagined as genuinely social and actively relational" (21). Indeed, Scully's relational scientific practice articulates the epistemological shift that Haraway envisions not only because it acknowledges the dialogism between scientific rationality and monstrosity but also because it involves regular engagement with the bodies and agencies of scientific objects.

Thus far, we have explored how Scully negotiates masculinized forms of knowledge/power—specifically, scientific rationalism and law enforcement—through her contact with the monstrous. Now, I would like to examine monstrous bodies as the site where feminization is put into process. Monsters are not essentially feminine; they are, however, a discursive site that is often articulated as feminine. In particular, *X-Files* monsters are feminized by processes such as reproduction and demonic possession. Moreover, some of these monsters are "mistakes" produced by federally funded scientific research within the military-industrial complex. The feminization of monstrosity, then, is symptomatic of the failure of historically masculinized and institutionalized scientific rationality, and as such works to initiate struggles over and contests between conventional scientific methods and agendas.

An episode entitled "Eve," for instance, features a group of girl DNA clones who live in suburban neighborhoods across the country and are programmed to kill their fathers. The girl monsters were the result of a federal research effort known as the Litchfield Project, headed by Dr. Sally Kendrick. Kendrick used the project to make clones of herself with extra intelligence and strength. The failure of the project resulted in Kendrick's eventual institutionalization in a state insane asylum.

The episode constructs both the little girl clones and their female scientist creator as monstrosities. In one scene, Scully and Mulder visit Kendrick to observe and interview the female scientist-turned-monster and encounter her curled up in the corner of a dark chamber, growling and hissing. Although the episode implicitly critiques the military-industrial complex's unethical experimentation on female bodies, it also positions Kendrick and the girl clones as coyotes—as scientific objects with tricky agencies that Scully and Mulder must ultimately confront. Kendrick escapes from the asylum and kidnaps her clone daughters. When in Scully and Mulder's custody, the girls try to poison the special agents at a fast food restaurant with a deadly serum they concoct. Indeed, the girl monsters are genetically coded by their "mother" to develop ingenious levels of scientific knowledge/power. Moreover, Kendrick deployed her own medical knowledge to produce and program them. In this instance, then, relational science is articulated the other way around—that is, the monster embodies and mobilizes scientific knowledge/power against a human object. Indeed, in "Eve," the feminized process of reproduction has a coyote dimension —its progeny play tricks with and on science and the law.

"The Colony" is another episode that feminizes the monstrous through reproduction. It features sets of male and female clones sent to earth by aliens during the 1940s to establish colonies. The clones (who have become medical doctors) occupy abortion clinics and combine human fetal tissue with alien DNA to produce human-looking aliens. The colonies' failure to proliferate, however, prompts the alien rulers to send a violent, constantly morphing mercenary to earth to terminate them. This episode focuses on the feminized reproduction process by which the aliens, both male and female, become monsters. The male clones figure most prominently in Scully's search, and the monstrous male body comes to represent more the possibility of perverse reproduction than masculinity. The bodies of these male clones are also feminized in contrast to the more heavily masculinized monstrosity (reminiscent of the shapeshifting character) who is sent to Earth to kill them. In one scene, several identical men in white lab coats slink from their hiding places and ask Scully to protect them after she bursts through the door of their lab with a gun; Scully takes the men into custody and places them under high security protection. Here again, Scully's relation to the monstrous is intensified as she is figured as the clones' protector.

In both "Eve" and "The Colony," Scully's legal agency is mobilized as a maternal force rather than as a punitive one. The power underlying her position as an FBI agent is feminized through her sympathy for and identification with the monstrosities she locates and investigates. The clones in both episodes have something in common with Scully in that they too test the limits of scientific rationalism. As scientists/doctors who have become monstrous through their own experimentation, they embody the continuum of scientific rationalism and monstrosity and thus partake in a relational scientific practice as well.

While some *X-Files* monsters are feminized through reproduction, others are feminized through demonic possession. The out-of-control, hysterical, hyper-sexualized, and evil female body is mobilized as monstrous in multiple episodes. "Die Hand Die Verletzt," for instance, presents the devil disguised as a seemingly innocent female substitute high school science teacher, who arrives in a small town community to punish a congregation of devil worshippers who have not sacrificed enough bodies. In one scene, the teacher, Mrs. Paddock, meets after school for a makeup final exam with a student named Shannon, whose parents participated in a local cult. Shannon's post-pubescent body had been used as a "breeder," yielding sacrificeable babies for the cult. Before the exam—a dissection of a fetal pig—Ms. Paddock asks Shannon to remove her jewelry. She carries the girl's bracelet to an adjacent office, where she creates a candlelit shrine. Closeup shots of Paddock's red, throbbing face are cross-cut with the face of nervous Shannon as she prepares to dissect the pig, and by extension to carve into her memory of the use of her own body to reproduce human fetuses for sacrifice. As the girl raises the blade to dissect the pig fetus, Paddock telepathically commands her to slice her two wrists instead of the pig's skin. We are left with a final aerial shot of Shannon lying on the lab floor in two pools of blood next to the dead animal. Scully arrives to investigate these traces of monstrous agency in the following scene, and after interviewing the teary-eyed, seemingly innocent Mrs. Paddock, whispers to Mulder, "There are some oddities to her story." Neither Scully nor Mulder, however, are able to resolve this narrative; the devil outsmarts them.

Another demonic possession episode, "Aubrey," features a local female detective, B.J. Morrow, who inherits the murderous genes of her serial killer grandfather. After a series of violent flashbacks, the pregnant detective develops pink blisters on her face and begins killing townspeople and carving the word "Sister" across her victims' chests. In one scene, B.J. tracks down one of her grandfather's rape victims, Mrs. Tibideau, now an elderly woman performing house work. B.J. enters Tibideau's house and tries to attack her with a hot iron. Chasing her up the stairs with a razor, B.J. says in a deep, husky voice, "Somebody's got to take the blame, little sister, and it's not going to be me." Tibideau screams, "You have his eyes . . . you're him! You're my grandchild!" B.J. rips open Tibideau's blouse and finds the word "Sister" already etched across her chest. Alarmed, B.J. tears open her own blouse to reveal the same red scar. As B.J.'s razor descends upon her, Tibideau screams, "You don't know what you're doing! He's the one to blame!"

In both of these episodes, monsters are feminized through both demonic possession and reproduction. In "Aubrey," B.J.'s drive to kill is the product of "bad genes," and her possession is operationalized through a reproductive cycle. Moreover, B.J.'s pregnancy raises questions as to whether this monstrous cycle of reproduction and genetic transference will be repeated. The episode ends ambiguously, with shots of a suicidal B.J. sitting in an insane asylum (not unlike Kendrick) rubbing her pregnant belly as Scully's voiceover narrates inconclusive findings. In "Die Hand Die Verletzt," the young student's reproductive capacity is made monstrous through its connection to devil worshipping and human sacrifice. At the moment Shannon engages in a "scientific" activity (fetal dissection) destined to invoke her memory of past atrocities, monstrosity takes over her body, denying her moment of "truth." Both Shannon, the science student, and Mrs. Paddock, the science teacher, are possessed by demons, locating monstrosity once again within the bodies of women engaged in scientific endeavors. Thus, in these episodes, a detective and a science teacher become monsters; these social positions are the same as Scully's, who teaches science as well as practicing it. Moreover, within the narratives, these monstrous characters are figured as Scully's partners. Before she is conscious of her possession, B.J. helps Scully gather evidence in an attempt to solve the case. Mrs. Paddock not only provides Scully with an interview after Shannon's murder but at the end of the episode leaves a devilish message on the chalkboard that reads, "Goodbye. It's been nice working with you." Indeed, Scully is allied with these monsters as she engages in the process of investigating them.

Ultimately, neither of the narratives in "Aubrey" nor "Die Hand Die Verletzt" are resolved scientifically. The X-Files constructs feminized scientific objects with agencies that test the limits of scientific rationalism and legal discipline, remaining beyond comprehension and control. Haraway would classify both B.J. and Mrs. Paddock as "coyotes"—as witty tricksters that outsmart the historically masculinized epistemologies that remain within scientific and legal discourse. The feminized *X-Files* monsters discussed here are not the passive objects of masculine scientific and legal control but rather are active agents that exist in dialogic relation to science and to the law. As such, they shape the very questions that they ask and attempt to answer.

Finally, an episode called "Ascension" features a scene in which science and monstrosity crystallize within Scully's body. This scene serves a significant function in making Scully's monstrosity visible. After interrogating Duane Barry about Scully's abduction, Mulder experiences a premonition that reveals Scully's abducted body as it is invaded by alien technologies. The segment opens with flashes of light followed by a closeup of Scully's tranquil, unconscious face. A tracking shot across her body shows it placed on a laboratory table beneath a spinning metal drill bit. As the probe pierces Scully's belly, her eyes abruptly open only to be blinded by bright ceiling lamps. The probe wedges itself inside her abdominal cavity and forces her belly to swell.

Although this scene is structured as a peek into Mulder's unconscious, it bears truth when, during Scully's subsequent hospitalization, we discover she has been implanted with modified DNA, the product of an alien experiment. The placement of alien matter within Scully's body constructs her monstrosity through both reproduction and possession. She becomes the carrier of another species and is stripped of her memory of the abduction. However, although Scully's body is monstrous, she is still a scientist and law enforcer. Scully thus becomes the very monstrosity she had previously set out to investigate; put another way, her body becomes the scientific object, the coyote, nature's actor/agent, which she—the scientist and lawmaker—is supposedly equipped to resolve. Scully's monstrosity, however, destabilizes her scientific rational and law enforcing agencies, rendering her unconscious on a hospital bed, where she experiences dreams that portray her on the threshold of death. Scully has, indeed, become a "special agent"—a monstrous scientist, a demonic dispenser of justice, a subjective object.

What are the feminist political implications of the convergence of these discourses at the site of the female body? On the one hand, Scully's monstrosity brings science and nature together and structures the relational science that Haraway, Fox-Keller, and others call for. On the other hand, it structures a hermeneutic relationship within the feminine that positions the female scientist as confronting a feminized monstrosity located ultimately within her own body. In this way, *The X-Files* constructs the feminine as ultimately in search of itself, never able to fully discover, much less combat, its subordinate position within scientific and legal institutions. What would happen if Agent Scully and the feminized monsters she investigates teamed up? What happens, in other words, if divergent, even antagonistic forms of feminized power materialize at specific moments to struggle against historically masculine forms of knowledge/power? Can such temporary microconcentrations of feminized power be mobilized for social and political change, or are they inevitably trapped in a struggle to define the feminine?

9

How to Talk the Unknown Into Existence

AN EXERCISE IN X-FILOLOGY

Alec McHoul

X is the kiss, the unknown, the fissure
In mystery stretching far back to the ape.
—Roy Fuller, *ABC of a Naval Trainee*

The Unknown as a Linguistic-Discursive Problem

There is an intimate relation between language and knowledge. Even if we can experience things nonlinguistically (by visual, tactile, and olfactory senses, for example), it is a moot point as to whether we can be said to *know* them unless they have a linguistic form. At least, if we can say or write something, we can usually also claim to know it. If so, language may well be said to come to an end, or to reach its limits, when it comes to expressing the unknown. That is, although it may be possible to refer to some general category of the unknown (as in the previous sentence), the particulars of some specific unknown thing by definition are not available to linguistic expression. However, language in actual situations of use (discourse) is more subtle than this. We know that it can hint, suggest, and imply, and through these mechanisms, it can arouse possibilities, vague ideas, and suspicions.

If we think of this as a problem (and a solution), we can see how pertinent it is to the science fiction writer. One of the unique qualities of SF is that it works by building up a puzzle and (at least in some cases) offering a solution to that puzzle in the course of events, or else (in other cases) leaving the reader/viewer with a conundrum to solve. In many instances, this is achieved through a disjunction between agents and practices. Ever since the early masters Wells and Verne started to refer to "the thing" or "the creature"—or else to describe peculiar events that could have no earthly agent—SF has worked in this way, and *The X-Files* is no exception to this time-honored technique.

With visuals to aid it, agents and practices in *The X-Files* can be made suitably mysterious—until we find out how, in the end, such a one (or ones) could do such a thing (or things)—or else we can be left, as before, with an imponderable mystery. Agents of a suspected alien or paranormal kind can be presented through mirrors, or from their own points of view (thus not revealing them), or else from the victim's distorted point of view. Actually-filmed frames can be skipped (as they were to great effect in the *Alien/s* movies), or the "thing" can be seen from the rear, through speed-ups or blurs, through incomplete scenes, half-views, and so on. On the other hand, we might see the effects of their actions but not the method of perpetration. Thus, in "Humbug," the first shot of the mysterious creature terrorizing Gibsontown is shown through a heavily greased lens. In this case, the agent could actually be any of the many possible suspects, from The Conundrum to the fabled Fiji Mermaid, and the action could involve anything from the victim being eaten to . . . well, whatever the Mermaid is supposed to do to its victims.

Over and above these remarkable televisual effects, however, the speculations of Scully and Mulder, as they talk together about the possible arrangements of weird agents and practices, add a considerable amount to the viewer's sense of a problem—and, sometimes, its solution. In fact the dialogue may be utterly crucial to such matters. (If there is any doubt about this, one might try watching a fresh episode with the volume off, to see whether anything like genuine puzzles and [proto-] solutions can be found at all.) What I want to show in this essay is the micro-discursive means by which this is achieved.

Routine Dialogue

If SF stories and films work with puzzles or problems about the connections between agents and practices—that is, if they pose the questions What is it? and What's been done? along with What's the connection between the two?—then it is also the case that, in everyday life, such questions are few and far between. In fact, in routine situations, if we are given a description of an agent, we can usually hear along with that description the sorts of expectable practices that she or he engages in, and vice versa.[1] Thus, if I describe someone as a postal worker, you will be able to hear, immediately, the sorts of practices they routinely undertake: sorting and delivering letters, wearing a certain uniform, and so on. Then again, if I tell you that someone exhibits their intimate parts on street corners while attempting to seduce passers-by, you will be able to tell me which agent-description is most plausible for that range of practices. For routine discourse, then, there may be a loose rule: if we know the agent-description, we will know the practice; and if we know the practice-description, we will know the agent. That is how life-as-usual proceeds. I'm a bass player (agent description)—so you know what I *do*. You dig flower beds and prune roses (practice description)—so I know what you *are*. In both cases, we can hear these things without being told in so many words; in ordinary talk, the doing tells us the being, and the being tells us the doing. It is as routine as knowing which predicate goes with which subject.

Examples of this routine kind of inference from practice to agent (or vice versa) can be found in *The X-Files* itself. In "F. Emasculata," when Mulder is on the trail of two escaped convicts and the trail leads to a gas station where the two have been holed up, the policeman leading the investigation is puzzled as to where they should look next. Mulder draws on a routine agent-practice connection and reminds the cop of how such commonsense techniques work:

> MULDER: If they [the escaped convicts he's tracking] had girlfriends they probably tried to call them. *(Walks to phone booth to check the last number dialed.)*[2]

The agent-practice connection is simple: if the agent is "boyfriend" or "girlfriend," a routine and expectable practice is that they will call each other, especially if they are apart and especially if there is news to tell (in this case, that the boyfriend is out of jail). The same thing

1. This analysis of what I am calling "agents" and "practices" is based on the conversation-analytic technique of membership categorization device (MCD) analysis pioneered by Harvey Sacks. Sacks uses the terms "category member" and "category-bound activity" for much the same things; I have simply altered this to get a slightly less cumbersome and less technical terminology for the general reader. Interested readers might like to look at Sacks' original formulations in "On the Analyzability of Stories by Children" and "An Initial Investigation of the Usability of Conversation for Doing Sociology."

2. Formal conversation analysis usually employs a more elaborate system of transcript notation, taking careful note of speech delivery features. For my purposes here, however, such features are not relevant, and so my transcripts will follow the standard format.

can work in reverse; that is, a practice can be *dis*associated from an agent if it is not routinely connected to it. Thus, in "Humbug," when Scully and Mulder discover that Sheriff Hamilton was once "Jim, the Dog-faced Boy" and then find him burying something in his garden at night beneath the full moon, they decide to see what he has buried. Just prior to this, however, Mulder cautions Scully about the assumption they are making by connecting a particular agent-description ("hairy faced person") with a possibly nonroutine practice-description for it ("lycanthropy," "aberrant behavior"):

> MULDER: Y'know Scully, hypertrichosis does *not* connote lycanthropy.
> SCULLY: What are you implying?
> MULDER: We're being highly discriminatory here. Just because a man was once afflicted with excessive hairiness we've no reason to suspect him of aberrant behavior.
> SCULLY: It's like assuming guilt based only on skin color, isn't it?
> *(Mulder nods. They start digging, only to find a potato.)*

This instance has a number of interesting features. First, as with the previous case, the agent-practice connections are made explicitly through such terms as "connote," "imply," "assume," "suspect," and so on. Second, if actions speak louder than words, then obviously both Scully and Mulder do not believe in the agent-practice disconnection they have just made explicit, given that they *do* exhume what the sheriff has buried—somewhat to their embarrassment, since the sheriff has merely buried the potato as a cure for warts. Third, the example shows how what may or may not count as a "normal" agent-practice connection can be the basis of many claims and struggles about political correctness or incorrectness. We cannot go from skin color to guilt (or innocence), and we cannot go from gender to, say, strength (or weakness) and so on. However, it is not entirely clear whether we can go from hirsuteness to lycanthropy. What counts as an acceptable agent-practice inference, then, is not fixed once and for all; rather, it is part of a particular historical conjuncture between discursive descriptions, morality, and politics. The ways persons are discursively categorized tell us not only about *their* moral positionings but also about those who make the categorizations.[3] (We will see another aspect of this later, in the case of "Fresh Bones.")

If this is how agent-practice inferences work in more or less routine situations, as soon as we move even slightly outside this sphere of

---

3. On the moral and political aspects of membership categorization, see Jayyusi, *Categorisation and the Moral Order* and "Values and Moral Judgment."

life-as-usual, things get more complex. They also get more puzzling and alluring. For example, newspapers would not be able to sustain themselves if they only reported routine conjunctions of agents and practices; that is why "Dog bites man" is less interesting (news-wise) than "Man bites dog." My favorite is an actual magazine headline: "Killer Nuns!" What is going on here—and it brings us close to *X-Files* territory—is a disjuncture: nuns may do all sorts of things except kill; and killing might be done by almost anyone except a nun. Hence, throughout "Humbug," Scully has to continually remind the sheriff that just because he regards his "freakish" townsfolk as "normal," this does not mean they cannot be killers—and she cites the fact that most relatives of serial killers think of them as perfectly normal persons until the truth about them comes out.

The question in SF is similar to that of news reportage: what is the practice, and who is the agent of that practice? Or: if one is supplied, how can the other be possible? These are the sorts of questions that *The X-Files* poses to viewers—and it is possible to watch episodes precisely as puzzles of this sort. True, certain episodes are quite disappointing if viewed this way, for sometimes both agent and practice are known to the viewer very early on and the only interest resides in seeing how Scully and Mulder manage to arrive at the same connection. By and large, at least the puzzle (and sometimes the solution) gets announced early on in the piece, during the scene-setting moments; given *The X-Files'* format, this usually means just after the (often mysterious) opening scene and the initial credits. At that point, we usually see Scully and Mulder in the lab or the morgue, examining the evidence, or else at the scene of the crime. It is at those crucial points that they set up—through their dialogue—the main pieces of the puzzle to be solved, and it is those "missing pieces" that are, precisely, unknown. It is then that they start to ask who and what agents and practices are involved, and to speculate as to how they can be related, thereby establishing the main narrative interest for the rest of the episode.

X-Dialogues

A brief but typical instance of the kinds of conjoint inference made by Mulder and Scully comes near the start of the "Fresh Bones" episode. A Marine working at the Folkstone resettlement camp, Jack McAlpin, has died after having driven himself into a tree: the audience know that McAlpin has crashed the car believing a strange disfigurement to have overtaken his face. Mulder and Scully investigate the crime scene, where they notice a strange marking on the tree itself.

MULDER: Most of the refugees at Folkstone are Haitian. *(Long pause.)*
SCULLY: Mrs. McAlpin believes that voodoo is behind her husband's
   death?

Given that the agents in this case are Haitian refugees and that a
strange death has occurred, Scully and Mulder have to find a practice
tied to the relevant agent-description that will render a plausible account of their (the Haitians') possible agency in the death. A practice
that is routinely bound to the national group in question is voodoo—
and that is the solution they hit on. This also gives Scully her chance
to deliver what has now become a standard line of skepticism in the
face of Mulder's belief in aliens and the paranormal: "You don't mean
to tell me that you think X is responsible for Y?" or variations on that
trope. (We will see another example of this later in connection with the
"Calusari" episode.) For now, we can note an interesting change in
the format: instead of charging Mulder with the expectable-but-weird
agent-practice solution, Scully attributes it to the dead man's wife,
Robin McAlpin. We can only speculate as to why this may be, but there
is at least one candidate reason here, namely that the Haitians-voodoo
connection has more than a slight element of "racial" or "ethnic" stereo-
typing about it. It is one of the possibly politically incorrect agent-
practice connections we noted above in the case of Sheriff Hamilton.
By attributing the connection to a third party, Scully is able to get the
(as it turns out correct) narrative solution off the ground, while at the
same time attributing any negative ethics it may connote to a minor
character.

The next instance is found in the post-credit lab scene in "Humbug." Following the death of the Alligator Man in Gibsontown (a
haven for practicing and former sideshow acts), Mulder notices a trail
of such inexplicable deaths around the country. Showing Scully a selection of photographic evidence, he goes on:

MULDER: The victims range from all different age groups, races, both
   male and female. The mutilations appear so motiveless that one
   would suspect some form of ritual. Yet they adhere to no known
   cult. No known serial killer would have been expected to escalate
   the level of violence of these attacks over such an extended period of time. So what do you think, Scully? What are your initial
   thoughts?

This again is a typical device for (what many think are the best)
episodes in which neither the FBI agents nor the audience know the
solution to a set of inexplicable events. Mulder describes the evidence,
looks for patterns in it, and then invites Scully to speculate on the

possible forms of agency that could have brought about those events. In this case, as well, he rules out lists of possible agents given his professional knowledge of the kinds of criminals to which the practices in question can be tied. Hence, the practice-description "ritual killing" goes with the agent-description "cults" and, somewhat less clearly, the practice-description "low escalation of violence" goes with the agent description "serial killer." These—among other things—can be ruled out in these cases, and Scully is invited to speculate. As is often the case, she refuses to be drawn into paranormal kinds of agent-practice solutions. Instead, she turns to the photo of the Alligator Man and comments, "Imagine going through your whole life looking like this."

Since the scene-setting in this episode does not yield a plausible agent-practice connection, Scully and Mulder have to probe more deeply. They visit Gibsontown itself, and going with Sheriff Hamilton to the shop of one Hepcat Helm, Mulder wants to check out an illustration he has found in one of Helm's manuals:

MULDER: Just hang on. I wanted to ask you about this manual illustration. I recognize most of the historical portraits you've drawn here. But what's this here? *(Pause.)*
HEPCAT: It's duh Fiji Mermaid. *(Pause.)*
HAMILTON: Is that what that thing is? *(Pause.)*
SCULLY: What's the Fiji Mermaid?
HEPCAT: The Fiji Mermaid—it's, it's the Fiji Mermaid.
HAMILTON: It's a bit of, er, humbug Barnum pulled in the last century.
HEPCAT: Barnum billed it as a real live mermaid. But—people went in to see it, all they saw was a real dead monkey sewn on the tail of a fish. *(Pause.)*
MULDER: A monkey? *(Pause.)*
HEPCAT: A mummified monkey.
HAMILTON: It supposedly looked so bad he had to exhibit it as a genuine fake.
HEPCAT: Ah, but see *(Pause.)*—that's why Barnum was a genius. You never know where the truth ends and the humbug begins. He came right out and he said this Fiji Mermaid thing is just a bunch of BS. That made people want to go and see it even more. So I mean—who knows. Maybe for box office reasons Barnum hawked it as a hoax but in reality . . .
MULDER: The Fiji Mermaid was a reality?
HEPCAT: *(Shrugs.)*

. . .

HAMILTON: . . . what's all this about?
MULDER: *(Showing him a photo.)* These tracks were found at several of the past few crime scenes. They've defied exact identification.

But one expert speculated that they might be *sim*ian *(Pause.)* in
nature.
HAMILTON: You don't mean to tell me you think these tracks were
made by the Fiji Mermaid?
SCULLY: *(To both men.)* D'you recall what Barnum said about suckers?

Here, a suspected agent gets inspected for the kinds of practice that
might be or could be tied to it. Because something called "the Fiji
Mermaid" is a complete unknown (except to sideshow insiders), its
possible range of tied practices is therefore equally unknown. It is
effectively "the thing" or "the creature." The question is, Could one
such tied practice be strange murders? Mulder, finding a suitably informed insider (presumably, as we find out a little later, because he
has his suspicions about a possible "simian" agent), gets the agent-
description mobilized: "But what's *this* here?" Then Scully attempts to
solicit a practice-description: "What's the Fiji Mermaid?" The answer
does not yield anything that might make the required connection. On
the contrary, as is almost typical of this episode (cf. Dr. Blockhead's
several assertions to the effect that some mysteries are better not
cleared up), the answer is of the "maybe yes, maybe no" variety:
perhaps it's a fake, perhaps it's real, who knows? Then it is left to
the Sheriff to articulate what is usually Scully's line: "You don't
mean to tell me . . . ?" This allows Scully an even more skeptical position, addressed to both men: "D'you recall what Barnum said about
suckers?"

"The Calusari" is more typical of the narrative structure in which
the audience has a fairly good suspicion of who the agent is and
what the strange practice is—even though we can't easily guess the
connection to start with. It begins with a fairly direct suggestion that a
young boy, Michael Holvey, has somehow "willed" the death of a
toddler, Teddy Holvey, to whom he is related. It is the "somehow" that
sets the narrative puzzle in this case; there is a suggestion of psychic
powers and a barely seen "attacker" whom Michael seems to control
—again, somehow. He appears to "think" the infant on to the track of
an oncoming showground train. Later, in the lab, Mulder spots a helium balloon behaving strangely in a photo taken just before the death.

MULDER: You see this is a helium balloon here, and the one thing I
did learn in kindergarten is that when you let them go they float
up up and away, but you see this is moving away from him—
horizontally.
SCULLY: Did you learn about *wind* in kindergarten?
MULDER: Well, I called the National Weather Service and they said on
the day that Teddy died the wind was blowing *north*, but you

see the balloon is moving *south*. As if it's being pulled against
the wind.

SCULLY: Pulled? By whom?

MULDER: Well, I don't know. That's why I came to Chuck, the king of
digital imaging.

. . .

CHUCK: *(Pointing to a shape holding the balloon by a string.)* Here it is.
(Pause.) It's clearly a concentration of electro-magnetic energy.
(Pause.)

SCULLY: Uh, so you're saying that, er, a ghost killed Teddy Holvey?
(Pause.) Has anyone checked the camera that took this photo?

Here, unlike the audience, Mulder and Scully have only the end event:
a toddler who has escaped an apparently escape-proof harness and, it
would seem, "wandered" onto a train track. (Did he wander or was
he led?) They have no agent and no possible practice that could cause
the event. In this computer-lab scene (again immediately following the
credits), they speculate first on the practice. It is somehow connected
with a helium balloon that we (although they do not) know Michael
wanted, having lost his own. It effectively becomes a substitute agent,
something that has "led" the toddler to his death. As an agent, it has
a set of typical predicates, which everyone knows: "when you let them
go they float up up and away." This agent description, however, de-
feats those standard preferences (as we saw the headline "Killer Nuns"
does). It has done something that helium balloons cannot do: it has
drifted horizontally against the wind. Ergo, there is another agent
responsible for its movement, for "pulling" it along—presumably to
lure the toddler onto the track. Enhancing the image, the computer
scientist, Chuck, is able to get a further visual unknown onto our
screens: "a concentration of electro-magnetic energy." Thus, a possible
quasi-human agent has been found, and Scully can introduce her (by
now completely expected) "You mean to tell me?" line plus the
(equally expected) dismissal of what she thinks Mulder might have in
mind: "Has anyone checked the camera that took this photo?"

As a final example, there is an interesting twist to these agent-
description conventions in the "F. Emasculata" episode. More than one
X-Phile has noticed and complained that this episode is anomalous for
the series, containing neither paranormal nor alien activities. Instead,
it is a straight conspiracy narrative about a big pharmaceutical company that secretly experiments on captive live populations. Given that
this part of the story is "outed" very early in the episode, the main
puzzle does not have to do with peculiar events or "beings"; rather,
the agents in this case are literally the agents, Mulder and Scully,

themselves, and the unknown practice is: why are they on this case? —apparently one in which two mere convicts have escaped from the state pen.

The episode begins with a biodiversity scientist in the jungle who finds a dead animal body with strange pustules and crawling with peculiar insects. Investigating, he is squirted in the face by one of the pustules. Later, a similar-looking piece of meat is delivered to a penitentiary. Some infected prisoners manage to escape, and Mulder and Scully are called in—but only with a brief to aid in the recapture of the convicts.

> MULDER: I thought this was about escaped prisoners.
> SCULLY: It is.
> MULDER: *(Indicating a medical crew in an adjacent room.)* Then who are the men in the funny suits? *(Pause.)*
> SCULLY: I don't know—it looks like some kind of decon. situation.
>
> . . .
>
> MULDER: Where did this case originate, Scully?
> SCULLY: Came out of Skinner's office.
> MULDER: Did he say why he gave it to us?
> SCULLY: No—why?
> MULDER: Well, this isn't the type of thing the FBI normally gets called in on—I have a feeling we're not being told the entire story here.
> SCULLY: I've got the same feeling.

Mulder's first line is interestingly self-reflexive here; it could just as easily refer to the episode itself as to his own narrative situation within it. He then raises a side-puzzle: What agent goes with wearing funny suits? Decontamination outfits, Scully speculates briefly. Then, Mulder gets to the main point of the puzzle: if the agent is an FBI agent, then getting called in on a fairly normal prison break is not a suitably tied practice to that agent-description. On the contrary, that cannot be a solution to the question "What are we doing here?" It must have to do with some other, more FBI-like, practice, presumably connected with the side-puzzle, the men in funny suits. Thus, while the audience can have pretty good suspicions about "the whole story" (and this is what makes the episode far from the best ever), Mulder and Scully are not "being told the whole story." Once they find out, of course, there is nothing much to do other than pursue it to its inevitable conclusion. Eventually it leads to the series' own continuing puzzle: Who is Cancer Man and what does he have to do with *The X-Files?* The solution to this master agent-practice puzzle may (or may not) have to wait until the fourth season. However, it remains a continuing instance of what each episode does, with varying degrees of success: it talks the un-known into existence.

Finally, is there another running puzzle in the *X-Files* that a mem-bership categorization analysis could partly illuminate? If this type of analysis connects agents with practices by offering a grammar (or set of rules) for connecting agent-descriptions with practice-descriptions, one puzzle for fans has been along the following lines: Is the sentence "Mulder and Scully have sex" grammatical? That is, is such an agent-practice combination legitimate within the narrative grammar of the *X-Files*? This is perhaps the longest-running *X-Files* "unknown" to date and a source of speculation in both fan and mainstream *X-Files* literature. Indeed, advertisers have begun to make the puzzle explicit; for example, as the third season started (in Australia), Fruitopia drinks ran a mid-episode ad with the following captions: "Scully and Mulder are always dealing with bad apples. When are they going to try some passion fruit?" *Who Weekly* magazine put the matter succinctly just prior to the opening of the third season (again in Australia):

> Not so easy in their affections are *The X-Files* FBI paranormal investi-gators Fox Mulder (David Duchovny) and Dana Scully (Gillian An-derson), who, although spending every waking hour joined at the hip, have so far resisted romantic entanglement. Each lives alone and is professedly in love with their work, but it's still the sexual chemis-try between the two that gives the plots added zest and keeps viewers turned on. (Casey, 35)

However, as the *Who* article acknowledges, there is almost no actual evidence for the possibility, except for one episode where Scully goes on a date (to Mulder's fairly apparent consternation) and a second involving Mulder's ex, recently arrived from the U.K. to assist in an investigation (eliciting barely-disguised jealousy from Scully). Bob Goodwin (co-executive producer) is quoted by *Who* as writing off the possibility altogether, comparing the agents to Matt and Kitty in *Gun-smoke:* "They just never quite connected. . . . They have a professional relationship."

In this sense, "professionality" and "sexuality" vie as candidate predicates for the description of Mulder and Scully's relationship, with the episodes themselves steering a course very close to the for-mer and the secondary literature continuously speculating on the latter. The contrast came to a head in the 1995 *Rolling Stone Yearbook* under the titles "*X-Files* Uncovered" and "Alien Sex Fiends" (see Denton). The cover shows Duchovny and Anderson in bed, possibly naked, and the article includes a double-page spread of Anderson, Duchovny and Chris Carter indulging the "complacencies of the peignoir," faking a postcoital threesome shot, and smaller stills of the two actors cavorting in bed with Duchovny's dog, Blue. The accompanying text makes it clear that this was no more than a sales pitch for the magazine and, perhaps, the series: the photos show the *actors* (and Carter) and clearly *not* Mulder and Scully.

The case is illuminating, however, for it shows that what I have identified as the show's peculiar narrative grammar (agent-practice puzzles and their full or partial solutions) is a quite conscious part of the *X-Files* production and marketing strategy. We keep watching the individual episodes because we want to know "Is it possible?"—for example, that the dead might return to seek revenge—but more importantly, we keep watching the *series* for a much broader development of the narrative grammar, where we want to know, again, "Is it possible?"—but in this case whether Mulder and Scully (will) fuck. In the first case, we routinely get hints, occasional conclusions, and from time to time, completely blank slates. In the second case, if there's any flirtation at all, it's between the production team and ourselves. As with strange happenings, alien possibilities, and the paranormal, sex appears to have most success (as in 40 million viewers) when subject to a tantalizing scarcity.

Throughout his work on membership categorization, Harvey Sacks insists that what I am calling "agent descriptions" are assembled into groups or teams (see footnote 1). He calls these groups "devices" and shows that when a member of a device is mentioned, we can routinely hear the other members. If someone is called "a cellist" or "a fullback," we can hear what other sorts of descriptions might be relevant to the context. What we have seen here is that there may be a rather peculiar device called "the unknown." It is peculiar in that by definition we cannot know in advance the sorts of agents or members that the device collects. This device is indefinite, fuzzy; it could range from having no members at all (hence Scully's occasionally total skepticism) to having infinite members (hence Mulder's occasionally crazy acceptances). The opening credits to *The X-Files* reveal or mention several possible members of the device: flying saucers, paranormal activity, and so on. However, the device is potentially much wider than this, and thus part of the puzzle in each episode is to identify possible device members—with the equally possible proviso that there may actually be none.

In addition to showing how agents are collected in devices, however, Sacks also finds that categories (agent descriptions) within such groups or devices have activities or practices bound to them. He calls these "category-bound activities." These can be very useful in routine discourse. To cite one of Sacks' own examples, the category "baby" can belong to two devices ("stage of life" and "family"). If "baby" is from the device "family," then the person so referred to could be in their twenties, thirties, forties, and so on, and would still be the baby of the family. However, if we hear an utterance like "the baby cried," we can hear that it is a reference to "baby" from the device "stage of life" because it carries a category-bound activity for *that particular variety* of baby (crying). What's more, if we hear the category-bound activity, we can usually infer the category from it, and vice versa. What we have discovered about possible members of the device called "the unknown" is that they do not have routinely bound activities or practices. Thus, one way in which Mulder and Scully can get to "the unknown" is through investigations that tie activities to agents in a piecemeal or case-by-case fashion, relying on assumptions and inferences quite different from the norm. This may be what "the unknown" is, then: a device that contains any members whose routine practices cannot be tied to them through any kind of commonsense or scientific inference. Making the unknown known therefore consists in seeing how it is a particular unknown agent, is tied to a particular practice. What this requires is a means of connection based on assumptions beyond both common sense and science; it invites us to imagine alternative sets of "rational" connections outside the ones we routinely use. In short, it invites us to imagine, via alternative rationalities, other *worlds:* not just the objects, beings, and activities of those worlds but also the alternative forms of knowledge that might inhabit them. This is one of the unique features of *The X-Files* and it might, in part, account for its currently massive fascination and following.

10

The Rebirth of the Clinic

THE BODY AS ALIEN IN *THE X-FILES*

Linda Badley

> Human beings are now such monsters of such sophistica-
> tion and complexity that we can't begin to know ourselves
> until we morph the human body, expand the bandwidth
> of our sensoria, permutate our brains, and strap on our
> add-ons!
>
> —R. U. Sirius

The truth may be "out there," as *The X-Files'* mantra asserts, but the alien (the other, the unknown) is found in or in relation to the body, albeit the body in multifarious and fantastic manifestations: decomposed, regenerated, transgendered, mutated, hybridized, implanted, cloned or doubled, invaded, possessed, colonized, vanished, vaporized, ensanguinated, cannibalized, dissolved and ingested, zombified, harvested, commodified.

The Alien-ated Body

The alien per se (as the extraterrestrial or monster) is neither natural or supernatural but fantastic, in between. It is often preternatural or anomalous, a permutation of the "natural" order such as the aptly designated Flukeman spawned in the sewer, one of a number of "genetically driven" species "deterministically acting out their survival needs" (Miller and Thorne, "*X-Files* Episode Guide," 10–11). As everything about the Flukeman suggests, the human body is equally (perhaps ultimately) the alien. It is the body of evidence, the abductee (Samantha, Duane Barry, Dana Scully), the medicalized body, the body infested by disease or parasite or "demon," the body as marginalized other (the Anasazi), the monstrous feminine, the body as "alien" invader of the territory designated as the self. When the body in question is not alien or invaded by aliens, it is "alienated" by the camera and by the narrative. It is made strange in the Brechtian sense, elided, or displaced within the mise-en-scène and represented allegorically or fantastically. The body in an enhanced sense becomes the "fantastic space" in which *The X-Files* often takes place.

The truth is not out there so much as "in there," as Allison Graham notes earlier in this volume—or rather, here, there, and everywhere. As Deep Throat replies to Mulder's "They're here, aren't they?" in the second episode, "*They* have been here for a very long time." We are alienated from within our systems. "We" are not ourselves. *The X-Files* follows on the 1980s postfuturist science fiction film, which has turned away from themes of space exploration and alien invasion. This shift occurred for reasons that go beyond Watergate and proliferating conspiracy theories. As Vivian Sobchack has commented on our postmodern condition of electronic space, today's world is subject not to invasion but " 'pervasion'—a condition of kinetic accommodation and dispersal associated with the experience and representations of television, video games, and computer terminals" (229).

Immune systems are information systems, adds Donna Haraway, in *Simians*. Biological space is pervaded and negotiated through exchanges of genetic data; biochemically, we are in a constant state of alienation from our "selves." The bipolar oppositions of self and other and the militaristic and colonial metaphors of body invasion and exploration that inform much of our popular immune system discourse have become obsolete.

Haraway also stresses our postmodern conflation of outer and inner space, seeing it exemplified in 1987 in the National Geographic Society's centennial history's positioning of Lennart Nilssen's biomedical photographs in correlation with the photocoverage of the Mercury, Gemini, Apollo, and Mariner voyages. The history's first chapter covers "Space," while the final chapter, "Inner Space," is subtitled "The Stuff of the Stars Has Come Alive" (Haraway, *Simians*, 222). As James Wolcott makes the point in 1993, we no longer study the sky for answers, and the "fascination with UFOs has flagged as the focus has shifted to alien abduction. . . . Even the starship voyages on '*Star Trek*' look nostalgic now" (98). The world of *The X-Files* is inverted on its own processes and intertexts. Its gaze is focused on the technologies of the body and on the intersections between the body and the mind, the body and the self.[1]

Alien Abduction and *Alien Autopsy*

The premise of *The X-Files* is the alien abduction scenario, which resembles the medical thriller or mad doctor genre more than the space opera or cyberpunk.[2] *The X-Files* recapitulates the primal scene of modern medical technology. It is Michel Foucault's *The Birth of the Clinic* 1990s-style, from the embodied patient's point of view ("Deep Throat," "Fallen Angel," "Little Green Men," "Fearful Symmetry," "Duane Barry," "Ascension," "The Blessing Way," "Nisei"): a blinding white light, invasive surgery, something taken out and put in, powerlessness, death and resurrection on a cold table. Lost time and cellular memories of the event reveal how the body does not lie when "mind" and science may. Medical surveillance is the equivalent to (or may be) the alien gaze. "Duane Barry" and "Ascension" have made this possibility horrifyingly clear, and "Nisei" suggests that "alien" abductions may be cover stories for government sponsored genetic experiments, with or without the collaboration of extraterrestrials. The "alien"/clinical gaze (the two inseparable in this scenario) is ultimately linked to the camera, which alienates the body as image from itself. Dana Scully is under this gaze; more often, though, she zealously employs it.

The obverse of the alien abduction is the alien autopsy over which Scully presides. *Alien Autopsy* is also the title of the "documentary" first aired on Fox in September 1995 during the 7:00 P.M. time slot (just before and implicitly in conjunction with *The X-Files*) and now widely available as a video cassette. *Alien Autopsy* features clips from two films purported to have been made at Roswell Air Force Base and at the autopsy center at Fort Worth in 1947, by a USAF film technician

---

1. For instance, the episode entitled "Space" gets no farther "out there" than a shuttle mission and a hostile alien "presence" that looks like the Turin Shroud. Wolcott emphasizes the intersection, in science fiction, between psychology and cybernetics: "As the world becomes . . . a giant cranium webbed with computer lines, it becomes too enmeshed in its own mental processes to extend an eye into the universe" (99). However, I find the *X-Files'* emphasis on biology and on the intersections between cybernetics and biology more insistent.

2. Brian Yamashuro noted after the first season (in an article in *Wrapped in Plastic*'s special issue on *The X-Files*) that the show "is often perceived as one that focuses primarily on UFOs" (28). However, the show's creator and executive producer Chris Carter has admitted that "I was never a science fiction fan," claims to have "never seen an episode of 'Star Trek,' " and is "really interested in personal experiences that could affect me in this place and time." Carter sees *The X-Files* as "a cross-genre show" (Van Syckle).

(Walker, B2). The longer of the films shows surgeons dissecting the body of a small, pubescent, perhaps pregnant female with a gigantic bald head and ovoid, reptilian eyes.

The "alien body" figures prominently in the series and seasonal pilots and finale: in the series premiere, "The X-Files, in "The Erlenmeyer Flask" (which opens and closes in a huge Pentagon warehouse as Cancer Man files away a canister containing what appears to be an alien fetus), in the two-part episode "Anasazi"/"The Blessing Way" (where Mulder "dies" and is resurrected in a mass grave of alien-human hybrids). The alien or alien-ated body—alienated from without and from within, the alien as predator and prey, colonized and colonizer—is the touchstone in a series that "speaks" in the discourses of the postmodern body. In the two-part "Nisei"/"731" and in "Jose Chung's *From Outer Space*," the alien autopsy videotape itself is the subject of investigation. As extraterrestrial-multinational conspiracy theories proliferate, in episodes set in railroad cars, mass graves, and conflagrations, the autopsied alien is increasingly identified with victims of covert medical, military, and government experiments. Reversing the alien invasion scenario, the alien body comes to stand metonymically for all marginalization and commodification of human bodies: the holocaust Japanese internment camps, a leper colony in North Carolina, Native American survivors. and implanted female abductees. The alien abduction and the alien autopsy are reverse mirror images proclaiming the same thing, that aliens R US. Ultimately, that which we call alien in *The X-Files* involves a separation of the body from the "self" and imagined as Other. The extraterrestrial alien becomes merely the farthest out in a number of biopolitically "extreme possibilities" contained in the X-Files. All together, these reflect a cultural moment in which bio-power is the issue.

On the one hand, the body has seemed increasingly within the realm of conscious human manipulation and control, through transplantation, genetic and reproductive technologies, cryonics, plastic surgery, transsexual surgery, cybernetics, and the electronic sensorium. On the other hand, these technologies have made the body a resource or commodity, alienating it from what is traditionally known as the "self." It is a display case of parts to be sold or spaces to be filled for commerce. Meanwhile, our cures have spawned new plagues, as in "The Host." The Flukeman, the product of "reproductive and physiological cross-trading," was born from Chernobyl, Scully explains, "in a primordial soup of radioactive sewage." Lacking sexual organs (like ordinary flukes), it regenerates spontaneously, insuring its survival. However, "Nature did not make this thing. We did." According to Laurie Garrett, AIDS "may well be just the first of the modern, large-scale epidemics of infectious disease" (xi). Moreover, "the age of antibiotics is giving way to an age of anxiety about disease," fostered by new viruses that mutate almost as soon as they have been identified (Ebola or hantavirus) or by antibiotic-resistant and/or "flesh-eating" bacteria (Lemonick, 66). "F. Emasculata," an episode that plays on such fears, has no need for the supernatural; in a visual pun on the word "bug," insects (whose larvae carry a deadly parasite) emerge from boils that erupt (*Alien*-style) in examiners' faces.

Pete Boss has noted how modern medicine have "recast the unknown" within the perimeters of the human body (19). The postmodern body has what Richard Corliss (describing the films of David Cronenberg) calls a "mind of its own" (84). It is a "haunted house whose rumblings trigger lust, misery and excruciating pain in the poor tenant. This property is condemned." Western expansionist medical discourse is hopelessly confused by autoimmune diseases in which the body "attacks" itself: the colonized is seen as the invader. *The X-Files* reflects an age in which, according to chaos theory, "the human immune system currently finds itself in the vicinity of a strange attractor. Which is to say that the biochemical aspect of humanity dedicated to distinguishing self from other is already on a greased slide . . . wherein things get weirder and weirder, faster and faster, until things change, quite utterly, signaling the emergence of a new order," (Gibson, xv).

It is no wonder that, like the medical dramas *ER* and *Chicago Hope* (or reality-based shows such as *Rescue 911* and *Trauma Center*), *The X-Files* returns to the image of the body on the procrustean bed of biotechnology, hooked up to, kept alive by, and at the mercy of machines ("One Breath," "Deep Throat," "The Erlenmeyer Flask," "End Game," "Dod Kalm," "Excelsis Dei," "The Blessing Way"). In "The Erlenmeyer Flask," Mulder finds a storage facility in which the bodies of five men are floating in huge tanks, part of an experiment using alien viruses on terminal patients. This image of the body so alienated recalls the film adaptation of Robin Cook's medical thriller *Coma* (1982), directed by Michael Crichton (*The Andromeda Strain, Terminal Man, Jurassic Park,* and *ER*), where a hospital system selects healthy patients for routine operations, renders them comatose, and maintains them for later dissection and sale for transplant operations. As the heroine (a Scully prototype) explores networks of air ducts, pipelines, crawl spaces, and corridors for evidence, the hospital comes to resemble the inside of a vast organic machine. In a shot that Foucault would have appreciated, the camera pans a bio-emporium where hundreds of perfect, rosy bodies surreally float, connected by a network of umbilical tubes.

Thus, in "Fearful Symmetry," in a zoo near a UFO spot, Scully and Willa Anderson perform an autopsy on a pregnant elephant, dictating their findings from the abdominal cavity. This scene speaks for the perspective of the show: we are embodied, our language on its terms, and the body (with the help of technologies of the body) is as alien as it is womb and home. As the title, an allusion to William Blake's poem "The Tiger" suggests, "Fearful Symmetry" concerns the alien power attributed to the animal/body. On yet another level, Scully is another alien invader in an episode about Diane Fossey, animal versus human rights, reproductive technologies and body rights, and power.

When the body is most incontrovertibly absent, as in "Soft Light" (in which victims appear to have spontaneously combusted), its absence is made physically, indeed biochemically and kinesthetically, present. Particle physicist Chester Banton has become through his own experiments a sort of walking black hole whose shadow deconstructs any body that crosses its path, leaving a small puddle of transparent black residue whose DNA may be identified. What Banton wants, moreover, is embodied knowledge: "I remember looking and seeing Chester," says Dr. Christopher Davy, a witness to the latter's transformation. "He was perfectly calm, as if he wanted it to happen, as if he was finally going to experience the dark matter he had theorized in some kind of physical way, as if the truth might come into him." The body conceived in such a fashion is fantastic. The truth of antimatter has to "come into" us in order to be known—the word made flesh.

The X-Files takes body invasion, mutation, and vampire motifs familiar from modern horror/sci-fi film to a postmodern level of cultural self-awareness, referring knowingly back to *Alien* (1979) through *Videodrome* (1983) and *The Silence of the Lambs* (1991). However, the show appeals to a culture whose major universities are known for their health letters (as well as their football teams) and recruit aggressively for organs and audiences—*The Harvard Heart Letter, The Johns Hopkins Health Letter, The Berkeley Wellness Letter,* and so on. Medically "privileged," endangered, and "dangerous" organs, parts, tissues, and fluids provide an amoral, ecologically, and biologically based mythology that *The X-Files* incorporates with increasing sophistication—for instance, blood in the second season's "3" and fat in the third season's "2Shy." The latter is about a vampire that feeds on fat; his kiss melts the normally too solid flesh of his victims and, in a perverse fulfillment of their heart's desire, pares them down to the bone. His specialty comments on a culture in which fat, like blood, is simultaneously fetishized and considered poison. The mutant Tooms requires five human livers every thirty years; driven by survival needs, his species converts biochemistry into a numerology with the mythical potency of vampire lore. (Now that the blood that was "the life" in the previous century is death, and as the heart becomes increasingly unworthy of mystification, the five livers resonate with connotations.) In the gambling ring of "Hell Money," the players do not bet on money but on their vital organs, with the losers becoming hapless donors. Hell is once again the steel table of the dissecting clinic.

In short, *X-Files* viewers are given a vitalistic world informed by the discourses and technologies of the body, by Foucauldian bio-power. The truth is in the genes.

Ufologist Budd Hopkins believes extraterrestrials are searching for a "certain kind of genetic structure" and have collaborated with the government and an international coalition in breeding experiments (quoted in Bader, 85). The pattern of recent abductions, moreover, presents a change from "a single random encounter to a purposeful, lifelong, genetic manipulation" to produce hybrid offspring (Bader, 86). Bio-power replaces sex (in the usual sense) as the characters' constant preoccupation, and it is what the conspiratorial powers (the aliens as the wielders of technologies of the body) want. Episodes take place in (or refer us to) institutions or outposts in which the production, reproduction, and manipulation of biological power is carried on: fertility clinics, abortion clinics, biochemistry labs, convalescent homes, leper colonies, psychiatric wards, prisons (infected with a deadly disease), reservations, refugee camps, military bases, military ships, zoos. The list sounds like it might have come from an index to the works of Foucault.

The far out "truth" that extraterrestrial aliens need human bodies (human genetic material and information) and vice versa makes the body both vulnerable and powerful, oppressed and oppressive. Whether one believes in this premise, however, makes little difference, because the alien abduction/autopsy scenario provides a metaphor for the way we perceive human and other biology at this particular cultural moment, as a "rebirth of the clinic." Ultimately it is a metaphor for the present fragility of the self, which biology, psychology, and cybernetics increasingly pronounce an illusion. At the same time, this tenuous, enhanced notion of the body provides a new arena for self-definition as the body "opens up" and is projected as an erotically charged fantastic space.

The Body as Fantastic Space

The X-Files explores the body as fantastic space and new frontier, opened up by Marie-Francois-Xavier Bichat's practice of pathological anatomy in the late eighteenth and early nineteenth centuries. According to Foucault, Bichat created the medical *perspective*, which envisioned the body as interiority and vital process. Bichat's advice to another physician in 1803 was to "Open up a few corpses; you will dissipate at once the darkness that observation alone could not dissipate." That "opaque mass in which secrets, invisible lesions, and the very mystery of origins lie hidden" would be revealed (Foucault, *Clinic*, 146). The clinical experience opened up a new conceptual "inner" space that was at once deep and visible, solid and enclosed, vital and accessible—in which a postmodern vitalism could be born.

What Foucault calls "the birth of the clinic" also alienated the subject from the body, producing a view of the body as fantastic. The clinic placed a new emphasis on seeing, and it was here that Foucault discovered the power-wielding, manipulative "gaze" (*Clinic* xii-xv). The clinical (probing, dissecting, defining) eye was like an "index finger palpitating the depths. Hence that metaphor of 'touch' . . . by which doctors will ceaselessly define their glance" (*Clinic*, 122). The emphasis on visualization, mapping, and surgical manipulation of the body led to what Foucault would term our modern "technologies of the body," a discourse of bio-power, whose terms were bodily fluids, organs, and parts, and identification of the human with the machine.

This alienation effect was intensified by the development of medical imaging technology, beginning with the X-ray. "Like the explosion of the first atomic bomb in 1945," writes Linda Henderson, the discovery of X-rays "produced a sense that the world had changed irrevocably" (336). Roentgen's X-ray images presented the viewing subject with a disturbing spectacle: "The X-ray's expressionism brought the subject closer to the image of the body, exposing its interiority to the eye. Rather than synthesizing the subject and its body, however, X-rays had the unintended effect of alienating the body from the self, recasting the body as a foreign object. . . . the X-rayed body exposed the subject to an aspect of itself it actively suppresses—namely, death" (Lippel, 6).

The birth of the X-ray in 1885 coincided with the birth of the cinema, as Lisa Cartwright notes (107). As the body's interior became a new frontier—particularly as it has been imaged and imagined in the last three decades—it has become the locus for a deeper Other self.[3] Spiritualists in the 1890s saw the X-ray as something like an image of the soul, the body stripped to its spiritual core (Cartwright, 21). Remythologized, biological innerspace becomes thoroughly *fantastic* in the sense in which Jean-Paul Sartre used the term. The fantastic denotes a liminal zone occupied by the embodied subject: "an entire world in which things manifest a captive, tormented thought . . . both

---

3. I consider the iconography and perspective of *The X-Files* as one indicator of a shift in the concept of the self from the Freudian psyche to the post-Freudian body—the body in an enhanced or "fantastic" sense derived from Lacan, French feminism, Foucault, and poststructuralist thought in general. The self or soul becomes the body conceived in the terms of bio-power.

whimsical and enchained" that never manages to "express itself" purely. One can imagine Mulder thinking (if not quite saying) that "matter is never entirely matter, since it offers only a constantly frustrated attempt at determinism, and mind is never completely mind, because it has fallen into slavery and has been impregnated and dulled by matter. All is woe. Things suffer and tend toward inertia, without ever attaining it; the debased, enslaved mind unsuccessfully strives towards consciousness and freedom," (Sartre, 58). Sartre proposed the fantastic as a language for existentialism, for the absurd; Tzvetan Todorov followed on him by extending the term to refer to a literary mode of hesitation between natural and supernatural explanations, as experienced by the situated, embodied subject.

Grounded, like Sartre and Todorov, in Western psychology and neurobiology, *The X-Files* sustains a Todorovian hesitation between the physical and the metaphysical that takes on an openly dialogic form. As Chris Carter explains, Scully and Mulder come from "Right out of my head. A dichotomy. They are the equal parts of my desire to believe in something and my inability to believe in something. . . . I want, like a lot of people do, to have the experience of witnessing a paranormal phenomenon. At the same time I want not to accept it, but to question it. I think those characters and those voices came out of that duality," (Bischoff, 44). However, Carter remains "a natural skeptic and tend[s] to doubt things until someone removes my doubt. So I write from the Scully point of view" (Kutzera, 53).

Scully is body knowledge in all senses: she is the female body as ground of being, as victim and test subject, as Other; she also represents the medical perspective, the clinical gaze, the self-and flesh-destroying X-ray. As object and bearer of the gaze, as test subject and medical authority, Scully (skull-y) is every body and a comment on "alien" pervasion. Swearing that the names of Scully and Mulder (mull over? molder?) have no "meaning," Carter tosses off the remark that he grew up in L.A., where "Vince Scully was the voice of God" (Bischoff, 44).

As Carter's comments suggest, *The X-Files* projects a fantastic space in which Todorovian hesitation can be prolonged indefinitely. This space is comparable to what David Gotlib, an anomalistic psychologist who works with abductees, calls (after Ken Ring and neo-Jungian psychologist James Hillman) "the imaginal." Gotlib argues that abductees are not psychotic, although he also does not think aliens are literally contacting them. Abduction reports are "real but . . . take place in an imaginal world . . . you can tune into if you have the right faculty of expression" (McLaughlin, 46). The imaginal experience is not imaginary but rather another dimension with its own form and reality; it is comparable to a lucid dream in which the dreamer "can feel every emotion and sensation that takes place." Ring and Gotlib put near-death experiences in the same category (McLaughlin, 46). They suggest that, psychologically speaking, the truth is neither purely physical or metaphysical: the truth of a phenomenon is validated by the body's experience of it. In the interzone of the "imaginal," the body cannot lie. In Hillman's psychology, the imaginal is a process of psychic accommodation to desire. The imaginal in all these senses corresponds with the quasi-biological, quasi-mythological territory presently occupied by alternative medicine and regressive hypnosis. It is a fantastic space in the Todorovian sense, one in which a creative, life-supporting dialogue of skeptic and believer can take place.

Throughout *The X-Files*, the body in this enhanced, fantastic sense is the site of truth. Its "voice" and vision are expressed through regressive hypnosis, accessing cellular memory, for instance—with Scully's flashbacks to her abduction a notable example. "Is *X-Files* dealing with the mythology of the twentieth century?" asks David Bischoff of *Omni*, and Carter admits "there is some kind of correlation." If so, it is a mythology that for whatever reason (perhaps the lack of a vital shamanistic tradition in the West) is based in the body, in neurobiology and Foucauldian vitalism mated with Lacanian feminism and alternative medicine. *The X-Files* projects a vision of the body "opened up" since the birth of the clinic, a new "inner" fantasy space in which a new myth, at once vitalistic and necrophilic, is trying to be born. Like the "aesthetic" of the X-ray as Cartwright views it (107), the "look" is gothic *and* postmodern, clinically detached and erotically charged.

Alien Sex

Fantasy space is eroticized space. In *The X-Files*, literal sex is displaced onto the body enhanced as fantastic or mythical space. This displacement tells viewers that sex is alien contact. Sex in the conventional sense is "safe" (nonexistent) on *The X-Files* because it is not safe in an age, like that of the Victorians, of anxiety about diseases; it must resonate from iconographies signifying its absence or alienation. Elaine Rapping has called *The X-Files* "the sexiest show on the air, despite— or because of—the fact that the relationship between the lead couple is almost wholly nonphysical" (36).

We see precious little "skin" in *The X-Files*. The erotic content of Mulder and Scully's relationship is communicated in subtle shifts in body position and eye contact, through closeups and cross-cuts (again reminiscent of *The Silence of the Lambs*) that leave out or elide the expected body images, a technique that was intensified in shooting around Gillian Anderson's pregnancy. The protagonists' bodies are eroticized indirectly, in terms of what is knowingly covered (by trench coats, dark, earth-toned suits, or surgical gowns), left out of the shot (Anderson's body), deflected self-referentially in shots emphasizing Scully's scopophilia (Anderson, in glasses and forensic garb, peering into a cadaver or a microscope, or lifting a stomach onto a scale), or strategically displaced by the pathological drive of the plot (Mulder's and Scully's examinations of each other for infection in "Ice").

Scully, speaking for 1990s Victorianism in "Genderbender," declares it "hard to believe in this day and age someone would have sex with a complete stranger." The episode concerns the Kindred, an isolationist religious sect whose members through some genetic mutation have developed the ability to change sex and secrete large amounts of pheromones (the chemical animals secrete for sexual attraction). The "animal" vitality repressed within this alien community is so potent that their touch can kill. Mulder, not so much jealous as appalled when Scully is drawn to one of the Kindred, reproaches her: "I saw you about to do the wild thing with some stranger." (Scully, aghast, asks, "Think he was trying to kill me?" Mulder replies. "Maybe it's the sex that kills.")

However, what Mulder most desires, like the renegade Kindred, is alien sex—alien contact, intimate proof that "we are not alone" in the universe. Like Victor Frankenstein, he seeks a friend for the alien soul in himself. The more negative side of his nature is suggested by Victor Klemper, the Nazi eugenicist who engineered Operation Paper Clip.[4] In a world of postmodern, international, and interplanetary biopolitics, Scully's "forensic zeal" competes with alien technologies of abduction. Much as the aliens are "turned on" by Scully, Samantha (presumably), and Duane Barry, Mulder is turned on by (and only by) alien bodies. To *U. Magazine's* Audette Fulbright, Duchovny explained that Mulder "thinks about UFOs the way other men think about sex" (Fulbright, 30).

Considering the erotic intensity and the scope of the sexual politics they cover up, *The X-Files* should be X-rated. For a frame of reference, we might go to Woody Allen's *Everything You Always Wanted to Know About Sex but Were Afraid to Ask* (1972), where we are inside the human body, embodied, identified with our organs and functions, and fascinated (simultaneously alienated and enamored) spectators of the same (Allen as spermatozoa yearning for the egg). As in Sartre's fantastic expressionism, a "topsy turvy" world in which means replace ends and existence essence, the relationship of body and soul are reversed (61). Critics often remark the series' famous "look"—of "a recogniz-

4. Klemper's name may combine references to Victor Frankenstein, M. Krempe (Frankenstein's icy science teacher at Ingolstadt), and the infamous Joseph Mengele and Heinrich Himmler.

able world gone slightly off," as Charles Taylor puts it. A conspiratorial, concealing cloud cover, a "negatively charged grayness hovers
over everything" (Taylor, 2). This peculiar alienation effect shifts into
overt, biologically grounded expressionism in certain episodes. These
become allegories about bio-power as the elixir every body has, needs,
desires, and fears.

The show's eroticized alienation effect derives from a projection of
visceral innerspace onto the world at large. The mise-en-scène is dark,
misty, and "moist." "Sex" is voraciously oral and anal, the two functions depicted as more or less inseparable. In episodes like "3," which
focuses on a vampire cult, you first notice the effect in a different color
coding: blood red clouds above a blackened skyscape, red fingernails
caressing a glass of red wine, red light, and so forth. In "Red Museum,"
the camera shows red and white cattle going to the slaughter, then the
marbled red and white sides of beef, then cuts to a scenario in which
a teenage boy is found wandering, branded with "He is one" on his
naked back. Next, with Mulder and Scully we view slides of similar
victims of "brandings" projected on a screen. Planted in the midst of
this already strange plot is the showpiece: the worship service of a
white-robed, red-turbaned *vegetarian* sect whose gods "speak" through
a computer text projected on a vast screen. The focus shifts back to
speculations about the effect of genetically engineered bovine growth
hormones on the oversexed local boys (beef). It shifts again as Mulder
finds evidence that aliens have turned this Wisconsin cattle country
into a genetic testing laboratory, using the vegetarian sect as a control
group. The use of teenage boys as test subjects is linked with child
pornography when Gird Thomas's private film studio is revealed. In
both instances, "alien" technologies abuse the boys, turning them into
beefcakes. (The boys, meanwhile, abuse girls, seven rapes having occurred over the past year.)

A self-referential sick joke is planted in the first ten minutes of
the episode in a scene in which Scully enthusiastically and messily
consumes a local restaurant's barbecued ribs. Similarly, in the chicken
processing plant in "Our Town"—where a worker dies in a trough of
chicken entrails, where human bones are found in the salmonella infested river, and where the townspeople are exposed as voodoo cultists
who practice cannibalism to extend their lifespans—Scully examines
the forensic evidence while snacking on a bucket of the local product.
In Our Town we are all what we eat.

"The Host" is shot from an excremental perspective; it takes spectators on an alimentary version of *Fantastic Voyage* in Mulder's repeated descents into the Newark, New Jersey, sewers. In one elaborate
scatological joke, the camera follows the Flukeman to the nether end
of an outhouse, where it gets stuck in the hose of a sewage suction

machine. This "monster" resembles nothing so much as the organ that it simultaneously inhabits and consumes. "Humbug"'s sheriff (formerly Johnny, the Dog-Faced Boy) tells Scully and Mulder, "It's what's inside that counts," and the platitude resonates with possibility. Like Eng of the famous Chang and Eng duo, Siamese twin Lenny dies when his brother disconnects from him permanently, having taken with him some essential information. The "inside self" as revealed in "Humbug" is overwhelmingly biological *and* anomalous. The sideshow acts are themselves allegories of the inner spaces and processes of the body.

The series mise-en-scène is perhaps a composite of Tim Burton (who like Carter began at Disney Studios), David Lynch, Jonathan Demme, and Carter's fellow Canadian David *(They-Came-From-Within)* Cronenberg. Where Burton specializes in the visual pun, Cronenberg is the master of squirmy eroticism and aestheticism (as in *Beetlejuice,* where the afterlife characters are visible and biologically acute embodiments of their respective deaths). A biology major before he became a filmmaker, Cronenberg has a character, Elliot Mantle, one of a set of twin gynecologists in *Dead Ringers* (1988), remark that "there should be standards of beauty for the insides of bodies as well as the outsides. You know, best kidney, most perfectly developed spleen." As Foucault has noted, the "sensible *truth* [of the medicalized body] is now open, not so much to the senses themselves, as to a *fine* sensibility," and the body's interiors are open to an aesthetic, with its prescriptions, rules, skills, and tastes (*Clinic,* 121). In Lacanian terms, *The X-Files* offers regression, a view from the womb that is erotically charged. Sex in *The X-Files* is deferred, displaced from skin shows to the interiors of the body, to its deep truths, as in Lynch's *Eraserhead* (1978) and *Blue Velvet* (1986).

In "Genderbender," creepier than the Kindred themselves are the flesh-colored, chthonian caverns where the sect members mine/absorb animal vitality and change sex. These caverns are marked on the earth's surface by crop circles. Like other alien landing sites—for instance, the mountain (in the third season's "Paper Clip") that contains the tunnels of medical records and tissue samples—the setting and mise-en-scène both signify and conceal layers of the deeper Truth within the body, the body's subtext.

Because Scully is the body *and* the doctor, the colonized and the colonizer, the woman and the gaze whose phallic technology opens "the fleshy secrets of normally hidden things" (Williams, *Hard Core,* 191), her victimization, scopophilia, and forensic zeal are useful indicators of where we live now. "Humbug," an episode that takes place in a community of retired sideshow performers, opens by presenting the

alien's (the Alligator Man's) point of view. Scully's scopophilia, which
is based in empathy, soon takes over, dominates, and solves the case.
Early in the episode, Mulder warns Scully that any medical or forensic
readings are meaningless in a town where the anomalous is the norm
—a point made by Tod Browning's horror film *Freaks*. Scully, however,
is undaunted. As a doctor and a woman, whose body is other to begin
with (for whom anatomy is destiny in numerous senses), she identifies
with and is "turned on" by anomalies. They allow her to return to the
site of abjection, the pre-Oedipal mother's body, to which she, more
than Mulder, is overtly attracted.[5] In the sideshow, a marginal space if
there ever was one, Scully finds her true home—as suggested in scenes
in Scully's trailer that seem located in the center of the carnival activity,
implicating her as a freak or alien. As in Cronenberg's *The Fly* (whose
title character accidentally splices his own genes with those of a house
fly), "freaks" in *The X-Files* may be anomalous but are not abnormal.
As mutations, they are maps or keys to biological past or future. Taking
the lead in this investigation, Scully is clearly stimulated by the sights,
the revelations culminating when she performs an autopsy on the
androgynous-looking Lenny and discovers vestigial umbilical functions in his esophagus and trachea.

    What is truly erotic is both out there and in here, as in Freud's
"uncanny," intimately familiar and therefore alien. Like *Dead Ringers'*
Beverly Mantle, who is obsessed with the reproductive organs of "mutant women," Mulder desires alien sex—or alienated sex. Dr. Blockhead (whose act features radical forms of body piercing and
manipulation) asserts that "You can train your testicles to draw up
into your body," and Mulder quips, "I'm doing this as we speak."
"You know," the psychic insurance salesman Clyde Bruckman (whose
single talent is to predict how people will die) confides to Mulder,
"there are worse ways to go, but I can't think of one more undignified
than autoerotic asphyxiation." "Why are you telling me that?" asks
Mulder. "Forget it. It's none of my business," replies Bruckman.

    During Scully's disappearance, Mulder has "ordinary" (human,
heterosexual, presumably missionary-position, offscreen) sex—with a
fascinating fledgling vampire named Kristen (Perrey Reeves, Duchov-

    5. Linda Williams argues that the heroine of the horror film returns the look of the
monster, with whom she has a curious rapport, a flash of "sympathetic identification"
based in their sharing a different and powerful sexuality that threatens phallocentrism
(*"Woman,"* 88–89). If the male gaze expresses "conventional fear" of what differs from
itself, the female look recognizes a "freakishness . . . similar to her own. For she too has
been constituted as an exhibitionist-object by the desiring look of the male" (*"Woman,"*
88). Scully turns the alienated role of the scientist into a more emphatic one based on
the woman's identification with the monstrous body.

ny's lover at the time), whose Thanatos is a match for his. Pricking her finger and offering it to him, she says, "This is my life. My name's Kristen" [Christian]. (Mulder's reply: "Aren't you afraid?") Mulder turns down the blood and "saves" her from vampirism (presumably using sperm as an antidote), but his real attraction is to her passion for the life of death. Decoded, of course, blood swapping is also just another kind of gene swapping.

Kristen (like Amy, the abuse victim Mulder confuses with his abducted sister in "Oubliette") has an androgynous, childlike appeal that extends to Mulder's romance with "little green men." The latter extends, in "Humbug," to little men in general. To Mr. Nutt, the dwarf who disparages Mulder's lanky, clonish good looks and asserts that "you'd be surprised how many women find my size intriguingly alluring," Mulder replies, "You'd be surprised how many men do as well."

"Ordinary" sex is small beans in a world in which body parts, tissues, and substances are ultimate terms—in which sexuality is aggressively pursued and constructed through discourses (and literal exchanges) of blood ("Blood"), "Fresh Bones," hormones, genetically engineered cow's milk, human livers, DNA, clones, Siamese twins that detach, "seeking . . . another brother" ("Humbug"), and vamps. Kristen is, of course, a surrogate for an absent Scully, whose body is (intimately) with the aliens—or at least Mulder believes her to be. Moreover, two of the sexiest episodes, from Mulder's point of view at least, are the two-part "Duane Barry"/"Ascension." In the first part, Mulder has intense empathetic relations with Duane Barry, the ex-agent and abductee with extraterrestrial microchips implanted in his sinuses, gums, and abdomen. Mulder thus shares Barry's experiences of alien presence, in which the violation and pain of alien surgery resembles rape (or a nightmare about dentists) and borders on revelation. In "Ascension," "aliens" (whether extraterrestrial, international, or governmental, we do not know) abduct Scully in place of Barry. Now, Mulder explicitly "becomes" or imagines Scully on an alien operating table, the shot framing a horrifically (or wondrously) swelling abdomen (which all X-Philes knew was Gillian Anderson's pregnancy). In his vision, shown from her point of view, her/his body is literally filled up with the alien presence, impregnated with the alien Word. Now that Scully has been touched by the sky gods, implanted with a microchip, and possibly (immaculately) conceived a half-Grey child, Mulder is enraptured. He stands—with one hand in the trench coat pocket where we just saw him put Scully's cross necklace—gazing at the stars, waiting for a sign.

Thus, in the third season episode "Paper Clip," Mulder insists that "the truth is in there, in the X-Files," referring to what might best (from the perspective of reproductive and genetic technologies) be called the

Sex Files. What Mulder and Scully desire, perhaps equally, is not much different from what Dr. Sally Kendrick (the brilliant geneticist and the original of all the Eve clones in "Eve") and the Nazi eugenicist Dr. Victor Klemper want: self-replication on a grand scale, transcendence of the body through the medium of the body.

Thanatopsis

In the 1990s Victorianism reflected in *The X-Files*, death is *not* alien. It is user friendly. Episode titles are revealing: "Born Again," "Tooms" (tombs?), "Ghost in the Machine," "Dod Kalm," "Fallen Angel," "The Blessing Way," and "Clyde Bruckman's Final Repose." As Barbara Ehrenreich has noted, death is in the 1990s "The Ultimate Chic." What I have called "alien sex" is, after all, death; when not literally life threatening, it undermines the illusion of the unity of the self, as "Genderbender" amply shows. The other side of sexual alienation and body panic is X generation and yuppie Thanatos.[6] Thus a typical *X-Files* episode begins, ends, or peaks in a scene in which Scully reads a corpse with the eager diligence and empathy of Clarice Starling. In "Irresistible" (aired for the second time on Friday, January 13, 1995), "death is a recorded event" and "the body has a story to tell," she elegizes, unzipping a body bag as she prepares to examine the victim of a necrophilic serial killer who takes as trophies body parts that "grow" after death (hair and fingernails). "Death like life itself is a drama with a beginning, middle, and end," she says as she looks at the victim's face and sees her own. As the episode concludes, Mulder's voiceover sermonizes: "The conquest of fear lies in the moment of its acceptance. And understanding that what scares us most is most familiar. . . . The fear of violent death and the primitive impulse to survive are as frightening [and as seductive] as any X-file—as real as the acceptance that it could happen to you."

As Navajo shaman Albert Hosteen says of the comatose Mulder in "The Blessing Way," his body is weak, and his spirit desires to be with his fathers, to transcend flesh, becoming alien entirely. Mulder's lust for alien bodies finally links him, like Scully, to Victor Frankenstein. "You still believe you can petition heaven and get some penetrating answers. If you found that answer, what would you do with it?" Skinner asks Mulder in "Paper Clip," echoing (perhaps) the editors of *Wrapped in Plastic*, who asked, "What would he do then? . . . Would

6. "Nothing concentrates the mind like Dr. Jack Kevorkian's gaunt visage on the TV screen as he is led away from yet another assisted-suicide site," or an image of the "throngs of his supporters . . . proclaiming the right to die swiftly and painlessly," Ehrenreich notes (695).

Mulder and Scully become genetically altered superhumans, or harness some other alien power?" (Miller and Thorne, "Rush to Judgment," 7). *The X-Files* is about transcendence of the body through the body—through alien biotechnology or what Cronenberg calls the "New Flesh."

Although or because of its squirmy sex appeal or its view of the body in a murky, pathological, Cronenbergian light, no body really dies in *The X-Files,* as James Wolcott notes (99). Nursing home residents suddenly become rapists, the citizens of "Our Town" extend their lifespans through cannibalism, and a mutant (Tooms) returns every thirty years. Death is replaced by transformation, reincarnation, regeneration, or hybridization and immunization through alien contact.

As in Cronenberg's New Flesh or Foucault's clinic, death has an alien life (and many processes) of its own. The clinical perspective, transgressing boundaries, relativized life and death, bringing the latter "down from that absolute in which it appeared as an indivisible, decisive, irrecoverable event; . . . volatilized it, distributed it throughout life in the form of separate, partial, progressive deaths, deaths that are so slow in occurring that they extend even beyond death itself" (Foucault, 145). While self-alienating, the new mortalism produced by the clinical perspective was anything but demystifying. It promised that the body could be manipulated, its processes reversed or suspended. On the popular front, since Mary Shelley's *Frankenstein,* the body armed with technology has replaced the soul and is presently displacing the psyche.[7] Viewed as primordial soup, bio-power, or cyborg, the body does not die; it reverts or converts, mutates or regenerates. Cyborgs in particular, Haraway tells us in "The Biopolitics of Postmodern Bodies," are "suspicious of the reproductive. . . . For salamanders, regeneration after injury, such as the loss of a limb, involves regrowth with the constant possibility of twinning or other odd topographical productions at the site of former injury. The regrown limb can be monstrous. . . . potent. We have all been injured . . . and require regeneration, not rebirth," (223). She dreams a "utopian dream of the hope for a monstrous world beyond gender" (223), sex, and death.

---

7. See Foucault, *Clinic,* 145: Victor Frankenstein's sequence of discoveries is similar to Bichat's. Frankenstein finds, like Bichat, that death is inseparable from life. "To examine the causes of life, we must first have recourse to death," he explains. And after "analyzing all the minutiae of causation, as exemplified in the change from life to death, and death to life . . . from the midst of this darkness a sudden light broke in upon me— a light so brilliant and wondrous, yet so simple" (Shelley, 51). As in today's versions of the Frankenstein myth, the power that no longer resided in Death (as absolute and supernatural) was invested in the revitalized inner space of the body. The new mortalism, as Foucault suggests, was really a new vitalism.

On *The X-Files*, there is always the possibility of transcendence of the body through the medium of the body, in near-death or out-of-body experiences as well as in regeneration and mutation. The ghost, as one episode title proclaims, is "in the Machine." In "The Walk," aired on Veterans' Day eve, astral projection is presented in terms of a paraplegic Gulf War veteran's phantom limbs. As Mark Leiren-Young notes, abduction by aliens is "*The X-Files'* version of maternity leave," after which Gillian Anderson's character returned to the show with a worldview more open to "extreme possibilities" (21). The "forensic zeal" (Wolcott, 98) of the show is such that the processes of death are studied for signs of alien—mutant, hybrid, transubstantiated, electronically charged, preternatural—life, which may be Mulder's and Scully's (and viewers') most intense (if also most sublimated) desire.

Embracing the alien seems to have brought Mulder and Scully together in their work if not in bed. In "Little Green Men," while instructing students at Quantico in performing an autopsy and preparing to open the cranium, Scully pauses, abstracted, and muses: "What this man imagined—his dreams, who he loved, saw, heard, remembered, what he feared, is all locked in this small mass of tissue and fluid." "Are you all right, Agent Scully?" asks a student. "For a minute there you seemed a little spooky." As Scully gets spooky, Mulder alters Deep Throat's "Trust no one" to "I trust no one but you, Scully." (He adds, "I am beginning to doubt that what I experienced ever really happened.")

In "Anasazi," Mulder is identified—like Scully—with the abductee when he is trapped in a boxcar full of "alien" bodies and appears to be exterminated in a fire. He joins the victims of all holocausts, particularly the Anasazi (the ancestors of the Navajos, whose name means "the ancient ones" or "the other ones" or even "aliens"). His body is linked with theirs in being penetrated and manipulated and as one of a throng of subjects/products of eugenics experiments involving alien-human hybrids. This link is confirmed in "Paper Clip," which ends with Mulder's reversal of terms, when he says to Scully, "The truth is *in* there. In the X-Files." He refers to the X-Files biologically enhanced to include miles of "an extremely elaborate filing system of medical records" stored in the inner recesses of a mountain. These contain (indeed *are*) tissue samples gathered with smallpox vaccinations from 1947 on and containing the essential genetic information to create an alien human hybrid. Not only is the truth in these X-Files; the alien is bodily or genetically contained in the X-Files. In the discourses of the body, *we* apparently *are* the "real" X-Files.

Scully and Mulder have met in another, perhaps more intimate way, however, in their parallel near-death/out-of-body experiences. In "One Breath," as Scully lies comatose, kept alive by machines, she is shown floating in a boat in the middle of a northern lake, kept from drifting off by a rope tethered to the shore (referring to the life support systems that sustain her). Her elements are earth and water. In "The Blessing Way," Mulder floats among the stars, but as the cross-cutting reminds us, the Navajo shaman has made this possible by taking him through the intensive body practices of the Blessing Way ritual. If Mulder communes with the spirits, as represented by the "fathers" in the sky (and including a darkly angelic host of alien/agents lined around his bier), he does so through the medium of the body. Restored after three days, Mulder recalls being "in a place." "Yes," says Hosteen. "You came *here*, to the origin point"—the origin point being no occupied site but an imaginal realm (or Lacan's Imaginary): a spiritual journey that can be made only in the body. "It wasn't a dream, was it?" asks Mulder. "Yes" is Hosteen's profoundly ambiguous reply.

In a waking dream that echoes and reverses her vision of her dying father in "Beyond the Sea," Scully meets Mulder and knows he is alive. More and more often, Scully and Mulder, skeptic and believer, flesh and spirit, meet and exchange information (as in the case of stigmatic) in the same liminal zone where *The X-Files* is projected. They connect, like two halves of the same person (Chris Carter?) in the text of the X-Files, which is after all the body—albeit the body enhanced with preternatural possibilities, the body as fantastic space between the empirical and the metaphysical. Together, and obsessed like Victor Frankenstein (or Victor Klemper, Sally Kendrick, and a host of others) by the urgency of their work, they convert the physical to the metaphysical, Eros to Thanatos.

I'd like to see Mulder die one day," Duchovny recently told Leiren-Young. "Not soon, but one day. . . . He should get laid, and then die" (22). "Can you see your own end?" Scully asks Clyde Bruckman (Peter Boyle) in "Clyde Bruckman's Final Repose." "I see *our* end," he replies. "We end up in bed together. . . . You holding my hand very tenderly. . . . Tears are streaming down my face and I feel so grateful." Later, Mulder asks if he ever has prophetic dreams. "I have only one dream," he says. "I dream it every night." We watch his dream as he narrates:

> I'm naked in a field of red tulips. . . . My body begins to turn a greenish white with spots of purple. . . . Next the insects arrive. Then the inevitable occurs, liquidity and putrescence. Before I know it, I'm

nothing but bones. . . . I lose whatever fear I still might have had about where my clothes are. . . . As I feel myself slipping away towards I know not what, I wake up.

When Bruckman (perhaps) finally dies, he has seen to it that both predictions come true. He has left a note, taken pills, and wrapped himself in plastic (which causes his body to produce tears through condensation). At his bedside, Scully sits and takes his hand, touched in recognition that every body ends the same way. The episode ends as we watch Scully watch the concluding scene of a Laurel and Hardy film that parodies an X-ray motion study. Skeletons from the neck down, the duo walk toward the screen as Hardy repeats the familiar closing, "Well here's another nice mess you've got me into," Laurel squeaks out "Well I couldn't help it," and they fade away to "The End."

The nice mess *is* the end—represented by the body as it is invaded by X-rays, pervaded by death, revealing the alien skeleton, decomposing and concealing the human. Scully knows that the alien is or must be "in there"—perhaps even visible on the screen into which she peers with an intensity equaling Mulder's as he gazes at the stars.

11

''You Only Expose Your Father''

THE IMAGINARY, VOYEURISM, AND THE
SYMBOLIC ORDER IN *THE X-FILES*

Elizabeth Kubek

> The unconscious is that chapter of my history that is marked
> by a blank or occupied by a falsehood: it is the censored
> chapter. But the truth can be rediscovered; usually it has
> been written down elsewhere.
>
> —Lacan, *Écrits*

> Mulder thinks about UFOs the way other men think about
> sex.
>
> —David Duchovny, *U. Magazine*

The recent popularity of *The X-Files* has given its long-term fans a
chance to say "I told you so" and also to speculate happily as to
why, when so many good but unusual shows disappear without a
trace, this one succeeded.[1] Although many things set this series apart,
its overall thematic unity helps make it compelling. Separate episodes
of *The X-Files* have addressed diverse topics, but the narrative formed

1. This article is dedicated to the members of the electronic mailing list The
Gravediggers' Union: Paula Vitaris, Ngaire Genge, Pat Gonzales, Cathy Kelty, Jennifer
Bills, Sandra Ballasch, Tonya Yount, "Friday," Leslie Jones, "Erzebel Bathory," et al. The
insights and information they have generously shared with me and their encouragement
to write this piece (without which it would not exist) are appreciated more than I can
say. My especial thanks to Ngaire, whose transcripts were an invaluable resource.

over the entire series returns persistently to observation and critique of authority and its abuses. A close examination of the series—especially of the episodes that develop what creator Chris Carter has called the "mythology" (Vitaris, 75)—reveals that distrust of (overwhelmingly masculine) authority informs not only the plot of the narrative, with its shadow government, but also its whole epistemology. The very production of meaning and knowledge is called into question by the show's discourse, which constantly represents "the truth" as something far from objective—a site of desire, conflict, and contestation.

From its pilot episode, *The X-Files* has had a double focus represented by two repeated phrases: the show's signature "The Truth Is Out There," and Special Agent Fox Mulder's personal theme, "I want to believe." In the course of its first two seasons, the show has established a complex network of signs relating the pursuit of "truth" to desire ("I want"), embedding these signs in a critique of patriarchal power structures. This critique, centering on the government, informs Mulder's relationships with other males; in the climactic episode of the second season, Mulder's own father is revealed to have participated in the conspiracy to conceal the truth Mulder so desires. The discovery that organized deception pervades the family itself, supposedly the heart of "privacy," makes literal the problematics of patriarchy that haunt the show.

What I term the problematics of patriarchy, as explored by *The X-Files*, concerns the relation of paternal or quasi-paternal authority to "truth," a theme explored in the show through its engaging and direction of the linked desires for belief and knowledge both in the characters and in the audience. These desires lead to relentlessly voyeuristic epistemologies at the levels of characterization, plot, and camera work. While Agents Mulder and Scully pursue the truth, they are under observation within the text by various shadowy powers as well as "outside" the text by their audience. Voyeurism also manifests itself in various "minor" aspects of the text—for example, Mulder's taste for pornography—that help construct the show's ethos of voyeurism (the desire to see) and epistemophilia (the desire to know).[2] For both the characters and the audience, a constant tension is maintained between

---

2. An e-mail conversation between Paula Vitaris and Cathy Kelty touched upon many of these points. Paula writes of "the continuing 'watching/looking/observing' theme that began with the very first X-Files episode (two-way mirrors in that one, not to mention Mulder's now-famous slide shows and all that fancy video equipment he has)." She points out the connections between psychology and voyeurism; Cathy agrees, and observes, "This watching/observing motif also ties in with the different views different characters frequently have of reality on the show." Paula also mentions "the SETI project" in connection with the "watching" theme.

satisfying the desire to know and leaving "the truth" unprovable; epis-temophilic desire is thus sustained, and with it the narrative. The truth is deeply desired yet endlessly deferred.

The erotics of knowledge, and of vision in particular, informs the search for "truth," which proceeds in defiance of patriarchal power structures but also reveals those structures in all their apparent immu-tability. Frequently, what Scully and Mulder discover through their investigations can only be observed; any "hard" evidence is destroyed or absorbed by the system, which maintains "deniability." The lack of evidence repeatedly throws them (and the viewer) back on alternative epistemologies: faith, memory, even dreams. Although these alterna-tives do not allow the agents to overcome the system within which they work, Scully and Mulder find in them, and in their faith in each other, the resources with which to continue resisting authority.

With its control over discourse and its assumption of absolute authority, the government that Scully and Mulder oppose can be seen as representing what Jacques Lacan calls the Symbolic Order: signifi-cation, which is presided over by the "dead" Symbolic Father and his Law. The human subject, having acquired language and thus entered into the Symbolic, knows everything only through images and signs, or representations; she or he is alienated, his or her desires framed according to the limits of the Law: "The father, the Name-of-the-Father, sustains the structure of the desire with the structure of the Law—but the inheritance of the father is . . . his sin" (Lacan, *Four Fundamental Concepts*, 34). The sins of the Father are repression—those things that are not represented within the Symbolic Order are lost to conscious-ness—and symbolic castration, which forces the subject to attribute meaning and wholeness not to him or herself but to an ideal. However, that which has been repressed or denied remains "out there" in the Unconscious or the Preconscious and frequently obtrudes upon con-sciousness in coded forms. Moreover, even though "desire becomes bound up with the desire of the Other, . . . in this loop lies the desire to know" (Lacan, *Écrits*, 301). Epistemophilia, the consequence of alien-ation, can threaten the reign of the Symbolic.

The X-Files marks the psychological potentials of its narrative by designating one of its main characters, Fox Mulder, as a psychologist, and by representing the family origins of both of its heroes as central to their motivations. As Paula Vitaris points out, the "backstories" of both Scully and Mulder involve their relationships with their families, developed over the course of the show's narrative (43–44). Moreover, according to creator Chris Carter, the show was partly inspired by a psychiatric study, John Mack's *Abduction*, a cogent discussion of the possible real and symbolic meanings of abduction narratives (Vitaris,

21). The use of psychoanalytic terminologies to theorize the show's underlying themes therefore is potentially fruitful. In particular, Lacanian terminology not only allows the examination of patriarchal authority as it is manifested at various levels of discourse but also provides a framework for describing the alternative epistemologies to which Scully (somewhat reluctantly) and Mulder (more willingly) must resort in order to understand or even perceive "paranormal" and/or "denied" phenomena—and to which the show itself must resort in order to bring these phenomena into representation. Over the course of the first two seasons of *The X-Files*, voyeurism is demonstrated to be an ambiguous tool for opposing the Symbolic Order because it is often in agreement with that Order's Law—the desire to know arises out of the subject's immersion in the Symbolic. Other psychological functions, however, bring the narrative closer to what has been repressed. Although its contents cannot be directly represented, the Unconscious manifests itself through gaps and inconsistencies.[3] Moreover, the Imaginary—the Preconscious site of ego identifications, ruled by similarities (as opposed to the Symbolic, which is concerned with differences)—serves in *The X-Files* as the site of alternative, benevolent images of paternity. For the characters, the Imaginary is accessed through dreams, visions, and memories; and for the viewer, the Unconscious is represented by various settings "outside" or "under" everyday experience (including the "space" of dreams). In these settings, *The X-Files* situates the possibilities of resistance and of approaching a return of that which has been repressed—which is often represented by Mulder's sister Samantha. The revelation that Mulder's father is implicated in Samantha's loss thus exposes one key secret of patriarchy: its repression of the feminine and the cost that that sacrifice exacts on all subjects.

The difficulty of resisting the Symbolic Order is made manifest by Fox Mulder's ambiguous relation to the government for which he works (Dana Scully at first seems less skeptical about her employers). Although references in "Fire" make it clear that the eccentric Mulder and the rational Dr. Scully as characters owe something to Sherlock

---

3. In keeping with the tenets of psychoanalysis, details that might appear to consciousness as "mistakes"—for example, the varying photographs of Samantha or the conflicting accounts of her abduction—will be treated as meaningful signs, as indicators of repression. Moreover, the show's narrative will be treated as a consistent psychological "text," despite its multiple sites of utterance, because according to Lacanian theory all subjects share the signifying networks of the Symbolic and thus share its tensions. However, it is worth noting that most of the episodes discussed in this paper bear the imprint of creator Chris Carter's close involvement; to a great extent, he is the "author" of the text.

Holmes and Dr. Watson, Mulder is not an independent investigator like Holmes but is part of the very structure he attempts to resist. In Mulder's first utterance in the pilot episode "*The X-Files,*" he characterizes himself wryly as "the FBI's most unwanted," and indeed the agency has "repressed" him into the basement (a first representation of the importance of unconscious elements); however, his continued access to the X-Files depends on his submission to the Bureau's authority. The problems of this relationship are further established in "Fallen Angel," when Mulder's mentor Deep Throat argues that Mulder is safely contained by his job: "Always keep your friends close, Mr. Mulder, but keep your enemies closer." In the same episode, Mulder argues eloquently that "no government agency has jurisdiction over the truth," but in "F. Emasculata," when he demands public disclosure of the escape of a prisoner exposed to a deadly disease, Mulder is shut down by Cancer Man: "You're a party to [the coverup] already. . . . What's the truth, Agent Mulder?" Unable to respond to this comment, Mulder must continue the investigation by questioning the prisoner's girlfriend, Elizabeth, who asks him, "Why should I tell the truth if you won't?" Elizabeth, exposed to the disease and probably doomed, is imprisoned in a transparent chamber that makes her the helpless object of his authoritarian gaze/discourse; thus, Mulder's complicity becomes uncomfortably clear to him and to the audience.

Mulder's ambiguous position relative to authority and its objects is addressed through the narrative's Imaginary, its metaphoric identifications, as Mulder's work brings him in contact with other searchers for truth operating outside the system. Often, the parallels are manifest enough to constitute an apparent identification on Mulder's part; "apparent" because David Duchovny plays Mulder as a subtle personality, whose reactions tend to be conveyed wordlessly. Duchovny's shifts of expression and the extensive use of reaction shots during Mulder's confrontations with his "doubles" are the visual devices through which the viewer's attention is drawn to Mulder's conscious shifts of identification. At the same time, clear textual parallels are established between Mulder and the doubles, often through the use of the word "truth" or its variants. However, because of the dangerous nature of the truths he and his doubles uncover, Mulder often finds himself unwillingly and/or unwittingly acting as indeed an "Agent" of the government he mistrusts. Mulder's destruction of the COS (in "Ghost in the Machine") and his attempt to help Chester Banton (in "Soft Light") both contribute to the imprisonment of his doubles.

The first-season episode "Ghost in the Machine" involves a computer genius, Brad Wilczek, whose Central Operating System commits several murders; Wilczek's company is called "Eurisko," which he translates as "I discover things." Wilczek's epistemophilia leads to his

being impressed into service by an undefined government agency—
"Let's just say our paychecks are signed by the same person," remarks
Claude Peterson to Mulder as he holds him at gunpoint. The abductee
Max Fenig, of "Fallen Angel," when asked by Mulder "what makes
[him] so sure" about the presence of the crashed UFO they both have
pursued to the Wisconsin woods, replies, "Same thing that makes you
so sure." The episode ends with Max being abducted again, despite
Mulder's attempt to save him. In "Space," Mulder's boyhood hero
Colonel Belt proves to have brought back with him from his space-
walks an extraterrestrial being, whom Belt can only exorcise by com-
mitting suicide. The parallels grow more detailed and ambiguous in
the second season. In "Duane Barry"/"Ascension," Mulder's identification with Duane, another abductee, ends when Barry connives in the
abduction of Scully. In "Firewalker," the brilliant vulcanologist Daniel
Trepkos' desire to "revisit the very origin of the earth and peer into
the fire where it all began" fatally exposes his team, including his
young mistress Jessie O'Neil, to a silicone-based parasite. Confronting
Mulder, Trepkos remarks, "You still believe you can petition heaven to
get some penetrating answer." Trepkos himself is convinced of the
need to destroy all evidence of his discovery. His glum comment when
looking at Jessie's body, " "I told her I would change her life," is a
clear reference to Mulder's comment about Scully, nearly killed by
prehistoric insects in "Darkness Falls": "I told her it was going to be a
nice trip to the forest." Mulder's guilt over Scully's abduction is clearly
reflected in Trepkos' responsibility for the death of Jessie. Finally, in
"Soft Light," scientist Chester Banton is "accidentally" exposed to a
barrage of subatomic particles; his partner muses that Banton seemed
to welcome the invasion, "as if the truth might come into him." After
the exposure, Banton finds that his shadow kills anyone who steps
into it. His quest for knowledge becomes desperate: "all I can do is
study [my shadow]—try to divine its true nature before they do."
"They," of course, refers to the government, which covets Banton's
power; we last see Banton a prisoner, subjected to endless observation
and testing while tears run down his face.[4]
    These episodes not only establish a comparison between Mulder
and various tragic truth-seekers but also reveal the erotics of the search
through repeated imagery of penetration. The extraterrestrial energy-

---

4. "F. Emasculata" is a somewhat unusual example of this identification in that it
uses a female "double," Elizabeth, who represents Mulder's "feminized" position of
frustration vis-à-vis Cancer Man (the title also suggests a feminized, "emasculated"
condition). Mulder's clear discomfort with his epistemological choices—the imprisoned
object or the oppressive interrogator—demonstrates the limits conscious identification
sets upon subjectivity.

being of "Space" painfully possesses Colonel Belt, the silicon-based parasite erupts from the throats of its cave-explorer victims like a phallus, the subatomic particles "come into" Banton's body. The "penetrating answer" turns upon, penetrates, and destroys its finder. That the truth is dangerous, even deadly, is of course the tenet of Mulder's opposition, as represented by Cancer Man's comment in "F. Emasculata" that "the truth would've caused panic"; Deep Throat also argues that "the world's reaction to such knowledge would be far too dangerous" ("E.B.E."). The logic of the show to some extent supports this warning, repeatedly representing the object of desire, the much-cited truth, as itself a phallic power with a will of its own.

Each of these episodes involves a dialogic movement between Mulder's similarity to these truth-seekers and the establishment of his difference from them, which most importantly consists of his persistence (or ability to persist) in pursuing the truth. The establishment of difference returns the narrative to the Symbolic, the realm of meaningful differences, and empowers Mulder as the signified to which the sacrificed doubles refer.[5] The theme of that which is sacrificed for truth or for Symbolic power also governs Mulder's relations with the representatives of the government: his "mentors," the paternal Deep Throat of the first season and the lethal Mr. X of the second; Assistant Director Walter S. Skinner, Mulder's immediate superior and sometime helper; and Cancer Man, tool of the shadow government. In the narrative's Imaginary—which on this point coincides with Mulder's—these men represent conscious sites of identification between which Mulder must choose. The stakes of this choice grow higher in "Anasazi," which reveals an ancient connection between Cancer Man and Mulder's father, thus literalizing the paternal function and revealing its role in the Symbolic.

By the end of the second season, both Deep Throat and Mulder's father are dead and thus (within the logic of the narrative) wholly withdrawn into his personal Symbolic and Imaginary; in other words, they become part of his characterization. These two Fathers and their deaths form a key connection in *The X-Files'* network of signifiers involving patriarchal power and Mulder's relation thereto. In "Deep Throat," the second episode of the first season, the mysterious title character follows Mulder into the men's room of a bar, where Mulder first catches sight of him as a reflection over his own shoulder in a mirror (the viewer has already glimpsed Deep Throat at the bar).

5. In the second season, Scully also acquires doubles whose death illuminates the cost of her own scientific and legal methodologies, a fellow-doctor in "F. Emasculata" and detective Kelly Ryan in "Soft Light."

"Deep Throat" ends with a conversation between the two men at an outdoor track; at one point, a framing shot shows them face-to-face with a railroad bridge running between and connecting them in the background. Although the episode visually insists on linking the two as equals, Deep Throat is verbally elusive: "Let's just say that I'm in a position to know quite a lot of things—things about our government." His "interest," he claims, is, like Mulder's, "the truth," but subsequent episodes reveal that Deep Throat does not always pass that truth on to Mulder. In "E.B.E.," he claims to have chosen Mulder as his confidant because "you were the one person I could really trust." However, in the same episode, Deep Throat admits to manipulating Mulder: "A lie is best hidden between two truths." Mulder is left "trying to decide which lie to believe." According to episode coauthor Glen Morgan, "[w]e said, 'This guy, you never know whether he's lying or not, so let's leave it ambiguous,' . . . The whole thing was written to get to the line, 'A lie is best hidden between two truths.' We worked the whole thing to get to that, which, in a way, is what doing these shows is about" (Vitaris, 49). Deep Throat's line establishes the central instability of truth in "these shows," a status as indeterminate as that of Schrodinger's famed cat; if truth is distributed between statements it is still true, but it ceases to function as something apprehensible. As Paula Vitaris writes of the episode, "The truth may be out there, but how do you know when it is the truth?" (49). The indeterminacy of "out there" becomes apparent.

"E.B.E." not only reveals that Deep Throat, despite his evocative name, has an ambiguous relation to the truth but also begins to erode our sense of his seemingly limitless powers. During a night meeting with Mulder, Deep Throat shows discomfort at the flash of a camera. Later, he meets Mulder at an aquarium. "I've spent years watching you from my lofty position," he remarks, but then he warns, "I'm not responsible for the electronic surveillance, but I do know they can still hear you." He is clearly both observer and observed, part of a network of watchers. The setting of this dialogue—the two men face each other in front of a giant shark tank—reiterates the image of enclosure and surveillance; like the sharks, both men are unwittingly the subject of a gaze that seems frighteningly alien (because of unspecified origin) and in which we as watchers are complicit. The fish tank image comes into play again at the climax of the episode, when Mulder arrives at the power plant where the "extraterrestrial biological entity" to which the title refers is supposedly being stored. Instead, Mulder finds an illuminated tank, clearly designed for display and surveillance but empty, and Deep Throat in attendance. Even as Deep Throat confesses to remorse for having previously executed an alien being, he seems vaguely implicated in another disappearance. "I'm wondering which lie to believe," Mulder reproaches Deep Throat at the episode's close.[6] Deep Throat's manipulations and his noncommittal comments eventually erode Mulder's faith, despite his desire to believe, and in the final episode of the first season, "The Erlenmeyer Flask," tension erupts between the two men. Importantly, Mulder's explosion is partly inspired by Scully's accusation that he "gets off on" Deep Throat's "game"—that is, that pleasure is somehow involved. The suggestion that the erotics of voyeurism and of power are becoming manifest in the relationship apparently motivates Mulder's anger in the next scene, when he confronts Deep Throat: "From day one, this has always been on your terms. I've gone along, been the dutiful son, but maybe this time we can cut the Obi-Wan Kenobi crap." However, Deep Throat responds to Mulder's demand for "something more to work with" by saying, "Trust me," thus leaving Mulder unsatisfied. Only when Mulder and Scully have found—and lost, through the vigilance of their opponents—evidence of experiments on human subjects does Deep Throat fill in the details of the sinister project called "Purity Control."

"The Erlenmeyer Flask" is in many ways a pivotal episode in *The X-Files'* argument about patriarchal power. Mulder's reference to the unequal father/son dynamics of his relationship with Deep Throat reflects shifts in the depiction both of paternal authority and of the need for more than a desire to believe. Scully's suspicion of Deep Throat opposes "hard" science, which she as a pathologist represents, to faith in human "fathers." "The Erlenmeyer Flask" provides Scully with a glimpse of evidence, through Deep Throat's knowledge: she will actually hold in her hand a cryogenically-preserved alien fetus, "the original tissue" as Deep Throat calls it, which is being used to create alien-human hybrids. Meanwhile, Mulder himself sees living hybrids floating in tanks of liquid. The tanks are stored in a warehouse owned by "Zeus Storage," with an address on Pandora Street—according to Deep Throat, "the room . . . where the first alien-human hybrid was created." The references to Greek mythology and to creation itself mark the transformation of paternal power into something both godlike and dangerous. At the same time, Deep Throat's personal power once again appears reduced; he claims, despite Mulder's skepticism, that he does not know which "black organization . . . unknown at the highest levels of power" has destroyed the hybrids and killed their creator: "There are limits to my knowledge, Agent Mulder." He has failed to "anticipate the speed and precision of their cleanup opera-

6. I am indebted in this paragraph to Cathy Kelty, who helped me fill in gaps in my discourse by supplying me with key quotes from "E B E."

tion.'' The increasing humanization of Mulder's manipulative mentor reaches its climax at the end of the episode: Deep Throat is shot while exchanging the alien fetus for the kidnapped Mulder. Without Deep Throat's protection, the X-Files are subsequently shut down and the two agents separated, leaving Mulder vowing, ''I'm not going to give up. I can't give up. Not as long as the truth is out there.''

Deep Throat's death serves several ends at the level of narrative. It provides a highly dramatic closure for the first season of the show; it also (at least temporarily) isolates Mulder and turns him back on his own agency. Perhaps most importantly, the death of Deep Throat—in ''The Erlenmeyer Flask,'' the culmination of a series of deaths—proves the value of the information he has provided. A vast and deadly conspiracy indeed exists and is directed against Mulder's search for a ''truth'' that also is proven to be real. If (as ''E.B.E.'' suggests) Deep Throat is indeed guilty of at least past complicity in this conspiracy, his death serves as his punishment (perhaps even a deliberate atonement) and passes the guilt on to his killers. His good intentions and final warning are validated by being absorbed into the prevailing logic of the narrative, as demonstrated by the extratextual use of his last words to Scully, ''Trust no one'': in the opening credits for ''The Erlenmeyer Flask,'' the usual ''The Truth Is Out There'' is replaced by these words. Moreover, in ''Little Green Men,'' Scully discovers that they have become another type of ''sacred'' text—Mulder's computer password.

Deep Throat's transformation into a sort of talisman, an extratextual presence, in this way underwrites the patriarchal mythology that informs *The X-Files'* depiction of authority and its problems. Through his death and his absorption into the text, Deep Throat enters the realm of the show's Imaginary, joining the masculine doubles discussed above. His murder, however, also reveals the presence in that text of the all-powerful Symbolic Father, possessor and wielder of phallic power. As Julia Kristeva puts it, ''symbolic and social cohesion are maintained by virtue of a sacrifice (which makes of a *soma* [body] a sign towards an unnamable transcendence, so that only thus are signifying and social functions clinched even though they are ignorant of this sacrifice) . . . the paternal function represents this sacrificial function'' (''From One Identity,'' 138). The death of Deep Throat is just such a sacrifice, for it restores meaning to Mulder's quest for truth while also revealing that the possessors of this truth indeed exist, although knowledge of their existence transcends even ''the highest levels of power.'' Transcendent, all-powerful, the shadowy ''black organization'' of the secret government becomes the Symbolic Father, who possesses and conceals the Truth. The source of ''the big lies'' with which Deep Throat has been involved, in whose name he has killed

("E.B.E."), is also the Truth of the Symbolic Order—the conspiracy of patriarchal culture itself.

The loss of Deep Throat leads not only to the temporary closing of the X-Files and the reassignment of Scully and Mulder but also to further exploration of the problematic ambiguity of voyeurism as a way of arriving at truth. Mulder's desire to know the secrets of the Law backfires when, as a way to keep him contained, Skinner assigns him to trivial surveillance operations; in "Little Green Men," we see Mulder wearily listening to two suspects discussing erotic dancers. The object of his unwilling voyeurism is now an undisguised and wholly mundane, objectifying masculine desire. This waste of Mulder's energies causes a crisis in his epistemophilia, as demonstrated by the voiceover that begins "Little Green Men," in which Mulder lists a series of "lost" surveillance projects, including Voyager and radio telescope scanning of deep space: "We wanted to believe. . . . We wanted to call out. . . . We wanted to listen. . . . I wanted to believe, but the tools have been taken away. The X-Files have been shut down. They closed our eyes, our voices have been silenced. Our ears now deaf to realms of extreme possibilities." When Scully, concerned about her former partner, arranges a meeting with him at the Watergate Hotel parking garage, she sees him approach as a backlit, trench-coated silhouette and murmurs, "From back there you looked like him . . . Deep Throat." Mulder replies, "He's dead, Scully. I attended his funeral at Arlington—through high-powered binoculars, from a thousand yards away." The distance from which Mulder turns his instruments of surveillance upon the dead Deep Throat marks the way his impulse to know and to see has been undermined. Instead of accepting Scully's identifying him with Deep Throat, Mulder compares himself to George Hale, who built "the largest telescope in the world" at the instigation of "an elf"; Mulder feels that he himself may have been "seeing" not elves but "little green men," and that "seeing is not enough," an insight he credits Scully with inspiring. It is Scully, however, who reminds him that "the telescope still got built." Her persistence signals us that voyeurism may have a value in itself, that there is still something to see, and that soon Mulder's search for the truth will begin again. The loss of Deep Throat is quickly surmounted when Senator Matheson sends Mulder to a radio telescope station in Arecibo, Puerto Rico, that has captured transmissions of apparently alien origin. Mulder's close encounter in Arecibo restores his determination, while the apparent success of the radio telescope in attracting and recording alien presences (although the evidence is destroyed) validates his epistemophilia.

Moreover, the appearance of the alien beings at the radio telescope station is preceded by a significant interplay between instruments of surveillance that reinvokes the guardian presence of Deep Throat. Mulder has been speaking frantically into a small tape recorder, narrating his discoveries, which include the activation of the telescope's long-dormant recording devices. The approach of the aliens is marked by a dialogue between Mulder's small recorder and the large reel-to-reel device that is part of the telescope's apparatus. First, the reel-to-reel deck comes to life and slowly drones "trust no one," repeating a remark Mulder made a moment ago to his own recorder; Mulder then rewinds his tape, which repeats, "I was sent here by one of those men. Deep Throat said trust no one." The reel-to-reel again echoes, more recognizably, "trust no one." Deep Throat's warning, spoken in Mulder's voice, thus presides over the moment when Mulder's faith will be renewed and prepares the way for Deep Throat's reappearance in "The Blessing Way" as an Imaginary Father.[7]

The links between the government of secrets and the paternal are revealed further in the second season, with the development of Mulder's relationship with his own "real" father. Initially a cold and unlikable figure, Bill Mulder, like Deep Throat, is first humanized and then killed in the climactic episode of the season. Also like Deep Throat, he is revealed as complicit in sinister government conspiracies and remorseful about that complicity. Bill Mulder's guilt is a central point of *The X-Files'* attack on patriarchal culture, for it focuses the viewer's suspicion on the site of the individual subject's indoctrination into the Symbolic Order—the family. With this shift of focus from the "public" sphere of government action to a "private" sphere in fact synonymous with that government and its actions, new light is cast on the possible fate of Mulder's missing sister and on what she represents within the symbolic economy of the show.

Mulder's relationship to his parents is an issue for the viewer beginning with the pilot, where we are told that Samantha's abduction broke up his family. In the first-season episode "Roland," the viewer catches a glimpse of this relationship as Mulder recounts a dream: "I dreamt I was swimming in this pool, and I could see my father under water, but when I dove down the water stung my eyes. And there was another man in the pool. He was watching me. He upset me. He was

---

7. Deep Throat and his warning will continue—through Mr. X—to preside over Mulder's search; the ambiguities of this hand-off of trust are examined verbally and visually in "Sleepless," where Mulder meets X in an empty stadium, a scene filmed partly in a long shot from the stands that gave the viewer the sense of an unattributed point of view—Deep Throat's? Or that of the Symbolic Order as Absent One (Silverman, 203–4), "speaking" through the camera, the instrument of surveillance whose presence is revealed by the POV's lack of attribution? Can Mulder trust X, despite his connection to Deep Throat? The shot remains unattributed, and thus unexplained, but it contributes to the narrative's overall sense of voyeuristic energies constantly in play.

asking me questions I didn't want to answer. I tried to leave, but I couldn't find my father." Ostensibly, Mulder recounts this dream in order to reassure Roland, the developmentally-disabled janitor who is being telepathically manipulated by the cryogenically-preserved brain of his twin brother. Mulder attempts to demonstrate this to Roland by having him operate a remote-controlled toy: "The way you work that toy is like what's happening to you. You're the spaceship, Roland, and your dreams are the controls." This statement marks the importance of dreams as "controls," keys to the unconscious motivations of the overall narrative. Mulder's dream represents the Father as a remote, inaccessible presence lurking in the Unconscious (water).[8] This possibility is strengthened by a reference in the second season's "Aubrey," where Mulder, discussing inherited traits, relates to Scully a childhood memory of awakening from nightmares of abandonment only to be reassured by the sound of his father crunching sunflower seeds in his study—which, he half-jokingly claims, explains his own "genetic" liking for sunflower seeds. However, the memory suggests a childhood marked by terrors, and the cracking of the seeds and spitting out of their shells is a strong image of oral aggression and the demarcation of the abject—that which is rejected, "spat out" by society. Mulder's assumption of his father's aggressive, authoritarian gesture (which we often see him perform when tense, as in "Little Green Men") emerges as a psychological compensation for the ambivalence towards his father apparent in both dream and memory.

Indeed, when we finally meet Bill Mulder (in the two-part episode "The Colony"/"End Game"), he seems unrelentingly cold to his son. Summoned unceremoniously to his father's house in "The Colony," Fox Mulder is met on the porch by a shadowy figure smoking a cigarette; the identification with Cancer Man is clear and, as later events demonstrate, deliberate. Bill Mulder speaks stiffly to Fox, seems unable to meet his eyes, and deflects a possible embrace with a handshake. Later, in "End Game," when the young woman who has claimed to be Samantha has vanished, Bill Mulder berates his son,

---

8. Mulder's "Roland" dream can be read as foreshadowing later revelations about Bill Mulder's involvement in Samantha's abduction. The difficulty Mulder experiences in seeing through the deep water indicates the blinding power (castration) the Symbolic holds over the subject, and it also probably represents his resistance to "seeing" the truth about his father—a truth the realm of dreams will eventually reveal. The watcher who asks unwelcome questions may represent a trace memory from the period of Samantha's disappearance; the figure reiterates the idea of resistance and makes it likely that Mulder's Unconscious "knows" that his father is somehow implicated, even though as the dreamer Mulder resents this line of thought. The watcher also represents the theme of surveillance and links Mulder's relation to his father with the voyeuristic power of the Symbolic—that is, with the government.

refusing to acknowledge the latter's obvious grief. It becomes clear that the father has compounded the trauma of Fox's loss, here briefly reenacted (although this "Samantha" proves to be an alien-human hybrid), and has unjustly added to his son's sense of guilt. Moreover, Bill Mulder's remark that "we bury our memories so deep after all that has been destroyed" allies him with repression and denial. He cannot even speak the whole word "sister" to his son after "Samantha" disappears: "Your sis-. . . Samantha," he falters.

In keeping with *The X-Files'* logic of shifting identifications, the problem of the father-child relationship is "doubled" by another family narrative, which reintroduces the daughter—this time as subject. The sad and distant relationship between Fox and Bill Mulder is in contrast to Dana Scully's close bond with her father, also named William. In the first season, "Beyond the Sea" introduces Navy Captain William Scully as a kindly but somewhat inarticulate man who has to be prodded by his wife Margaret before he asks his daughter about her job (of which he disapproves). We also learn that he and Dana affectionately call each other "Starbuck" and "Ahab," an identification that relates them as age-and rank-differentiated males. Their relationship is clearly one of silences and playful codes that simultaneously cover and mark their differences. Captain Scully represents a seemingly benevolent paternal repression, but the unspoken gains an unexpected significance when he suddenly dies of a heart attack and Dana is left to figure out how he felt about her. "Beyond the Sea" allows Scully to demonstrate her complete faith in her father, a faith Mulder cannot comprehend.

Before hearing of her father's death, Scully awakens from a nap on the sofa to see him sitting in an armchair across the room; he looks glassy-eyed, and his lips move silently. The apparition vanishes with the ringing of the phone, and Dana's mother delivers the news of William Scully's death. Scully must then decide if this apparent visitation was "real." Her dilemma is worsened by Luther Boggs, a self-described psychic on death row, who briefly takes on her father's appearance and claims the ability to "channel" his spirit. Consumed by the desire to talk to her father—and sadly asking her mother, "Was he at all proud of me?"—Scully nevertheless resists the temptation to listen to Boggs. When Mulder asks her why, she claims to be "afraid to believe." "Even if it meant never knowing what your father wanted to tell you?" "But I do know," she replies, and repeats her mother's answer: "He was my father." For Scully, to be a father is apparently to transcend the need for any other speech; the paternal preempts signification.

Even more than Deep Throat, then, William Scully potentially represents the paradoxical embodiment—through death—of the Symbolic Father and of his control over his children, especially his daughter. Scully in effect silences her father by refusing to hear the message Boggs claims to carry, but she does so because (she claims) there is no longer any need for speech on his part. The dead father's authority is absolute, his feelings represented by a tautology ("he was my father"). Apparently, Scully's loyalty and subordination to her father is only strengthened by his death; indeed, in "The Blessing Way," when Scully believes that her actions have led to Mulder's death, she sobs to her mother, "Dad would be so ashamed of me."

It is tempting in this light to read Dana Scully—rational, law-abiding, skeptical—as a phallic woman, a fetishized figure. As a forensic pathologist, she is a modern Antigone whose role is to minister to the dead according to the Law (although in her case Law is represented by science rather than religion). The second-season episode "Irresistible" explores Scully's connection with the dead, showing her emotional identification with the mutilated female victims of a fetishist who eventually chooses Scully herself as an object. Indeed, the whole logic of the show risks fetishizing Scully. An attractive woman, she makes available the easy, commercially-safe narrative route of the "fem-jep" (woman in jeopardy) formula, a problem that episodes such as "Irresistible" attempt to address by showing her aggressively defending herself. Scully also shows her awareness of Mulder's protective feelings towards her, thus exposing another narrative problem: the danger of her becoming an object of her partner's concern and care, a mere signifier for the vanished Samantha. The logic of the visual medium also contributes to the risk of fetishization, because cinema traditionally reduces the feminine to attractive object (a tendency that sometimes infects the promotional spots for the show, which have too frequently featured images of Scully in distress). However, *The X-Files* resists reducing the feminine either visually or through narrative; in fact, its resistance to enclosing woman in the Symbolic is at the heart of the show's denunciation of patriarchy.

The fetish, the object that "stands for" the mother's missing phallus, is one of the props of patriarchy and its logic of sexual difference; it is that which both covers over and marks the "castration" of the woman, thus allowing the masculine subject to feel temporarily secure in his illusory superiority. By (re)assuring men that women are dangerous but inferior, the Symbolic Order locks men into "masculine" stances of control, authority, and hierarchy. In order for gender difference to become negotiable, therefore, the feminine must become visible as living subject rather than as static image.[9] These linked issues—the

9. For a discussion of fetishization and its role in visual narrative, see Laura Mulvey's classic essay "Visual Pleasure and Narrative Cinema."

daughter's relation to the father, the "freezing" and "killing" of the feminine into a fetish-object, and the problematic role of Scully/Samantha as the object(s) of Mulder's search for "truth"—inform the arc that began the second season: the two-part "Duane Barry"/"Ascension," the bridge episode "3," and the climactic "One Breath." These episodes reveal the sadistic and oppressive practices that underwrite the patriarchal Law and begin to suggest an alternative, benevolent mode of paternal and masculine knowledge, rooted not solely in the Symbolic but also in regression through the Imaginary.

"Duane Barry"/"Ascension" makes clear parallels between alien abduction and government surveillance, using repeated images of voyeurism and violation. In the first episode, Chris Carter deliberately creates a visual resemblance between a circular diagram on the operating table on which Duane Barry recalls being splayed, his teeth drilled into by lasers, and the penciled circles that surround a spy-hole being drilled in the ceiling of the room where Duane is holding Mulder and another man hostage (Vitaris, 63). In this scene, Mulder's own body has become an instrument of surveillance—he is wearing a wireless microphone and a receiver in his ear—while Duane Barry's body contains an implanted tracking device. In "Ascension," Mulder traces an abducted Scully with the help of audio tapes (Scully's message on his answering machine, recordings of Duane Barry's ramblings) and of a video image from a police car, and he is tormented by visions of his partner subjected to invasive "alien" medical procedures. The discovery that the disappearance of Scully and the "hard and damning evidence" she possessed (Duane's implant) has been arranged by whatever mysterious agency employs Cancer Man seems to signal a victory not only for that agency but for the Symbolic Order. From being not only Mulder's friend but his critic, whose insistence on evidence makes his discoveries more effective ("Little Green Men"), Dana Scully is reduced to a photographic image of a gagged and frightened woman—a feminine fetish. Voyeurism works here in the service of the Law and against the heroes.

Deprived of his partner, who from the beginning has pulled him out of his role as "most unwanted" eccentric, Mulder is left in danger of sinking into a merely personal epistemophilia. In "Little Green Men," Scully implies that the building of the telescope is more important than whether George Hale actually saw elves—in other words, that Mulder's work with the X-Files is perhaps separable from the question of Samantha's fate. Although the narrative will eventually reunite the two issues, Scully's comment points out the problem of fetishization. Samantha's photograph has repeatedly been shown in Mulder's hands, as a reminder of his dedication to her memory. In "Little Green Men," the photograph is used as a signaling device between Scully and Mulder—an interesting violation of its fetish-value, given that a fetish is not supposed to be "desecrated" by being made useful. After "Ascension," however, Scully herself is no more than a photograph, and "3" shows us the results of this loss: Mulder no longer sleeps, he wears Scully's cross, and his behavior has become, as the L.A. coroner remarks, "upsetting . . . on several levels." Dream-like, tragic, and deeply unpleasant, "3" exposes the dangers of voyeurism and the sadistic energies it can activate when used for personal ends.

"3" begins by showing Mulder reopening his basement office; in the process, a disturbing connection is made between his sexual voyeurism—he turns the leaves of a pin-up calendar—and his search for the missing Scully, as he files her belongings among the X-Files and fingers her cross (entrusted to him by Margaret Scully in "Ascension"). Searching Los Angeles for a group of murderous "vampires," Mulder becomes attracted to one of their followers, Kristen, and his surveillance of this woman also takes on an air of perversity.[10] His observation of Kristen's erotic meeting with a man she met at a bar ends on a darkly comic note when the man sees Mulder looking in the window and punches him down the steps, calling him "freak." Later, a cop searching the scene hands Mulder a blood-smeared pair of women's panties in an evidence bag; Mulder then joins in the search of Kristen's house. We see him surreptitiously open the oven, find a loaf of bread, and tear it open to reveal a pool of blood inside. When Kristen later finds him lurking in the shadows of her house, he offers to protect her, and she confronts him: "Why are you here alone? . . . Because you have to know?" She recounts her victimization by an abusive father: "I was dead. . . . The blood poured from my mouth onto the floor. And down my throat. It was the only way I knew I was alive." However, Kristen —despite her pleasure in blood—is not a vampire, refusing to join in her lover John's "unnatural" behavior. Instead, she makes love with Mulder; unfortunately, John is watching from outside. Although she

10. My discussion of "3" in regard to voyeurism is influenced by the observations of my colleagues in the Gravediggers' Union, who expressed discomfort with the "personal" nature of Mulder's pursuit of Kristen and also repeatedly raised the issue of the viewer's voyeuristic pleasure. Cathy Kelty remarks, "I think the line gets drawn with use vs abuse of power When Mulder is spying on people in his official capacity, he is working for the greater good of the many . . . even if it does coincide with his own personal search for truth. . . . With Kristen, it was not just his official capacity, or his morally defensible search for truth; the spying fed into his own sexual interest, which gets dangerously close to abuse of power. (Makes his pornography hobby more sad in a way, that watching is the only power he has most of the time)." Cathy also points out that Mulder's anger at the voyeur/pedophile Gert in "Red Museum" may stem from identification with him.

and Mulder successfully fight off the "real" female vampire, Kristen dies, apparently sacrificing herself in order to ensure the death of John and his companions. Mulder is left clutching Scully's cross.

In some ways, "3" is a classic example of the use of the visual to demonstrate the castration of the woman, thus enclosing her within the Symbolic Order. Kristen is "the bearer of the bleeding wound" (Mulvey, "Visual Pleasure," 432), suspected of being "unholy," spied on, made to tell her story, and punished by death. Of course, patriarchy is the villain in her story, but in "3" women consent to their victimization. Kristen's father begins the cycle by abusing her, turning her into a masochist, but she accepts the role. The vampires who use her as bait to attract victims are a parody of the Symbolic Order—Father, Son, Unholy Spirit—with the latter, a whorish-looking woman with a distorted voice, the most frightening of the three: the feminine as monster of desire. Even Mulder, although he wants to protect Kristen and discourages her perversity, succumbs to desire for her and then to sleep; the price of his release is her death when the vampires catch up with her. However, "3" carries with it an air of elaborate, nightmarish unreality, from its setting in La-La Land to the mysterious absence of bruises on Mulder after his beating. Paula Vitaris speaks of "3" as a trip to "Hell," and the comment captures the mood of the episode, originally written (for Halloween and the start of sweeps month) as even more "kinky," according to writers Morgan and Wong. The writers also saw Scully's absence and Mulder's grief as key elements in the episode (Vitaris, 73), which operates as an exploration of the negative possibilities of voyeurism and epistemophilia—especially in terms of the repression and victimization of the feminine.

In "One Breath," however, Scully's return restores Mulder to epistemological health. Significantly, this episode contains a denial of the visual connection made at the beginning of "3" between Scully's image and Mulder's pornography: a shot of Mulder's living room shows us the picture of a gagged Scully from "Ascension," tossed aside on the table, before panning to Mulder on the couch, remote in hand, watching what sounds like a pornographic film. That the photograph of Scully is out of Mulder's line of sight operates as a denial of the connection between it and the image of a sexually consenting woman Mulder is watching (we hear what sounds like a woman's voice saying "please don't stop"). At the same time, we as watchers connecting the images are confronted with our own voyeurism. Much of "One Breath" reflects on our privileged voyeuristic status as we watch Mulder wrestle with his desire for revenge on Scully's abductors—a desire that if indulged will make him like them and more importantly will continue to treat Scully as an object.

"One Breath" begins with a voiceover: Margaret Scully tells

Mulder a story about Dana's first confrontation as a child with death,
that of a snake that she and her brothers shot. Mrs. Scully appropriates
the image of a weeping Dana forced to resign the snake to death,
claiming that "at this moment I know how my daughter felt." The
camera then follows Mrs. Scully and a reluctant Mulder as they examine a gravestone bearing Dana's name and two inscriptions, "Loving
Daughter and Friend" and "The Spirit is the Truth—1 John 5:07."
This opening seems to solidify Dana Scully's image as that of the lost
daughter, become an illustration of the "truth" of patriarchal religion:
only God has the answers. However, Scully's reappearance and her
struggle for life return *The X-Files'* narrative to the question of "spirit"
from a different angle. In "3," woman was the "unholy spirit," connected with the perverse and contaminating power of blood lust, but
"One Breath" envisions a spiritual realm in which gender and familial
differences are bridged by constructive desires. This Imaginary realm,
signified by dreams and by near-death states, evolves throughout *The
X-Files* as a regressive alternative that predates the Symbolic Order
and as a "back door" to that which the Symbolic has repressed or
denied.

At the hospital, a gendered opposition quickly develops between
Dana's sister Melissa, who urges Mulder to "feel" Dana's presence,
and Mulder, who is consumed by the need to act. It is Melissa who is
on the right track, as we learn when we see a representation of Scully's
mental state: she sits silently in a boat on what looks like a pond,
apparently observing Mulder and her sister on a dock. As in Mulder's
"Roland" dream, the water represents the Unconscious; floating on its
surface, Scully is in a liminal state, which in the language of *The X-Files*
means she is open to Imaginary influences. Thus, Scully sees not only
Mulder and Melissa on the dock but also Nurse Owen, who later
proves to be fully "Imaginary." Dana Scully is also visited by her
father, dressed in a dazzlingly white full-dress uniform. Captain Scully
addresses his daughter lovingly as "Starbuck," and confesses that his
career became meaningless "[at] the moment I knew—I understood—
that I would never see you again, my little girl. . . . I never knew how
much I loved my daughter, and I could never tell her. . . . At that
moment, I would have traded every medal, every commendation,
every promotion, for one more second with you. We'll be together
again, Starbuck, but not now. Soon." William Scully's confession that
he longed to speak to his daughter again makes sense of his visitation
in "Beyond the Sea" (where he mouthed the words "I had to tell you"):
far from fading into symbolic sanctity, the father has died with a desire
(towards his daughter) unmet. However, as Imaginary Father, he is
free to admit his longing and his guilt and to postpone the desired
reunion with his daughter because, as Nurse Owen tells Dana, "your

time is not over." Instead of the brutal figure who objectifies the daughter for his own pleasure seen in "3," this Imaginary Father desires the wholeness of the feminine subject, her reintegration and return to consciousness. As Lacan writes of Alcibiades' Imaginary image of Socrates, he has been robbed of phallic aggressivity and thus idealized as a mentor (*Écrits*, 323).

"One Breath" also adjusts Mulder's relation to patriarchy and to the feminine away from sadism and objectification, in part through the open representation of his "choice" between Imaginary "fathers." This episode inscribes clear similarities and differences on the images of Skinner, Mr. X, and Cancer Man as possible identifications for Mulder. As Scully lies near death, Skinner voices Mulder's deepest fear: if Mulder, as he confesses, "knew the potential consequences" of his pursuit of the truth but "never told her," then he is "as much to blame for [Scully's] condition" as Cancer Man. Mulder thus confronts (but does not "solve") the consequences of his pursuit of truth. Skinner also tells Mulder that a near-death, out-of-body experience in Vietnam has left him open to possibilities, but "I'm afraid to look any further. . . . You are not" (in a later episode he will tell Mulder, "I stand right on the line that you keep crossing" ["F. Emasculata"]). Mr. X has crossed a line of another sort: "I used to be you. I was where you are now. But you're not me, Mulder. I don't think you have the heart," X says in "One Breath," after which he executes another shadow-agent with cool brutality. Indeed, both Skinner and X offer Mulder a chance at waylaying his enemies, demonstrating their patriarchal willingness to make Scully the object of masculine vengeance. Instead, Mulder first resists Cancer Man's taunts, which dare Mulder to shoot him, and then accepts Melissa Scully's challenge to go to the hospital and "express to [Dana] how you feel . . . at least she'll know. And so will you." Sitting by her motionless body, Mulder tells his partner, "I feel, Scully, like you believe you're not ready to go. And you've always had the strength of your beliefs. . . . I'm here." Apparently some part of Scully hears him, for the next day, when she awakens, she apologizes for not being able to "remember anything" but tells Mulder, "I had the strength of your beliefs." Mulder's ability to speak to her, instead of making her the object of his vengeance, contributes to Scully's reconstitution as a subject, a living being rather than a dead image. Mulder also returns Scully's cross, thus aligning himself with Scully's mother (who originally gave it to her daughter) and erasing the fetishistic meaning with which "3" invested the token.

"One Breath" closes with the revelation that Nurse Owen, whom Scully remembers, is not a "real" nurse; both Scully and the viewer must accept that this figure, who was only seen in the hospital or with "real" people, in fact bridges the gap between dream and reality. The

Imaginary cannot be dismissed as mere fantasy, for it is the treasure-house of identifications and metaphors, the site of the ego's ideal reflections (Silverman, 157–58). Here, the father is at last able to speak of his love for his daughter and to confess the guilt of his silence. Although William Scully's apology to Dana might seem like a minor device, *The X-Files* persistently returns to what might be termed "true dreams" as a site for healing the symbolic wounds that patriarchy opens in the father/child relation. Through dream and memory, moreover, the feminine (as represented by Samantha, among others) emerges as no longer a fetishized object but rather the site of a visible and criminal act of repression.

The question of the truth value of dreams and memories is an important theme beginning with the pilot, when Mulder recounts to Scully his attempts to recall the night of his sister's abduction through "deep regression hypnosis": "I've been able to go into my repressed memories to the night my sister disappeared. I can recall a bright light outside and a presence in the room. I was paralyzed, unable to respond to my sister's calls for help." In the third episode, "Conduit," Mulder explains that "when I was a kid, I had this ritual: I'd close my eyes before I walked into my room, because I thought that one day, when I opened them, my sister would be there, just lying in bed like nothing ever happened." This episode closes with a double surveillance trained on Mulder and his sister: we see first Scully listening to a tape and looking at Samantha's picture from her file, then Mulder alone in a church, holding another picture of his sister and grieving. Meanwhile, the tape provides a voiceover of Mulder under hypnosis, describing himself lying paralyzed in bed and hearing Samantha "calling out my name over and over" while a "voice in my head" urges him "not to be afraid. It's telling me that no harm will come to her, and that some day she'll return." Asked by the hypnotist if he believes the voice, Mulder replies, "I want to believe."

The first-season account of Samantha's abduction thus represents Samantha as a lost object, an image on film whose recovery is a fantasy of Fox Mulder's childhood; she is in danger of becoming a fetish, an object that signifies a lost plenitude in whose return he "wants to believe." The odd suggestion that the siblings shared a bedroom signifies the lack of separation between Fox and his sister as subjects in this account. However, in the first episode of the second season, "Little Green Men," Fox Mulder has a dream that gives the viewer the first visual account of Samantha's abduction, and it differs significantly from the hypnotic version: here, Fox is babysitting his sister when the house is invaded by a brilliant light that lifts her out the window. The Samantha of the dream is no ideal image but rather a spirited child who (before the aliens appear) screams in her big brother's face just to annoy him. The writers describe the difference in the descriptions as accidental, although James Wong claims that "it plays into the idea of memory being screwed up" (Vitaris, 58). Still, the idea that the "dream" is more reliable fits the show's overall skepticism about paternal authority. Lacan, in his discussion of the therapeutic power of anamnesis (the return of repressed material through speech), compares hypnotic recollection to "the drama in which the original myths of the City State are produced" and argues that hypnotically-and narcotically-induced states produce an untrustworthy catharsis: "because it comes to [the subject] in an alienated form, even a retransmission of his own recorded discourse . . . cannot have the same effects as psychoanalytic interlocution" (*Écrits*, 47–49). Mediated through the intervening technologies of hypnosis and the analyst's direction, Mulder's initial account lacks the continuity with his life that would make it "true" in the only sense that matters to the subject. However, his dream arises naturally out of his need to know that he is not merely pursuing "little green men" and out of the material of his waking life—the picture of Samantha leads to her memory, just as the Watergate Hotel sign in the garage leads to a memory of the televised Watergate hearings the night of the abduction. Moreover, this dream in its details coincides with Mulder's later encounter with the alien beings at the Arecibo telescope. In Arecibo, when Mulder tells Scully "They were here," she asks, "Here? Or here," touching his head; the viewer knows that the present setting and dream/memory have become one. The dream is a valid anamnesis in that it restores to the subject his own history as a meaningful "story" that connects to the future: "in psychoanalytic anamnesis, it is not a question of reality, but of truth, because the effect of full speech is to reorder past contingencies by conferring on them the sense of necessities to come" (*Écrits*, 48).

In "The Colony"/"End Game," the abduction of a false Samantha by an alien presence is fully reenacted and brought into "reality," but this episode also involves Mulder's entry into a dreamlike realm from which he nearly fails to return alive. The Imaginary again obtrudes into the external world, as Mulder pursues the Pilot, an alien shapeshifter who apparently knows the real Samantha's fate, into the frozen "underworld" of the Arctic. Significantly, "The Colony" begins with a voiceover from the perspective of the unconscious and (for the moment) dying Mulder; as in "Little Green Men," "One Breath," and other key episodes, the initial "point of view" is timeless, caught up in memory or reflection. Visually and audibly, this effect is communicated by the disembodied voice, accompanied by shots with no character visible to whom the shot can be attributed as visual field—the Voyager and telescope in "Little Green Men," clouds and then the actions of other, oblivious characters in "One Breath" and "The Colony." "The Colony" is thus linked by the semiotics of its photography and soundtrack to the two earlier episodes that invoked dream and memory as epistemological sites. Mulder's remarks in the voiceover also connect key terminologies: "I have lived with a fragile faith built on an ether of vague memories. . . . This belief [in Samantha's abduction] sustained me, fueling a quest for truths that were as elusive as the memory itself." Belief, truth, and memory come together: "What happened to me out on the ice has justified every belief." The encounter with the Pilot completes what "Little Green Men" started: the return of Mulder's belief that his "story" will have meaning.

The Pilot's shape-shifting ability marks him as a denizen of the Imaginary, the site of shifting identifications; one of the forms he takes is that of Mulder himself. Like Mulder, the Pilot is searching for that which has been lost, and his repeated demands "Where is he?" and "Where is she?" are echoed by Mulder's "Where is she?" when the two confront each other "on the ice." Also like Mulder, the Pilot (according to the false Samantha) is pursuing those who have committed specifically genetic crimes—a parallelism that will become more meaningful with the revelations of "Anasazi"/"The Blessing Way"/"Paper Clip." The hybrids whom the Pilot destroys are guilty of "unsanctioned" experiments combining human and alien DNA; "Samantha" describes this in terms ("a pollution of their race") that cast the senders of the Pilot as bigots, but genetic experimentation is not given a positive value in the overall narrative. Mulder is never clearly convinced by the false Samantha—"That's a good story, but I've heard a lot of good stories lately," he comments. Even his distress at informing his father of her loss may have more to do with his parents' belief than his own. However, he pursues the Pilot as if convinced that this being knows where Samantha is to be found, on the slim evidence of the false Samantha's apparent knowledge. His faith is rewarded. "I could have killed you many times before," the Pilot warns, and then nearly does so, saying, "She's alive. Can you die now?" The answer, according to Mulder's voiceover, is yes: "If I should die now, it would be with the certainty that my faith has been righteous." He has found, as he says to Scully, "faith to keep looking."

The encounter with the Pilot thus validates and reactivates Mulder's voyeurism by invoking the energies of the Imaginary and bringing them back into consciousness. That the Imaginary realm (represented by the Arctic) belongs to Mulder himself is hinted by the Pilot's taking on Mulder's form, for a key content of the Imaginary is a self-image arrived at (metaphorically at least) through vision: the famous "mirror stage" of Lacanian psychoanalysis, in which the infant recognizes and idealizes itself as reflected in a mirror. The subject's confrontation with the Imaginary's contents—especially with the Imaginary self—is according to Lacan the goal of psychoanalysis, although its achievement amounts to the discovery of the subject's alienation within/because of the Symbolic Order. The Imaginary self is really an imitation of an ideal, complete Other (the mirror-self) that will "be taken from [the subject] *by another*" (the Symbolic Father) when the subject accepts its own lacking state and enters into the Symbolic Order (*Écrits*, 42). The bringing into consciousness of Imaginary material reveals the powerlessness of the subject—as absolute as Mulder's powerlessness to escape the Pilot, who as an Imaginary (alienated) self confronts him with the alienating power of patriarchal Law. However, access to the Imaginary also reactivates a relation to the maternal that circumvents patriarchy; at the mirror stage, the origin of the Imaginary, the infant wishes to become the ideal object of the mother's desire. *The X-Files'* narrative fantasizes a return through dreams to this lost relation and the reconstruction of paternity in the image of the loving mother.[11]

In the three-part arc written to bridge the gap between the second and third seasons, *The X-Files* splits the father between Symbolic guilt and Imaginary redemption. In the central episode of the arc, "The Blessing Way," the moment comes for Mulder (as it already has for Scully in "One Breath") when the Imaginary Father, by admitting his longing and love for his child, becomes the Mother, reintegrating the feminine into the heart of masculinity. At the same time, "Anasazi"/ "The Blessing Way"/"Paper Clip" also provide a final and damning demonstration of the guilt of the father, especially as it pertains to the daughter's disappearance. The arc returns to the issue of memory in very explicit ways, while using Navajo culture as an alternative site on which to develop the possibility of a masculinity without patriarchy— a masculinity that can oppose the repression of the feminine and heal the wounds opened by the Symbolic Order.

"Anasazi" opens by introducing the viewer briefly to three generations of Native American males: the elder Albert Hosteen, his adult son, and his grandson Eric. A recent earthquake is glossed by Albert in Navajo (translated in subtitles): "The earth has a secret it needs to tell." In fact, upon venturing into the desert, Eric does find a partially-buried boxcar, from which he retrieves a body that does not look human. The themes of burial and of the speech of the earth alert the viewer that this arc will focus on the return of the repressed; Albert's use of Navajo here is also a warning that perhaps English has no way of expressing what this earth desires. Albert is not the only speaker who will need translation in "Anasazi," for the other half of the secret that is emerging from repression is a document (stolen by a hacker and given to Mulder) that describes a secret international project. The

---

11. For discussion of the "maternal Father," see Oliver.

document itself is in Navajo, a product of the World War II Code-Talkers. The theft of the document brings together a consortium of aging men—the Fathers of several nations, including former Axis powers—determined to recover the document and kill anyone who has seen it. Navajo is represented as the language of truth, while the lying Fathers (including Cancer Man, who speaks fluent German) speak the "dominant" tongues of the First World.

In "Anasazi," the Symbolic Order emerges from the shadows with startling clarity. About to show Scully the document, a feverish (and, it turns out, drugged) Mulder describes it in terms of "the ten commandments": "the one where God made heaven and earth but didn't bother to tell anyone about his side projects—the biggest lie of all." The invocation of God, the ultimate image of patriarchal authority, foreshadows the "big lie" that the arc reveals—the vast conspiracy set in motion to cover a new "creation" through genetic experimentation. To Mulder, however, the stolen document looks like "b.s. and double-talk"; it is Scully who recognizes it as "coded" in Navajo, a language so nearly destroyed by Western patriarchy that it has itself become a sign for the repressed.

As in "F. Emasculata," *The X-Files* here approaches an analogy between gender and other sites of repression and difference, namely race and class. In the earlier episode, the challenge to the conspiracy of silence came from the lower-class Elizabeth; in "Anasazi"/"The Blessing Way"/"Paper Clip," racial/class differences operate not only between the "global consortium" of Fathers (represented, aptly, by the class-marked, British-accented "Well-Manicured Man") and the rural Navajo but also in the whole scenario Scully and Mulder uncover: a joint project of U.S. and former Axis scientists to create human-alien hybrids. The hideous secret that emerges from the earth is the extent to which the system of differences that is the underlying structure of the Symbolic has been connived at and exploited by a society that supposedly stands for equality in diversity. Moreover, the revelation that Mulder's father has been part of this project brings home the way that the Symbolic Order originates in the family and sets its members in opposition.

The viewer is the first to know of Bill Mulder's guilt, for we see Cancer Man arriving at his house in West Tisbury—appearing first, evocatively, as a silhouette against the frosted glass of the door—to warn him that his son has the dangerous document. "My name is in those files," Bill Mulder worries; and then, "You wouldn't harm him." It is half a question, and Cancer Man replies, "I've protected him this long, haven't I?" Has he? The viewer is unsure, but for the first time, we see Bill Mulder as a sympathetic figure—he looks ill and fright-ened. This side of the father emerges more strongly when Bill calls his son (who is also in poor health from the drugs being put in his water). We see a feverish Fox gulping water before his phone rings, and then the camera cuts to Bill, clutching a glass of alcohol. The camera thus establishes a parallel between father and son, then writes over it with another identification as Fox, standing on his father's porch, sees him approach as a silhouette through the glass of the door—which aligns Bill Mulder visually with Cancer Man. This identification is suspended, however, as Bill greets his startled son with the embrace that he withheld in "The Colony."

The father's confession, when it comes, is fragmentary, incomplete:

> BILL MULDER: It's—it's so clear now—simple—it was so complicated then—the choices that needed to be made.... You're smarter than I ever was.... Your politics are yours—you've never thrown in.... You're going to learn of things, Fox, you're going to hear the words, and they'll come to make sense to you.
>
> FOX MULDER: What words?
>
> BILL MULDER: The merchandise.

Bill Mulder, a coward to the end, can say no more; he goes to the bathroom to take his medication and to try (unsuccessfully) to face himself in the mirror, until Alex Krychek shoots him. Cradling his dying father, Fox Mulder catches his last words: "Forgive me."

As in "End Game" (where he was unable to say "your sister"), Bill Mulder is unable to speak (of) what he has repressed; instead, he makes a final appeal for the love of his son. (This, as "Paper Clip" will reveal, mirrors an earlier act of betrayal: the exchange of the daughter for the son.) Fox Mulder, however, is aware (from the final scenes of "Anasazi") that his pursuit of what the earth has hidden will damn his father. Cancer Man warns Mulder: "Your father may have told you things.... He was never an opponent of the project—in fact, he authorized it. Expose anything and you only expose your father." The identification of Bill Mulder as "author" of the horror his son finds in the buried boxcar—a pile of bizarre-looking corpses—is strengthened by Scully's telling Mulder over his cell phone, "In these files I found references to experiments conducted by Axis-power scientists on humans" and confirming that the files contain the term "merchandise." The clear references to the Holocaust (the boxcar, the marks on the dead creatures' arms, the Nazi connection) anchor the story in the history of genocide. Whatever the beings in the boxcar might be— aliens or mutated humans—the Symbolic Father has objectified, killed, and buried them. Moments later, at the orders of Cancer Man, Fox Mulder is (temporarily) buried with them.

The cliffhanger ending of "Anasazi" (the second-season finale) invites the viewer's fantasy, through a long summer of reruns, about the arc's resolution, leading us to dwell on Bill Mulder's guilt and the fate of his son. It also leaves Fox underground, once again in the realm of the Imaginary. Judging by conversations on the Internet, the question that summer for many viewers was how Mulder would escape from the boxcar, but the two remaining parts of the arc concentrate very little on the mechanics of plot. Instead, "The Blessing Way" and "Paper Clip" focus on what is to be "exposed" and on the Imaginary economies that allow the guilt of the father to be demonstrated —at least to the viewer. Like "3" or "End Game," these two episodes unfold in a space that is less "logical" and more dream-like, one in which important psychological conflicts are played out.

This time, the voice that presides over this transition to the "dream" realm belongs to Albert Hosteen, who represents an epistemology that the dominant Order has repressed. As a Native American, Albert represents an Other who has come to be very important of late in the cultural Imaginary: the spiritual man. In "Anasazi," Albert's oracular comments provide Mulder with the outline of an answer to the questions that drive him:

ALBERT: In the desert things find a way to survive. Secrets are like that too. They push their way up through the sands of deception so that men can find them.
MULDER: Why me?
ALBERT: You are prepared to accept the truth . . . to sacrifice yourself to it.
MULDER: What is the truth?
ALBERT: Nothing disappears without a trace.
MULDER: (Pause.) What's buried out there?
ALBERT: Lies. You will see for yourself.

This dialogue, ritualistic in its question-and-answer format, begins Mulder's relation to the new model of masculinity that Albert represents. It also introduces the themes that govern the metaphysics of the arc: the return of the repressed (through what Lacan calls the "trace"), sacrificial exchange, and the "lie" of false creation.

Fittingly, then, it is Albert's voiceover that opens "The Blessing Way," once again providing thematic structures that will inform the episode.

ALBERT HOSTEEN: (*Voiceover.*) There is an ancient Indian saying that something lives only as long as the last person who remembers it. My people have come to trust memory over history. Memory, like fire, is radiant and immutable, while history serves only those who seek to control it, those who would douse the flame of memory in order to put out the dangerous fire of truth. Beware these men, for they are dangerous themselves—and unwise. Their false history is written in the blood of those who might remember and those who seek the truth.

Where in the first-season episode "Fire" that element was revealed as the subject of a phobia on Mulder's part, in "The Blessing Way" fire is given a traditional positive meaning: rebirth. Having survived the burning of the boxcar, Mulder is revived through the Blessing Way ritual, which involves fire and smoke. During this ritual, according to Albert, Mulder "suffer[s] great fevers, and his body burn[s] like fire," but on his recovery Albert "sense[s] in him a rebirth." Moreover, this ancient symbology is drawn into the semiotics of the antipatriarchal theme through its connection with truth and memory, a connection made not only by Albert in the opening voiceover but also (later) by the image of Deep Throat. The equation of fire with memory posits Mulder's fire phobia as resistance to anamnesis, suggesting that his "forgetting" exactly what happened to his sister may not have been entirely imposed upon him from the outside. The trauma that Mulder undergoes in the Blessing Way ritual is the acceptance of his father's (always-already) unconsciously-known guilt. For this reason, in "Paper Clip," Mulder apparently does not need "time to process" what he has learned about his father, despite Scully's misgivings.

Albert's voiceover also establishes a key structuring opposition between history and memory. As discussed above, Lacan suggests that the "truth" elicited by anamnesis is not primarily verifiable "reality" but rather the subject's creation of a meaningful "story" of his own life; when he speaks of the subject's "history" Lacan qualifies the term by adding "in so far as history constitutes the emergence of truth in the real" (Écrits, 48–49). Lacan's subjective "history" is thus Albert Hosteen's "memory." The truths of the Unconscious are "radiant and immutable" because they are embedded in an atemporal stratum of the mind but nevertheless send their "fire," their influence, into consciousness, so that they can be reintegrated into the subject's consciousness. "History," meanwhile, is defined as a dominant, ideo- logically-motivated discourse—the discourse of the Symbolic Order, the discourse of the Other. As such it is "false," alienating and murder- ous. Now it becomes clear why Albert (in "Anasazi") refers to the bodies in the boxcar as "lies." Even the "evidence" that the discourse of history creates is a lie written in blood: the "big lie" of the Fathers' attempt to become sole creators, gods, by eliminating the feminine from reproduction.

Mulder is physically reborn when Albert and his people pull him out of the rocky tunnel where he has taken shelter; the theme of the

Unconscious recurs when Albert remarks, still in voiceover, "The FBI man would have surely died had he not stayed underground, protected like the jackrabbit or the fox." The symbolic resonances of Mulder's unusual first name are here exploited: the Symbolic Order has attempted to bury him, but the Unconscious is somehow his natural habitat. However, he must then emerge from death/the Unconscious through the Imaginary, that is, through a Preconscious order of protosignification that predates the repressive regime of the Symbolic. The Imaginary is formed before the Symbolic but only manifests itself in consciousness retrospectively, after the subject enters the Symbolic (Silverman, 161); thus, this journey is a true regression, as opposed to the dubious regression represented by hypnosis.

The healing of Mulder's wounded body (feverish, damaged in unspecified ways by the boxcar fire, and also bearing a bullet-wound in the shoulder) and that of his mind are linked; the journey through the Imaginary and back to life is marked by "hysteria," the physical mirroring of mental trauma. This dual suffering is the only road to truth: "The ambiguity of the hysterical revelation of the past is due not so much to the vacillation of its content between the imaginary and the real, for it is situated in both. Nor is it because it is made up of lies. The reason is that it presents us with the birth of truth in speech, and thereby brings us up against the reality of what is neither true nor false" (Lacan, *Écrits*, 47). During the Blessing Way ritual, Mulder's identification with his father puts him at risk, as Albert points out: "my fear for the FBI man was that his spirit did not want to be healed, that it wished to rejoin the spirit of his own father who had died." However, Mulder instead confronts both of his "fathers"—the biological one and Deep Throat—as Imaginary images. As was the case with William Scully, these Imaginary Fathers are now able to say what they could not in life—what the dreamer needs to hear them say.

The Imaginary Deep Throat, who speaks first, appears both more than and less than human, filled both with wisdom and with what he calls "the dull clarity of the dead"—his image carries a diminished affective charge, having been drained by "the perpetual night which consumes purpose, need, all passion, will." He retains only the impulse "to feed on your fire, the intensity that still lives in you." Purified from phallic aggressivity, he is an ideal mentor, whose affection for Mulder can be expressed in terms of a reversal of the infant's relation to the mother ("feeding"). "Deep Throat" warns Mulder that the afterlife contains "truth," "But there's no justice or judgment, without which truth is a vast dead power." The contents of the Imaginary must be brought into consciousness and subjected to the differentiating functions of the Symbolic—that is, to language—before they can "live." Mulder's strategy of overcoming the patriarchal order from within the Law is thus validated, although to do so he must give up his desire to join his father in the all-revealing afterworld (a fantasy Mulder's voiceover has previously alluded to in "The Colony").

The Imaginary Bill Mulder will also speak to his son, but his comments are separated from those of "Deep Throat" by a horrific vision of the gassing of the hybrid beings in the boxcar. The identity of the agent who "remembers" this vision is unclear, but it seems to be "seen" by Mulder as well, as a repressed truth emerges through the Imaginary. However, at this point the barrier between the Unconscious and the Imaginary asserts itself: Mulder cannot access the Unconscious directly—he must "go back" without "look[ing] into the abyss or let-[ting] the abyss look into [him]," the Imaginary Deep Throat warns.[12] As Lacan points out, the "truth" of the Unconscious "has been written down elsewhere": in the hysterically-inscribed body; in "childhood memories," which Lacan calls "archival documents"; in personal "vocabulary" and "legends"; and in the gaps and "distortions" that mark the missing "chapter" (*Écrits*, 50). The "legends" of the Imaginary and of Mulder's "little green men"—transformed in the Imaginary into the beings murdered in the boxcar—are inscriptions of what has been denied. But the Imaginary Bill Mulder cannot speak directly of what has been repressed—he still cannot speak of Samantha. The ellipses in his speech indicate her presence behind a veil of words.

> "BILL MULDER": Hello son. I did not dare hope to see you again so soon, or ever again hope to broker fate with a life to which I gave life. The lies I told you were a toxic poison to my soul and now you are here because of them—lies I thought would bury forever a truth I could not live with. I stand here ashamed of the choices I made so long ago, when you were just a boy.
>   You are the memory, Fox—it lives in you. If you were to die now, the truth would die and only the lies survive us.
> FOX MULDER: My sister—is she here?
> "BILL MULDER": No! *(Pause.)* The thing that would destroy me, the truth I felt you must never learn, is the truth you will find if you are to go forward.

This Imaginary Father admits his guilt, his role as author of "lies" and as repressor of memory and truth. He also expresses his "hope" to rejoin his son and refers to "giving life," asserting a biological connection usually associated with the maternal (given that paternity is typically aligned with culture rather than nature). However, the Imaginary Bill Mulder is still unable to speak of the daughter, except through a

---

12. For the distinction between the Unconscious and the Imaginary, see Lacan, *Seminar* III, 115–16.

negative—that explosive "No!"—and silence. There is no signifier in the Imaginary for the "thing" Fox Mulder must find. Nor is this "thing" itself in the Unconscious (death/the abyss); what has been repressed is not the "thing" but a signifier with no fixed signified—in other words, an X (a "thing"). The X of *The X-Files* is the fate of the feminine (the daughter) under patriarchy; the Imaginary Father's confession reveals that the daughter herself survives because she is elsewhere.

What Paula Vitaris calls "the central question of [Mulder's] life" (32)—Where is she?—will of course not be answered in this three-part arc, but traces and doubles of Samantha Mulder will begin to fill in the blanks in memory. The Imaginary Bill Mulder's reference to "again . . . broker[ing] fate with a life to which I gave life" (at which the dreaming Mulder opens his eyes and looks at his Father) and to a "choice" establishes another structuring theme of "The Blessing Way" and "Paper Clip," the exchange/sacrifice. Inevitably, what is exchanged or sacrificed in these episodes is the feminine. Before he can learn what his Imaginary Father's comments mean, however, Fox must return to life and begin rebuilding his memory. The process begins with his awakening from unconsciousness; he is unwilling or unable to speak at first, but soon he is able to ask Albert about his journey:

> MULDER: During my fever, I left here and traveled to a place—
> ALBERT: *(Indicating a sand painting.)* This place. You carry it with you.
>   It is inside of you. *(Touching Mulder's chest.)* It is the origin place.
> MULDER: It wasn't a dream?
> ALBERT: Yes.

The sand painting, which Albert wipes out after answering Mulder's questions, is of a starry sky—the backdrop to Mulder's Imaginary visions—and Albert's ambiguous and ungrammatical "yes" reiterates the Imaginary status of this "place." What Mulder has seen, according to Chris Carter, isn't "that Deep Throat" (personal communication from Ngaire Genge)—the Imaginary Deep Throat is a construct. Moreover, the Imaginary's identification as "the origin place" relates both to the idea of extraterrestrial life and to the concern with origins that underlies the scopophilic and epistemophilic drives, which are ultimately directed at the question Where did I come from? The answer is the feminine, the X to which the truths found in "the origin place" point. However, returning from "the fire where it all began" is not easy, as Mulder's unfortunate doubles discover; it requires the help of the loving father, the father whose love and desire cause the conception of the child (the father/place of "origin"). Holding Mulder in the starry womb of night, the Imaginary Fathers become Mothers enough to give (re)birth to the son.

Scully, meanwhile, is located somewhat ambiguously in terms of the thematic economies of the arc. While Mulder is dreaming of Fathers, she has discovered evidence of their voyeuristic power not only in the stolen document (which names her) but in her own body, in the form of an implant, a small computer chip embedded in her neck. Distressed, she shows the extracted chip to her sister Melissa, who advises her to seek "access to your own memory. . . . obviously you've buried this so deeply you can't consciously recall it!" At Melissa's urging, Scully undergoes regression hypnosis, but her resistance is too great and (as Lacan warns) the process is too alien for her to be able to integrate the material into consciousness. She then visits the Imaginary, dreaming of Mulder speaking to her from that same place of origin, the starry night sky; he describes her as having come "here today, looking for a truth that was taken from you, a truth that was never to be spoken, but which now binds us together in dangerous purpose." Scully is thus both the seeker and the object of the search, the carrier of memory and that which has been repressed, and her access to the Imaginary is still mediated through masculine images. Still, as in "One Breath," Scully is reassured by her "dream."

Although Scully and Mulder will not be physically reunited until "Paper Clip," in "The Blessing Way" their paths cross at Mulder's mother. Scully contacts her at Bill Mulder's memorial service, to reassure her of her son's safety; Fox Mulder then tracks his mother down at his father's house. Here the repression that the father has enjoined on his family is clearly evidenced. Mulder tells his mother, "I need you to remember," and asks her about the identities of a group of men shown in a photograph—the first "archive" that holds the truth. Mrs. Mulder refuses even to look at the photograph: "I don't know. . . . I don't remember, Fox! Please! . . . Don't do this to me." Her every intonation, however, her every gesture, signify her knowledge—Lacan's "distortions" that mark the missing chapter. Finally, she admits that she has seen the men—"But I don't remember their names anymore." She asks, "What does this have to do with, Fox?" Mulder replies, "I think it has to do with Samantha. I think it has to do with what happened to my sister." He has said what "was never to be spoken," leaving Mrs. Mulder speechless. "The Colony," which showed Fox Mulder tucking his exhausted mother into bed as if she were a child, established her essential helplessness, but "The Blessing Way" demonstrates that that weakness stems from denial.

In "Paper Clip," the gaps begin to be filled in by the Lone Gunmen, who can identify one of the men in the photograph: the former Nazi geneticist Victor Klemper. Reunited, Scully and Mulder trace Klemper, finding him in a greenhouse pollinating his orchids—an appropriate image for the Fathers' attempt to co-opt reproduction. Klemper is not very forthcoming. "History bores me," he proclaims, claiming a scientific immunity from responsibility; "Our experiments changed the world . . . progress demands sacrifice." "Like my father?" Mulder angrily demands. "Was he a murderer too?" Klemper's cool assumption of his right to trade lives for "progress" echoes a remark made to Scully by the Well-Manicured Man at Bill Mulder's funeral: "We predict the future. The best way to predict the future is to invent it" ("The Blessing Way"). Klemper's attitude also foreshadows what Mulder will learn about the fate of his sister. Klemper does give Scully and Mulder an important clue—the location of an abandoned mine in West Virginia (perhaps the state most "sacrificed" to "progress," and another site of great class differences). Here, the agents find acres of files containing medical records and tissue samples, including Scully's and Samantha Mulder's. The crisis comes when Mulder peels away the name label on his sister's file to find his own name underneath: "This file was originally mine."

The abandoned mine is another version of the Unconscious, and what it contains is a set of "traces"—the files, mysterious small beings, a UFO. The latter two remain unexplained, as Mulder pursues the meaning of the changed labels. The Well-Manicured Man provides a partial explanation: when Bill Mulder "objected strenuously" to Klemper's attempts at creating alien-human hybrids, Samantha was taken as "insurance." When Mulder asks, "Why not me?" he is told that his father chose to sacrifice Samantha. Mulder, however, is unsure whether or not to believe this man, who represents the "consortium" of Fathers.

The real site of memory proves to be his mother. Significantly, Mulder confronts her at night, waking her from sleep, when repression is in abeyance; finally, her resistance crumbles.

> MRS. MULDER: Oh, Fox, I don't remember anything. I told you before.
> MULDER: Mom, listen to me. When Samantha—before she was gone, did Dad ever ask you if you had a favorite? . . . did he ever ask you to make a choice?
> MRS. MULDER: Fox, don't do this to me!
> MULDER: Mom, listen to me—I need to know! Did he make you make a choice?
> MRS. MULDER: No. I couldn't choose. It was your father's choice. I hated him for it. Even in his grave, I hate him still.

With this, the crime of the Father is fully exposed. He has sacrificed the daughter in exchange for the son—an exchange signified by the otherwise-unnecessary detail of the two labels. In other words, the feminine has been repressed in favor of the masculine, in keeping with the values of the Symbolic Order. At the same time, the fact that Samantha's name "overwrites" her brother's also indicates the degree to which the brother's whole identity has become veiled beneath the sign of her loss. Samantha's loss is also the sacrifice of something in masculinity itself.

This insight in effect "overwrites" the image of alienation as castration, on which the Symbolic Order is based, with the idea that the lost "thing" is neither masculine nor a signifier. Samantha's visual image has always suffered from a strange indeterminacy: the photographs and "visions" used to represent her in various episodes have varied greatly. The false Samantha of "The Colony"/"End Game" proves to be nonhuman, either an alien or an alien-human hybrid; she simultaneously vanishes (her body dissolves) and is replicated as multiple clones and an "original." This "Samantha," whose presence signifies the possible survival of the "real" sister, is both nonexistent and multiple at the same time. The many images of Samantha thus operate as what Julia Kristeva locates as a challenge to signification, "a heterogeneity with respect to system, operating within the practice and one which is liable, if not seen for what it is, to be reified into a transcendence" ("System," 31). She is an otherness within the system—not transcendent but radicalizing, "allowing the subject to get pleasure from [the social/signifying code], renew it, even endanger it" ("System," 30).

However, the signifying code constantly works to recapture this straying energy, to contain it—thus the exchanges of Samantha, the establishment of her value relative to another, which recaptures her (at least briefly) within the signifying network of the narrative. Even Fox Mulder is implicated in the exchange of women: he has risked Scully's life in order to find truth ("One Breath") and chosen to trade the false Samantha for Scully in "End Game," a trade that despite his doubts about the clone's identity plainly fills him with guilt. Seen in the light of "Paper Clip," Bill Mulder's rage at his son in "End Game" is marked as an identification: Fox has repeated his father's crime. In "Paper Clip," the Well-Manicured Man, after reporting Bill Mulder's use of Samantha as "insurance," tells Fox Mulder that "you have become your father"—perhaps not only in his unwillingness to remain silent but also in risking the lives of others. The exchange/sacrifice theme returns us to the parallel between Mulder and his truth-seeking doubles, and to the problematic gendering of the sacrifice explored in "3."

Clearly, in this narrative at least, participation in the symbolic economy of exchange cannot be used as the sign of difference between villains and heroes. From the beginning, the search for truth has been seen as involving loss and guilt; the gathering of evidence, of (visual/

visible) objects, feeds back into the Symbolic Order and its logic of sacrifice. Albert Hosteen also accepts these terms: "For something to live another thing must often be sacrificed" ("Paper Clip"). We are reminded that in "Anasazi," he and Cancer Man both observe that "nothing disappears [vanishes] without a trace"—and Lacan would agree: "the truth can be rediscovered" through "the traces that are inevitably preserved by the distortions necessitated by the linking of the adulterated chapter to the chapters surrounding it, and whose meaning will be re-established by my exegesis" (*Écrits*, 50). In other words, the buried lies reappear as inconsistencies, holes in the face of the earth, silences that function as signifiers saying "dig here." However, their shared maxim signifies that both Albert and Cancer Man accept the existence of repression and exchange as part of order. Masculinity is always in danger of being recapitulated into patriarchy, even as it employs strategies of resistance.

In "Paper Clip," the trade in lives is brisk as the text arrives at meaning and closure. Albert's comment about sacrifice applies not only to the white buffalo calf, whose fortunate birth leads to the death of its mother, but to Melissa Scully, shot (in "The Blessing Way") when she is mistaken for her sister. In "Paper Clip," she dies without regaining consciousness. "She died for me," Dana Scully tells Mulder. Scully's desire to visit her sister in the hospital has led to another exchange, the disk that holds the stolen document for her and Mulder's lives. Melissa's sacrifice identifies Scully with Mulder and ensures the continuation of the narrative, as the agents, deprived of other evidence, turn again to the X-Files: "The truth is in there," Mulder urges his partner. The demands of "exegesis" turn the energies of the show inward upon signifiers—files, evidence—and reason: "I've heard the truth, Mulder," Scully comments bitterly. "Now what I want are the answers."

Still, as has been the strong point of *The X-Files* from the beginning, there are loose ends, possibilities unforeclosed by the narrative. The culture of memory has one clear triumph over that of history. Despite having been robbed of the disk, Skinner thwarts Cancer Man: Albert Hosteen's memory, he claims, contains "everything on your precious tape . . . [and] in the ancient oral tradition of his people he's told twenty men the information on that tape" ("Paper Clip"). As Skinner points out, only another act of genocide could destroy this signifying network. Moreover, the world of true dreaming remains available as a source of strength. Comforting Scully, who has "tried to tell [Melissa] I was sorry," Mulder refers obliquely to the narrative's Imaginary logic, with its transformation of the dead into allies: "She knows." "Paper Clip" also offers a brief visual allusion to another non-Symbolic source of hope. When Scully and Mulder revisit Victor Klemper's greenhouse, the Well-Manicured Man informs them that its owner is no more. The viewer already knows this, for the first shot of the scene shows us (although not the agents, who are in the background) a bee happily pollinating one of the orchids we saw Klemper jealously tending earlier. Nature has reclaimed the work of generation.

In that the three-part arc reveals that the "sacrifice" required by the Symbolic Order is in fact the daughter rather than the father, "Anasazi"/"The Blessing Way"/"Paper Clip" succeeds in exposing one of the secrets of patriarchy: that which is secretly sacrificed by others (rather than openly sacrificing itself, like the Imaginary Father) is the feminine. This discovery draws into its web not only the female figures who die or are lost in these episodes but other characters that haunt the overall narrative. In the first season, these include abductees Darlene and Ruby Morris in "Conduit"; the "primitive" woman murdered by the police in "Jersey Devil"; the psychotic female clones who are the government project of "Eve"; and the woman and little girl who become vehicles for masculine vengeance in "Shadows" and "Born Again." The second season sees sacrificed not only "3' "s Kristen and "Firewalker' "s Jessie but also B.J. Morrow in "Aubrey," possessed by her murderous grandfather (another story in which repressed memory is represented as "underground"); a teenage girl driven mad by her father's satanic rituals in "Die Hand Die Verletzt"; and a series of female animals experimented on in "Fearful Symmetry." The sexual/reproductive focus of Mulder's version of alien abduction in "Duane Barry," where he comments on "what they do to a woman's ovaries," is justified not only by actual abductee narratives but by the logic of patriarchy that these episodes expose: the feminine is a privileged site of the father's sadistic observation and introjection.[13]

The X-Files thus exposes the father's use of the repressed "daughter" as a site of (his own) creation and rebirth. On another level, it subverts "order" by engaging voyeurism (ours as well as the characters') to avoid "making sense—that is, it consistently shows us more than it explains (the UFO and the tiny skittering beings in the mine in "Paper Clip," for example). The camera and the narrative, whether or

---

13. The theme of the daughter's sacrifice and exchange receives its most comprehensive treatment to date in the third-season episode "Oubliette." In this episode, the empathic bond that forms between Lucy Householder and Amy Jacobs, both victims of the same voyeur/pedophile, allows Mulder and a skeptical Scully to locate Amy but also leads to Lucy's death from trauma inflicted upon Amy. Significantly, while the voyeur Carl Wade represents a Symbolic logic of duplication (the girls he kidnaps are the same age, and he photographs them obsessively), Mulder is able to resist reading Amy/Lucy/Samantha as simple equivalents (he denies that his sympathy for Lucy is strictly related to his sister's loss and suggests that Lucy's death is an escape as well as an exchange).

not they "name" what they expose, insist that there is something to be discovered: "Even if it communicates nothing, the discourse represents the existence of communication; even if it denies the evidence, it affirms that speech constitutes truth; even if it is intended to deceive, the discourse speculates on faith in testimony" (Lacan, *Écrits*, 43). By constantly deferring the question of Samantha (the prototype for all unanswered questions), by refusing to stabilize her as signifier or signified, *The X-Files* resists the functional aspect of signification ("the answers" Scully desires). Instead, its refusal to give answers and its portentous repetitions, visual (flashlight beams in darkness, glimpses of alien beings, forests and large echoing interiors) as well as narrative (doubling, plot recycling) add up to a subversive poetics: in Kristeva's words, "the subject of poetic language continually but never definitively assumes the thetic function of naming, establishing meaning and signification, which the paternal function represents within reproductive relation" ("From One Identity," 138). In style as well as in content, *The X-Files*—like its heroes—struggles, from within representation, against patriarchal convention.

Appendix
Works Cited
Index

Appendix

Episode Summary, 1993–1996

First Season

Episode	Air Date	Writer(s)	Director
1. Pilot	Sept. 10, 1993	Chris Carter	Robert Mandel
2. "Deep Throat"	Sept. 17, 1993	Chris Carter	Daniel Sackheim
3. "Squeeze"	Sept. 24, 1993	Glen Morgan and James Wong	Harry Longstreet
4. "Conduit"	Oct. 1, 1993	Alex Gansa and Howard Gordon	Daniel Sackheim
5. "Jersey Devil"	Oct. 8, 1993	Chris Carter	Joe Napolitano
6. "Shadows"	Oct. 22, 1993	Glen Morgan and James Wong	Michael Katleman
7. "Ghost in the Machine"	Oct. 29, 1993	Alex Gansa and Howard Gordon	Jerrold Freedman
8. "Ice"	Nov. 5, 1993	Glen Morgan and James Wong	David Nutter
9. "Space"	Nov. 12, 1993	Chris Carter	William Graham
10. "Fallen Angel"	Nov. 19, 1993	Howard Gordon and Alex Ganza	Larry Shaw
11. "Eve"	Dec. 10, 1993	Kenneth Biller and Chris Brancato	Fred Gerber
12. "Fire"	Dec. 17, 1993	Chris Carter	Larry Shaw
13. "Beyond the Sea"	Jan. 7, 1994	Glen Morgan and James Wong	David Nutter
14. "Genderbender"	Jan. 21, 1994	Larry Barber and Paul Barber	Rob Bowman

15. "Lazarus"	Feb. 4, 1994	Alex Ganza and Howard Gordon	David Nutter
16. "Young at Heart"	Feb. 11, 1994	Scott Kaufer and Chris Carter	Michael Lange
17. "E.B.E."	Feb. 18, 1994	Glen Morgan and James Wong	William Graham
18. "Miracle Man"	Mar. 18, 1994	Howard Gordon and Chris Carter	Michael Lange
19. "Shapes"	Apr. 1, 1994	Marilyn Osborn	David Nutter
20. "Darkness Falls"	Apr. 15, 1994	Chris Carter	Joe Napolitano
21. "Tooms"	Apr. 22, 1994	Glen Morgan and James Wong	David Nutter
22. "Born Again"	Apr. 29, 1994	Howard Gordon and Alex Ganza	Jerrold Freeman
23. "Roland"	May 6, 1994	Chris Ruppenthal	David Nutter
24. "The Erlenmeyer Flask"	May 13, 1994	Chris Carter	R. W. Goodwin

Second Season

Episode	Air Date	Writer(s)	Director
1. "Little Green Men"	Sept. 16, 1994	Glen Morgan and James Wong	David Nutter
2. "The Host"	Sept. 23, 1994	Chris Carter	Daniel Sackheim
3. "Blood"	Sept. 30, 1994	Glen Morgan, James Wong, and Darin Morgan	David Nutter
4. "Sleepless"	Oct. 7, 1994	Howard Gordon	Rob Bowman
5. "Duane Barry"	Oct. 14, 1994	Chris Carter	Chris Carter
6. "Ascension (Duane Barry Part 2)	Oct. 21, 1994	Paul Brown	Michael Lange
7. "3"	Nov. 4, 1994	Chris Ruppenthal, Glen Morgan, and James Wong	David Nutter
8. "One Breath"	Nov. 11, 1994	Glen Morgan and James Wong	R. W. Goodwin
9. "Firewalker"	Nov. 18, 1994	Howard Gordon	David Nutter

10. "Red Museum"	Dec. 9, 1994	Chris Carter	Win Phelps
11. "Excelsis Dei"	Dec. 16, 1994	Paul Brown	Stephen Surjik
12. "Aubrey"	Jan. 6, 1995	Sara B. Charno	Rob Bowman
13. "Irresistible"	Jan. 13, 1995	Chris Carter	David Nutter
14. "Die Hand Die Verletzt" ("The Hand that Wounds")	Jan. 27, 1995	Glen Morgan and James Wong	Kim Manners
15. "Fresh Bones"	Feb. 3, 1995	Howard Gordon	Rob Bowman
16. "The Colony"	Feb. 10, 1995	David Duchovny and Chris Carter	Nick Marck
17. "End Game	Feb. 17, 1995	Frank Spotnitz	Rob Bowman
18. "Fearful Symmetry"	Feb. 24, 1995	Stephen DeJarnatt	James Whitmore Jr.
19. "Dod Kalm"	Mar. 10, 1995	Howard Gordon and Alex Ganza	Rob Bowman
20. "Humbug"	Mar. 31, 1995	Darin Morgan	Kim Manners
21. "The Calusari"	Apr. 14, 1995	Sara B. Charno	Michael Vejar
22. "E. Emasculata"	Apr. 28, 1995	Chris Carter and Howard Gordon	Rob Bowman
23. "Soft Light"	May 5, 1995	Vince Gilligan	James Contner
24. "Our Town"	May 12, 1995	Frank Spotnitz	Rob Bowman
25. "Anasazi"	May 19, 1995	David Duchovny and Chris Carter	R. W. Goodwin

Third Season

Episode	Air Date	Writer(s)	Director
1. "The Blessing Way"	Sept. 22, 1945	Chris Carter	R. W. Goodwin
2. "Paper Clip"	Sept. 29, 1995	Chris Carter	Rob Bowman
3. "D.P.O."	Oct. 6, 1995	Howard Gordon	Kim Manners
4. "Clyde Bruckman's Final Repose"	Oct. 13, 1995	Darin Morgan	David Nutter
5. "The List"	Oct. 20, 1995	Chris Carter	Chris Carter
6. "2shy"	Nov. 3, 1995	Jeffrey Vlaming	David Nutter
7. "The Walk"	Nov. 19, 1995	John Shiban	Rob Bowman

8. "Oubliette"	Nov. 17, 1995	Grant Craig	Kim Manners
9. "Nisei"	Nov. 24, 1995	Chris Carter, Howard Gordon, and Frank Spotnitz	David Nutter
10. "731"	Dec. 1, 1995	Frank Spotnitz	Rob Bowman
11. "Revelations"	Dec. 15, 1995	Kim Newton	David Nutter
12. "War of the Coprophages"	Jan. 5, 1996	Darin Morgan	Kim Manners
13. "Syzygy"	Jan. 26, 1996	Chris Carter	Rob Bowman
14. "Grotesque"	Feb. 2, 1996	Howard Gordon	Kim Manners
15. "Piper Maru"	Feb. 9, 1996	Frank Spotnitz and Chris Carter	Rob Bowman
16. "Apocrypha"	Feb. 16, 1996	Frank Spotnitz and Chris Carter	Kim Manners
17. "Pusher"	Feb. 23, 1996	Vince Gilligan	Rob Bowman
18. "Teso dos Richos"	Mar. 8, 1996	John Shiban	Kim Manners
19. "Hell Money"	Mar. 29, 1996	Jeff Vlaming	Tucker Gates
20. "Jose Chung's From Outer Space"	Apr. 12, 1996	Darin Morgan	Rob Bowman
21. "Avatar"	Apr. 26, 1996	Howard Gordon	James Charleso
22. "Quagmire"	May 3, 1996	Kim Newton	Kim Manners
23. "Wet Wired"	May 10, 1996	Mat Beck	Rob Bowman
24. "Talitha Cumi"	May 17, 1996	Chris Carter	R. W. Goodwin

Works Cited

Alexander, David. *"Star Trek" Creator: The Authorized Biography of Gene Rodden-berry.* New York: Rock, 1994.

Allen, Robert D., ed. *Channels of Discourse, Reassembled: Television and Contemporary Criticism.* Chapel Hill: Univ. of North Carolina Press, 1992.

Anderson, Kevin J. *Ground Zero.* New York: Harper/Prism, 1995.

Bacon-Smith, Camille. *Enterprising Women: Television Fandom and the Creation of Popular Myth.* Univ. of Pennsylvania Press Series in Contemporary Ethnography. Philadelphia: Univ. of Pennsylvania Press, 1992.

Bader, Chris D. "The UFO Contact Movement from the 1950s to the Present." *Studies in Popular Culture* 17 (1995): 73–90.

Barber, Paul. *Vampires, Burial, and Death: Folklore and Reality.* New Haven, Conn.: Yale Univ. Press, 1988.

Beam, Alex. " 'Mack Attack': Harvard Takes No Action." *MUFON UFO Journal* 329 (1995): 13, 15, 19.

Beerman, Frank. *"Star Trek:* Conclave in NY Looms as Mix of Campy Set and Sci-Fi Buffs." *Variety,* Jan. 19, 1972, 1.

Behrens, S. "Technological Convergence: Toward a United State of Media." *Channels of Communication 1986 Field Guide,* 8–10.

Ben-Amos, Dan. "Toward a Definition of Folklore in Context." *Journal of American Folklore* 84 (1971): 3–15.

Bischoff, David. "Opening *The X-Files:* Behind the Scenes of TV's Hottest Show." *Omni,* Dec. 1994, 42–47, 88.

Boss, Pete. "Vile Bodies and Bad Medicine." *Screen* 27, no. 1 (1986): 14–24.

Bowie, Malcolm. *Lacan.* Cambridge, Mass.: Harvard Univ. Press, 1991.

Broadcasting-Cable Yearbook. Annual. Washington, D.C.: Broadcasting Publications, 1935–.

Brooks, Tim, and Earle Marsh. *The Complete Directory to Prime Time Network TV Shows, 1946–Present.* 4th edition. New York: Ballantine, 1988.

Brunvand, Jan Harold. *The Vanishing Hitchhiker: American Urban Legends and Their Meanings.* New York: Norton, 1981.

Butler, Judith. *Bodies That Matter.* New York: Routledge, 1993.

———. *Gender Trouble.* New York: Routledge, 1991.

Caerwyn Williams, J. E. *The Court Poet in Medieval Ireland.* Sir John Rhys Memorial Lecture. London: The British Academy, 1971.

Camera Obscura 20/21 (1989). (Special issue on female spectatorship.)

Carter, Chris. Notes to *Songs in the Key of X*. Sound recording. Burbank, Calif.: Warner Brothers Records, 1996.

Cartwright, Lisa. *Screening the Body: Tracing Medicine's Visual Culture*. Minneapolis: Univ. of Minnesota Press, 1995.

Casey, Simon. "The Sex Factor." *Who Weekly* (Australian edition), Feb. 5, 1996, 35–37.

Castleman, Harry, and Walter J. Podranzik. *Harry and Wally's Favorite TV Shows: A Fact Filled Opinionated Guide to the Best and Worst on TV*. New York: Prentice Hall, 1989.

Caudwell, Sarah. *The Sirens Sang of Murder*. New York: Delacorte, 1989.

Cawelti, John G. *Adventure, Mystery, and Romance: Formula Stories as Art and Popular Culture*. Chicago: Univ. of Chicago Press, 1976.

Chen, Cliff K. "Newbie FAQ: Please Read Before Posting!" Posted regularly to alt.tv.x-files.

Clerc, Susan. "Estrogen Brigades and 'Big Tits Threads': Media Fandom Online and Off." In *Wired Women: Gender and New Realities in Cyberspace*, edited by Lynn Cherny and Elizabeth Weise. Seattle: Seal Press, 1996.

Clover, Carol J. *Men, Women, and Chain Saws: Gender in the Modern Horror Film*. Princeton, N.J.: Princeton Univ. Press, 1992.

Collins, Jim. "Television and Postmodernism." In *Channels of Discourse, Reassembled: Television and Contemporary Criticism*, edited by Robert C. Allen, 327–49. Chapel Hill: Univ. of North Carolina Press, 1992.

Condit, Celeste. "The Rhetorical Limits of Polysemy." In *Critical Perspectives on Media and Society*, edited by R. Avery and D. Erason. New York: Gilford, 1991.

Corliss, Richard. "A Terminal Case of Brotherly Love." Review of *Dead Ringers*. *Time*, 26 Sept. 1988: 84.

Crichton, Michael. *Jurassic Park*. New York: Ballantine, 1990.

Cross, Tom Peate, and Clark Harris Slover, eds. *Ancient Irish Tales*. Totowa, N.J.: Barnes and Noble, 1968.

D'Acci, Julie. *Defining Women: Television and the Case of Cagney and Lacy*. Chapel Hill: Univ. of North Carolina Press, 1994.

Daly, Steven, and Nathaniel Wice. *alt.culture: An A-to-Z Guide to the '90s—Underground, Online, and Over-the-Counter*. New York: HarperCollins, 1995.

David Duchovny Estrogen Brigade World Wide Web home page. http://www.egr.uh.edu/~escco/DDEB.html.

Davis, Mike. *Prisoners of the American Dream: Politics and Economy in the History of the U.S. Working Class*. London: Verso, 1986.

Denton, Andrew. "Alien Sex Fiends." *Rolling Stone Yearbook* (Australian edition), Dec. 1995, 66–76.

Derrida, Jacques. *Margins of Philosophy*. Translated by Alan Bass. Chicago: Univ. of Chicago Press, 1982.

Dolan, Marc. "The Peaks and Valleys of Serial Creativity: What Happened to/on *Twin Peaks*." In *Full of Secrets: Critical Approaches to "Twin Peaks*," edited by David Lavery, 30–50. Detroit: Wayne State Univ. Press, 1994.

Donald, Adrienne. "Working for Oneself: Labor and Love in *Silence of the Lambs*." *Michigan Quarterly Review* (Summer 1992): 347–60.

Dowd, Maureen. "Looking For Space Aliens (And Denying Yale)." *Washington Post,* Mar. 2, 1995.

Doyle, Arthur Conan. *The Complete Sherlock Holmes.* 2 vols. Garden City, N.Y.: Doubleday, 1930.

Duchovny-1 World Wide Web home page. http://www.webcom.com/ ~walterh.

Dumézil, George. *The Destiny of the Warrior.* Translated by Alf Hiltebeitel. Chicago: Univ. of Chicago Press, 1970.

———. *Mitra-Varuna: An Essay on Two Indo-European Representations of Sovereignty.* Translated by Derek Coltman. New York: Zone, 1988. [Originally published in French in 1984.]

Dyer, Richard. "White." *Screen* 29, no. 4 (1988): 44–64.

Ehrenreich, Barbara. "The Ultimate Chic." *Nation,* 6 Dec. 1993: 681–95.

Emery, Eugene. "Paranormal and Paranoia Intermingle on Fox TV's *X-Files.*" *Skeptical Inquirer,* 19, no. 2 (1995): 18–19.

Facts on File Dictionary of Television, Cable and Video. New York: Facts on File, 1994.

Fandom Directory. Annual. Springfield, Va.: Fandata Publications, 1995. [Note: This directory covers fans, fan clubs, and research libraries.]

Feuer, Jane. "Genre Study and Television." In *Channels of Discourse, Reassembled: Television and Contemporary Criticism,* edited by Robert C. Allen, 138–59. Chapel Hill: Univ. of North Carolina Press, 1992.

Fisher, Kim N. *On the Screen: A Film, Television, and Video Research Guide.* Littleton, Colo.: Libraries Unlimited, 1986.

Fiske, John. *Power Works, Power Plays.* London: Verso, 1993.

———. "Television: Polysemy and Popularity." In *Critical Perspectives on Media and Society,* edited by R. Avery and D. Eason, 391–408. New York: Gilford, 1991.

———. *Television Culture.* New York: Routledge, 1987.

Foucault, Michel. *The Birth of the Clinic: An Archeology of Medical Perception,* translated by A. M. Sheridan-Smith. New York: Vintage, 1975.

———. *Discipline and Punish: The Birth of the Prison,* translated by Alan Sheridan. New York: Vintage, 1979.

———. *A History of Sexuality. Volume One,* translated by Robert Hurley. New York: Vintage, 1990.

Fraina, Georjean M. Letter to the Editors. *Wrapped in Plastic* 1, no. 14 (Dec. 1994): 19–20.

Frazer, James George. *The Golden Bough: A Study in Magic and Religion.* Abridged ed. New York: Collier, 1922.

Freud, Sigmund. *The Interpretation of Dreams.* Translated and edited by James Strachey. New York: Basic Books, 1953. [Originally published in German in 1900.]

Fulbright, Audette. "Phile Under Phenomenon." *U. Magazine,* Oct. 1995: 30.

Fuller, John G. *The Interrupted Journey: Two Lost Hours Aboard a Flying Saucer.* New York: Dial, 1966.

Fuller, Roy. *New and Collected Poems, 1934–84.* London: Secker and Warburg, 1985.

Gallup, G., and F. Newport. "Belief in Psychic and Paranormal Phenomena Wide-spread among Americans." *The Gallup Poll Monthly* 299 (Aug. 1990): 35–44.

Garrett, Laurie. *The Coming Plague.* New York: Farrar, Straus, and Giroux, 1995.

Genge, N. E. *The Unofficial X-Files Companion: An X-Phile's Guide to the Mysteries, Conspiracies, and Really Strange Truths Behind the Show.* New York: Crown, 1995.

Gianakos, Larry James. *Television Drama Series Programming: A Comprehensive Chronicle.* Metuchen, N.J.: Scarecrow, 1980– . [Note: The series covers from 1947–84 at this point. It also lists episode titles when available.]

Gibson, William. "Foreword: Strange Attractors." In *Alien Sex: Nineteen Tales by the Masters of Science Fiction and Dark Fantasy,* edited by Ellen Datlow, xv–xvi. New York: Dutton, 1990.

Gilligan, Carol. *In a Different Voice: Psychological Theory and Women's Development.* Cambridge, Mass.: Harvard Univ. Press, 1982.

Gitlin, Todd. *Watching Television.* New York: Pantheon, 1996.

Gliatto, Tom, and Craig Tomashoff. "X-Ellence." *People Weekly,* Oct. 9, 1995, 73–78.

Glynn, Kevin. "Tabloid Television: Popular Culture and the New 'Reality' Programming.' " Ph.D. diss., Univ. of Wisconsin-Madison, 1995.

Grant, Charles. *Goblins.* New York: Harper/Prism, 1994.

———. *Whirlwind.* New York: Harper/Prism, 1995.

Griffin, Peni R. "The Sum of the Partners." *Spectrum* 1, no. 4 (July 1995): 29–30.

Hague, Angela. "Infinite Games: The Derationalization of Detection in *Twin Peaks.*" In *Full of Secrets: Critical Approaches to "Twin Peaks,"* edited by David Lavery, 130–43. Detroit: Wayne State Univ. Press, 1995.

Hall, Stuart. "Encoding/Decoding." In *Culture, Media, Language,* edited by Stuart Hall et al., 128–39. London: Hutchinson, 1980.

———. "The Rediscovery of 'Ideology': Return of the Repressed in Media Studies." In *Culture, Society, and Media,* edited by M. Gurevitch et al., 56–90. London: Metchuen, 1982.

Hampton, Howard. "Rest in Peaks." *Artforum,* Sept. 1991, 103–5.

Haraway, Donna. "The Actors are Cyborg, Nature is Coyote, and the Geography is Elsewhere: Postscript to 'Cyborgs at Large.' " In *Technoculture,* edited by Constance Penley and Andrew Ross, 21–26. Minneapolis: Univ. of Minnesota Press, 1992.

———. *Simians, Cyborgs and Women.* New York: Routledge, 1991.

Harvey, David. *The Condition of Postmodernity: An Inquiry into the Origins of Cultural Change.* Oxford: Basil Blackwell, 1989.

Henderson, Linda D. "X-Rays and the Quest for Invisible Reality in the Art of Kupka, Duchamp, and the Cubists." *Art Journal* 47, no. 4 (1988): 223.

Herring, Susan. "Politeness in Computer Culture: Why Women Thank and Men Flame." Forthcoming.

———. "Posting in a Different Voice: Gender and Ethics in Computer-Mediated Communication." Forthcoming.

Herring, Susan, Deborah Johnson, and Tamra DiBenedetto. " 'This Discussion Is Goinig Too Far': Male Response to Female Participation on the Internet." Forthcoming.

Hess, David J. *Science in the New Age: The Paranormal, Its Defenders and Debunkers, and American Culture.* Madison: Univ. of Wisconsin Press, 1993.

Hirschman, Elizabeth C. "Using Consumption Imagery to decode *Twin Peaks.*" *American Journal of Semiotics* 9, nos. 2–3 (1992): 185–218.

Hopkins, Budd. *Intruders: The Incredible Visitations at Copley Woods.* New York: Avon, 1987.

———. *Missing Time.* New York: Ballantine, 1981.

Hyman, Ray. "Scientists and Psychics." In *Science and the Paranormal: Probing the Existence of the Supernatural,* edited by George O. Abell and Barry Singer, 119–41. New York: Charles Scribner's Sons, 1981.

Infusino, Divine. "Paranoid About the Paranormal." *TV Guide,* Jan. 15, 1994, 20.

International Directory of Film and TV Documentation Collections. London: Federation Internationale des Archives du Film (FIAF), 1994.

Jacobs, David M. *Secret Life: Firsthand Documented Accounts of UFO Abductions.* New York: Simon and Schuster, 1992.

———. *The UFO Controversy in America.* Bloomington: Indiana Univ. Press, 1975.

Jameson, Frederic. "Postmodernism, or the Cultural Logic of Late Capitalism." *New Left Review* 145 (July/Aug. 1984): 52–92.

Jayyusi, Lena. *Categorization and the Moral Order.* London: Routledge and Kegan Paul, 1984.

———. "Values and Moral Judgment: Communicative Praxis as a Moral Order." In *Ethnomethodology and the Human Sciences,* edited by G. Button, 227–51. Cambridge: Cambridge Univ. Press, 1991.

Jenkins, Henry. " 'Do You Enjoy Making the Rest of Us Feel Stupid?': alt.tv.twinpeaks, the Trickster Author, and Viewer Mastery." In *Full of Secrets: Critical Approaches to "Twin Peaks,"* edited by David Lavery. 51–69. Detroit: Wayne State Univ. Press, 1994.

———. *Textual Poachers: Television Fans and Participatory Culture.* New York: Routledge, 1992.

Jones, Leslie. "The Bad Anthropology Film Festival: How the Other Sees Us." Paper presented at the American Folklore Society Conference, Milwaukee, Wis., Oct. 19–23, 1994.

———. "The Function of the Otherworld in the Middle Welsh Arthurian Romance, *Owein, neu Chwedl Iarlles y Ffynnawn.*" Ph.D. diss., Univ. of California at Los Angeles, 1992.

———. "The Truth Is in Here: On Electronic Literary Criticism in General, the *The X-Files* in Particular." Paper presented at the American Folklore Society Conference, Lafayette, LA., Oct. 12–15, 1995.

Kaplan, E. Ann. "Feminist Criticism and Television." In *Channels of Discourse, Reassembled: Television and Contemporary Criticism,* edited by Robert C. Allen, 211–53. Chapel Hill: Univ. of North Carolina Press, 1989.

Keller, Evelyn Fox. "Feminism and Science." In *Sex and Scientific Inquiry,* edited by Sandra Harding and Jean F. O'Barr, 233–46. Chicago: Univ. of Chicago Press, 1987.

Kennedy, Dana, "The *X-Files* Exposed: Strange-But-True Tales Lurk Behind the Scenes of TV's Creepiest Cult Hit." *Entertainment Weekly,* Mar. 10, 1995, 18–24.

King, Stephen. *Danse Macabre.* New York: Everest House, 1981.

Kinsella, Thomas, trans. *The Tain: From the Irish Epic Táin Bó Cuailgne.* Oxford: Oxford Univ. Press, 1969.

Kozloff, Sarah. "Narrative Theory and Television." In *Channels of Discourse, Reassembled: Television and Contemporary Criticism,* edited by Robert C. Allen, 66–100. Chapel Hill: Univ. of North Carolina Press, 1992.

Krantrowitz, Barbara, and Adam Rogers. "The Truth Is X-ed Out There." *Newsweek,* Dec. 1995: 66.

Kristeva, Julia. "From One Identity to An Other." In *Desire in Language: A Semiotic Approach to Literature and Art,* edited by Leon S. Roudiez, translated by Thomas Gora, Alice Jardine, and Leon S. Roudiez, 124–47. New York: Columbia Univ. Press, 1980.

———. "The System and the Speaking Subject." In *The Kristeva Reader,* edited by Toril Moi, 24–33. New York: Columbia Univ. Press, 1986.

Kutzera, Dale. "*X-Files:* TV Series Creator Chris Carter on His Homage to Kolchak." *Cinefantastique,* 26, no. 2 (1995): 52–53.

Lacan, Jacques. *Écrits: A Selection.* Translated by Alan Sheridan. New York: Norton, 1977.

———. *The Four Fundamental Concepts of Psycho-Analysis.* Edited by Jacques-Alain Miller, translated by Alan Sheridan. New York: Norton, 1981.

———. *The Seminar,* Book 3. Translated by Russell Grigg. New York: W. W. Norton, 1993.

Lavery, David, ed. *Full of Secrets: Critical Approaches to "Twin Peaks."* Detroit: Wayne State Univ. Press, 1994.

Ledwon, Lenora. "*Twin Peaks* and Television Gothic." *Literature/Film Quarterly* 21, no. 4 (Fall 1993): 260–70.

Leiren-Young, Mark. "X-Treme Possibilities: How *The X-Files* Built a Franchise on Aliens." *Shift,* Nov.–Dec. 1995: 18–22.

Lemonick, Michael D. "The Killers All Around." *Time,* 12 Sept. 1994: 62–69.

Lentz, Harris M., III. *Science Fiction, Horror and Fantasy Film and Television Credits.* Jefferson, N.C.: McFarland, 1983.

Lepselter, Susan. " 'I'm Not at Home on Earth': Earth as Region in UFO Discourse." Paper presented at the American Folklore Society Conference, Milwaukee, Wis., Oct. 19–23, 1994.

Lévi-Strauss, Claude. *The Raw and the Cooked: An Introduction to a Science of Mythology.* Vol. 1. Translated by John and Doreen Weightman. Chicago: Univ. of Chicago Press, 1969.

———. "The Story of Asdiwal." Translated by Nicholas Mann. In *The Structural Study of Myth and Totemism,* edited by Edmund Leach, 1–48. A.S.A. Monographs. London: Tavistock, 1968.

———. "The Structural Study of Myth." In *Myth: A Symposium,* edited by Thomas Sebeok, 81–106. Bloomington: Indiana Univ. Press, 1965. [Originally published in 1955.]

Lippit, Akira Mizuta. "The X-ray Files: Alien-ated Bodies in Contemporary Art." *Afterimage* 22, no. 5 (1994): 6ff. *Expanded Academic ASAP.* Online. Infotrack. 18 Sept. 1995.

Lipton, Michael, and Craig Tomashoff. "His X-Cellent Adventure." *People Weekly,* June 19, 1995, 11–13.

Littleton, C. Scott. *The New Comparative Mythology: An Anthropological Assessment of the Theories of George Dumézil*, 3d ed. Berkeley: Univ. of California Press, 1982.

Lovece, Frank. *"The X-Files" Declassified: The Unauthorized Guide.* Secaucus, N.J.: Carol, 1996.

Lowry, Brian. *The Truth Is Out There: The Official Guide to the X-Files.* New York: Harper/Prism, 1995.

MacDonald, J. Fred. *Television and the Red Menace: The Video Road to Vietnam.* New York: Praeger, 1985.

Mack, John E. *Abduction: Human Encounters with Aliens.* New York: Scribner's, 1994.

———. "Foreword." In David M. Jacobs, *Secret Life: Firsthand Documented Accounts of UFO Abductions,* 9–13. New York: Free Press, 1992.

———. "The Politics of Ontology." *Center Review: A Publication for the Center for Psychology and Social Change* 2 (1992): 6.

Malach, Michele. " 'You Better Dust Off Your Old Black Suit': Agent Cooper, *Twin Peaks,* and the Rewriting of the FBI Agent." *Wrapped in Plastic* 1, no. 14 (1994): 2–7.

Markovsky, Barry, and Anne F. Eisenberg. "An Exploratory Study of Belief Structures." Unpublished study, Univ. of Iowa, 1995.

Masello, Robert. "Romance Writers Pick TV's Hottest Moments." *TV Guide,* Aug. 5, 1995, 22–23.

McConnell, Frank. "The X-Files." *Commonweal,* Sept. 9, 1994, 15–17.

McLaughlin, Paul. "ET: The Extraterrestrial Therapist." *Saturday Night* 110, no. 5 (1995): 44–48, 50, 52.

Miller, Craig. "An Appointment with Dr. Scully." *Wrapped in Plastic* 1, no. 12 (Oct. 1994): 3–5.

Miller, Craig, and John Thorne. "Rush to Judgment? WIP Conspires to Reexamine *The X-Files.*" *Wrapped in Plastic* 1, no. 12 (Aug. 1994): 6–27.

———. "The World Spins." *Wrapped in Plastic* 1, no. 7 (1993): 29–32.

———. "*The X-Files* Episode Guide [First Season]. *Wrapped in Plastic* 1, no. 12 (Oct. 1994): 9–26.

———. "X-Files Extra!" *Wrapped in Plastic* 1, no. 15 (Feb. 1995): 29–31.

———. "*The X-Files* Second Season Episode Guide." *Spectrum* 1, no. 4 (July 1995): 7–29.

Mulvey, Laura. *Visual and Other Pleasures.* Bloomington: Indiana Univ. Press, 1989.

———. "Visual Pleasure and Narrative Cinema." In *Feminisms: An Anthology of Literary Theory and Criticism,* edited by Robyn R. Warhol and Diane Price Herndl, 432–42. New Brunswick, N.J.: Rutgers Univ. Press, 1991.

Nabokov, Vladimir. *Pale Fire.* New York: Putnam, 1962.

Nagy, Joseph Falaky. "Hierarchy, Heroes, and Heads: Indo-European Structures in Greek Mythology." In *Approaches to Greek Mythology,* edited by Lowell Edmunds, 199–238. Baltimore: Johns Hopkins Univ. Press, 1990.

Newcomb, Horace. "*Magnum:* The Champagne of TV?" *Channels of Communications* (May/June 1985): 23–26.

——, ed. *TV: The Most Popular Art.* New York: Anchor, 1974.

Nichols, Nichelle. *Beyond Uhura: "Star Trek" and Other Memories.* New York: Putnam, 1994.

Nochimson, Martha. "Desire Under the Douglas Firs: Entering the Body of Reality in *Twin Peaks.*" In *Full of Secrets: Critical Approaches to "Twin Peaks,"* edited by David Lavery, 144–159. Detroit: Wayne State Univ. Press, 1994.

——. *No End to Her: Soap Opera and the Female Subject.* Berkeley: Univ. of California Press, 1992.

Nollinger, Mark. "20 Things You Need to Know about *The X-Files.*" *TV Guide,* Apr. 6, 1996, 18–29.

Oliver, Kelly. "Kristeva's Imaginary Father and the Crisis in Paternal Function." *Diacritics* (Summer/Fall 1991): 43–63.

Ostria, Vincent. "Le Polar Psychotrope." *Cahiers du Cinema* 446 (July/Aug. 1991): 74–75.

Parish, James Robert. *Complete Actors' Television Credits, 1948–1988,* 2nd ed. Metuchen, N.J.: Scarecrow, 1990. [Note: A particularly valuable resource as it lists supporting actors as well as stars.]

Penley, Constance. "Feminism, Psychoananlysis, and the Study of Pop Culture." In *Cultural Studies,* edited by Lawrence Grossberg, Cary Nelson, and Paula Treichler, 479–94. New York: Routledge, 1992.

Penley, Constance, and Andrew Ross. "Interview With Donna Haraway." In *Technoculture,* edited by Constance Penley and Andrew Ross, 1–20. Minneapolis: Univ. of Minnesota Press, 1992.

Powers, Richard Gid. *G-Men: Hoover's FBI in American Popular Culture.* Carbondale: Southern Illinois Univ. Press, 1983.

Progoff, Ira. *Jung's Psychology and Its Social Meaning.* New York: Dialog House, 1953.

Puhvel, Jaan. *Comparative Mythology.* Baltimore: Johns Hopkins Univ. Press, 1987.

Rapping, Elaine. *"The X-Files." Progressive,* Jan. 1995, 34–36.

Rees, Alwyn, and Brinley Rees. *Celtic Heritage: Ancient Tradition in Ireland and Wales.* New York: Thames and Hudson, 1961.

Reeves, Jimmie L., and Richard Campbell. *Cracked Coverage: Television News, the Anti-Cocaine Crusade, and the Reagan Legacy.* Durham, N.C.: Duke Univ. Press, 1994.

Reeves, Jimmie L., Elizabeth Brent, Richard Campbell, Herb Eagle, Jennifer Jenkins, Mark C. Rogers, Lis Saaf, and Nabeel Zuberi. "Postmodernism and Television: Speaking of *Twin Peaks.*" In *Full of Secrets: Critical Approaches to "Twin Peaks,"* edited by David Lavery, 171–95. Detroit: Wayne State Univ. Press, 1994.

Rhys, John. *Celtic Folklore: Welsh and Manx.* London: Wildwood, 1980. [Originally published in 1901.]

Ross, Jonathan. "Talking with Aliens." *Sight and Sound,* June 1995: 61.

Sacks, Harvey. "An Initial Investigation of the Usability of Conversation for Doing Sociology." In *Studies in Social Interaction,* edited by D. Sudnow, 31–74. New York: Free Press, 1972.

——. "On the Analyzability of Stories by Children." In *Directions in Socio-*

linguistics, edited by J. J. Gumperz and D. Hymes, 325–45. New York: Holt, Rinehart & Winston, 1972.

Sahl, Mort. *Heartland.* New York: Harcourt Brace Jovanovich, 1976.

Sartre, Jean-Paul. " 'Aminadab': Or the Fantastic Considered as a Language." 1927. Reprinted in *Literary Essays.* New York: Citadel, 1955: 56–72.

Schatz, Thomas. *Hollywood Genres: Formulas, Filmmaking, and the Studio System.* New York: Random House, 1981.

Schwartz, John. "Technology's Magic Can't Make Pseudoscience Disappear." *Washington Post,* Oct. 31, 1994, A3.

Sexton, Jim. "No Rest for the Eerie." *USA Weekend,* May 12–14, 1995, 4–6.

Shelley, Mary Wollstonecroft. *Frankenstein; or, the Modern Prometheus, the 1818 Text,* edited by James Rieger. Chicago: Univ. of Chicago Press, 1982.

Silverman, Kaja. *The Subject of Semiotics.* New York: Oxford Univ. Press, 1983.

Stacey, Jackie. *Star Gazing: Hollywood Cinema and Female Spectatorship.* London: Routledge, 1994.

Stout, Rex. "Watson Was a Woman." In *The Baker Street Reader: Cornerstone Writings About Sherlock Holmes,* edited by Philip Shreffler, 159–65. Contributions to the Study of Popular Culture 8. Westport, Conn.: Greenwood, 1984.

Strieber, Whitley. *Breakthrough: The Next Step.* New York: HarperCollins, 1995.

———. *Communion: A True Story.* New York: Avon, 1987.

———. *Transformation: The Breakthrough.* New York: Avon, 1988.

Suttell, Seth. "*X-Files* Doing Buffo in Japan." *Tennessean Showcase,* Apr. 21, 1996, 22.

Svetkey, Benjamin. "No Wonder He's Called Fox: The Teeny Bikini, the Big, Um, Brain, Why X-Filer David Duchovny is TV's New Pinup Boy." *Entertainment Weekly,* Sept. 29, 1995, 20–26.

Takei, George. *To the Stars.* New York: Pocket Books, 1994.

Tannen, Deborah. *You Just Don't Understand: Women and Men in Conversation.* New York: Ballantine, 1990.

Tarvers, Josephine Koster. *The Writer's Library: Science and Society.* New York: HarperCollins, 1992.

Taylor, Charles. "Truth Decay: Sleuths After Reagan." http://www.bgsu.edw/ckile/popc290/truth/decay.html.

Television Programming Source Books. Annual. New York: BIB Channels, 1949–.

Thompson, Stith. *The Motif Index of Folk Literature: A Classification of Narrative Elements in Folktales, Ballads, Myths, Fables, Medieval Exempla, Fabliaux, Jest-Books, and Local Legends.* 6 vols. Bloomington: Indiana Univ. Press, 1932–36.

———. *The Types of the Folktale: Antti Aarne's Verzeichnis der Märchentypen Translated and Enlarged.* Folklore Fellows Communications no. 74. Helsinki: Folklore Fellows, 1928.

Thorburn, David. "Television as an Aesthetic Medium." *Critical Studies in Mass Communication* 4, no. 2 (June 1987): 161–173.

Todorov, Tzvetan. *The Fantastic: A Structural Approach to Literary Genre,* translated by Richard Howard. Cleveland: Press of Case Western Reserve Univ., 1973.

Truzzi, Marcello. "Zetetic Ruminations on Skepticism and Anomalies in Science." *Zetetic Scholar* 12/13 (1987): 7–20.

Vallee, Jacques. *Confrontations: A Scientist's Search for Alien Contact.* New York: Random House, 1990.

———. *Dimensions: A Casebook of Alien Contact.* Foreword by Whitley Strieber. New York: Random House, 1988.

———. *Passport to Magonia: On UFOs, Folklore, and Parallel Worlds.* Chicago: Contemporary Books, 1993. (Originally published in 1969.]

———. *Revelations: Alien Contact and Human Deception.* New York: Random House, 1991.

Van de Walle, Mark. "Fear and Present Danger." *Artforum,* May 1995: 18.

Van Syckle, Richard. "An Interview with *X-Files* Creator Chris Carter from C/net. Online. C/net Central. 12 Aug. 1995.

Vitaris, Paula. *"The X-Files."* Special issue of *Cinefantastique,* Oct. 1995.

Walker, Martin. "What on Earth?: Truth May Be Stranger Than Science Fiction." *The Ottawa Citizen,* 19 July 1995: B2.

Warlick, Debra. "Mulder & Scully: Actors David Duchovny and Gillian Anderson Talk about Playing the F.B.I. Probers of the Unknown." *Cinefantastique,* Oct. 1995, 23–24.

Watson, James D. *The Double Helix.* New York: Doubleday, 1968.

Whitehead, Don. *The F.B.I. Story.* New York: Random, 1956.

Wilcox, Rhonda V. "Beyond the Borders: Living on (the Edge) in *Twin Peaks.*" *Wrapped in Plastic* 1, no. 17 (June 1995): 20–25.

Wild, David. *"X-Files* Undercover." *Rolling Stone,* 16 May 1996: 38–42.

Williams, Linda. *Hard Core: Power, Pleasure, and the "Frenzy of the Visible."* Berkeley: Univ. of California Press, 1989.

Williams, Linda. "When the Woman Looks." In *Re-Vision: Essays in Feminist Film Criticism,* edited by Mary Ann Doane, Patricia Mellencamp, and Linda Williams, 83–97. Los Angeles: American Film Institute, 1984.

Winslow, Harriet. *"The X-Files:* Fox's Frightening Friday Series." *Washington Post,* June 5, 1994, final ed., Y6.

Wolcott, James. " 'X' Factor." *New Yorker,* Apr. 18, 1994, 98–99.

Yamashiro, Bryan. "The Truth Is Way Out There." *Wrapped in Plastic* 1, no. 12 (Aug. 1994): 28–31.

Index